Dark
Like
Under

Dark
Like
Under

Alice
Chadwick

First published in the United Kingdom in 2025 by
Daunt Books
83 Marylebone High Street
London W1U 4QW

I

Copyright © Alice Chadwick, 2025

The right of Alice Chadwick to be identified as Proprietor
of this work has been asserted by her in accordance with
the Copyright, Designs and Patents Act 1988

A CIP catalogue record for this title is available from
the British Library

ISBN 978-1-914198-90-8

Typeset by Marsha Swan

Printed and bound by Bell & Bain Ltd, Glasgow

www.dauntbookspublishing.co.uk

MIX
Paper | Supporting
responsible forestry
FSC® C007785

Dark
Like
Under

I

The Weir

solar midnight

It was only the second time Robin had walked the weir. The first time had been the summer she met Tin and Tin had made the hot, empty days sparkle like broken glass. 'Let's walk the weir,' Tin said one slack afternoon, and they had, their bare feet on the cold stone, the fine green waterweed combed straight by pulling water. Coming out numb on the other side, they had walked the long way around, past the chip shop and over the bridge, to reclaim their shoes. Robin had wanted to push her. She would have pushed her, but Tin was always too quick.

The second time was Sunday night, the night of the last-minute party. Why Tin wasn't there, nobody knew.

Sometimes she came to things, sometimes she didn't. Robin had gone around to find out and seen her from the street, upstairs at her desk, wearing glasses that Robin didn't even know she owned.

'What are you doing?' Robin shouted up. Three storeys. Tin pushed the sash of the window higher. Above the glasses, her eyebrows arched black. She held a piece of paper out, a bright blank in the softening dusk, revved a lighter and, when the corner took, flames darting up, she let it go. The blazing paper sat in the air, borne up by a rising sheet of fire, held down by its own weight, until the flare sharpened to a point, ash swallowing the whiteness, and it began to sink, breaking up, burning itself out, landing in flakes on the channel of dark water that ran in front of Tin's house.

'I-love-you letters,' Tin said. 'Mostly hot air.'

'To you or from you?' Robin called up, but Tin was already back at her desk. In Robin's mind, 'Fire in Cairo' was on the record player, although she might only have imagined that. Tin attracted coincidences, fire and fire, but it was Robin, really, who always played The Cure. She stood for a moment, beside the narrow stream, below the tall house, its darkening glass, then walked away alone.

To Tin, obviously, Robin thought later, following Jonah back down the hall, into the party. From Jonah, probably. If it had been a letter. If it hadn't only been Tin's homework, an essay Robin hadn't written yet. Comedy in *Hamlet*. Robin was two weeks late with that.

'You're so nice,' Jonah kept saying, trying to untangle Robin's earring from the net of her jumper. 'Why are you so nice to me?' She hadn't, in truth, been nice to him, no more than any other night. She had offered him a swig of a bottle. She had sat down with him against the wall and listened to him talk. Francis Bacon, SLR cameras. David Bowie's suits. She had followed him up through the crush on the stairs and back down again. But Tin wasn't there. They were both aware of that.

They left the party. Often they wandered around, any combination of them, between the pub that let them in, the off-licence that sold them vermouth and the rounda-bout where they drank it. Jonah turned into a back lane Robin didn't know. It was dark, without streetlamps, a rough track, and even though she was with Jonah, she felt lost in her own town and somehow afraid. They walked between high banks of nettles and into a gravelled opening. Motorbikes in pieces, pallets stacked square like forts. Skirting some dark buildings, they went in around the back.

Later, he wanted to go to the park. They crossed the humpback bridge and turned into the narrow strip of grass that runs along the river. The lights of the football club yellowed the darkness. The willows draped their hair into the moving water. It was then that she realised how out of it Jonah was. He staggered, and more than once fell down and she had to pull him up. They were laughing, but it wasn't how she'd imagined it would be. They made it to the weir, where he folded himself to the ground, his long legs and arms unwieldy. The water slid shiny in the dark, then plunged down in boiling confusion.

'Do you want to walk it with me?' he asked, rolling over, his head dropping sideways to his arm. A button-down collar but his shirt wide open.

'Ok-ay,' she agreed, but she knew that they shouldn't. He was stoned and she wasn't a swimmer. She hadn't been the kind of kid who ever got taken to lessons. But Jonah had already unlaced his boots. He tugged off his socks and threw them away.

The water was high, its pull strong and the flat stones thicker than she remembered with soft, traitorous waterweed.

'Hold my hand,' he instructed. 'I need you to keep me upright.' And they started out, her feet burning with cold, across the rushing black.

Could he feel what she felt, the humming between the skin of their hands? A skateboard vibrating over loose ground, a car engine idling. But he stopped, not even halfway across, and released his grip. He was trying to turn around. He was giving at the knees as if to sit down.

'You know she doesn't give a fuck?' he shouted, over the drumming volume of water. 'Not about you. Not about me.' He threw an arm around her, clumsy like a heavy rope. She thought he would kiss her but his head landed hard on her collarbone. 'I can't anymore, but she has to let somebody.'

'What?'

'Let somebody in. Her heart's—'

Robin didn't want to hear what Tin's heart was. She was tired of Tin's heart. She stopped trying to hold them up. She and Jonah were unevenly matched, he much taller than her, and when her foot slid and balance failed, she gave her body to his falling weight. Why not fall? she thought, as he collapsed in stages like a building and they went over into the shocking cold, the water hitting hard, legs and arms flung down.

How cold and dark and big underneath, a liquid roar closing over her head. It can't, she knew, be this deep, but she couldn't find a footing. The weir kept battering, pushing her down. She felt a punch through the thickness of the pounding water, then his hand firm around her chin, yanking her skull upwards, sideways, dragging her spine, her beating limbs with it; Jonah pulling her out, lifesaving, like they were supposed to have learnt at school. A choking gulp of air. A crash to the back of her head: the concrete edge of the weir pool. She knew this rough platform. She had stubbed her toes, scraped her knees sitting here many summers. Already out, he hauled her up by a wrist and an elbow.

'Why the fuck did you do that?' he asked. On the bank, flooding the grass with water, he seemed pin-sharp sober.

'I didn't mean to.' Her clothes hung heavy. The back of her brain felt thick.

'Let's go,' he said, turning, hooking up his boots.

Casting around for her shoes, she saw the shadow of someone, a man, approaching.

'Hello, Robin. Jonah.' A quiet voice. Mr Ardennes.

'Evening,' said Jonah, gathering himself together, a sturdy citizen. 'You're up late.'

'Late, or too early,' Mr Ardennes said. 'I wondered if the heron was here.'

Jonah looked around. 'Is it?'

'No. The water's too high, perhaps.'

'Maybe we frightened it away,' said Robin.

'I don't think so.'

Mr Ardennes had come to a stop. He seemed different in the dark. Not older, exactly, but less, as if the night had worn him thinner. He stood with his head at a tilt, courteous but appraising. His hair, cut like a boy's, looked trampled like grass. The soft fabric of his jacket drew the darkness to him. His arms were bound to his sides, his hands like weights in his pockets.

He walked around at night, Robin knew. She had seen him before. And when he had to take school assembly, he spared them God and talked about birds, their nocturnal calls, the dark respiration of trees, the sudden shifts in the town's water meadows, fragile and complicated, as if night was a younger wayward sibling they should all look out for.

'Are you both okay to get home?' he asked them.

'We're heading off now,' said Jonah.

Mr Ardennes nodded.

'School tomorrow,' Robin said conversationally, or trying to excuse herself, and immediately the church clock began to strike, its low, dull thuds vibrating as much in the wet ground as through the air.

'It might already be tomorrow,' Mr Ardennes said.

Robin smiled, then shivered. Her teeth and bones rattled with cold.

Mr Ardennes wished them goodnight and made a sidestep around them. But it seemed that until they went, he could not go, and so they started off and he, released, walked away at pace.

'Take it easy,' Jonah called after him.

It was the wrong thing to say, Robin felt, to someone like Mr Ardennes. To someone so spare and occupied, who looked like he might walk and keep walking and never be easy.

'He didn't say anything,' she reflected, weighing the dripping hem of her jumper. It had stretched almost to her knees.

'He looked a bit rough.'

'Worse than us?' Under the faint sulphur cast of the night, Mr Ardennes had looked drawn, even for him, and bruised around the eyes. Yet his voice in the dark had been the same. Steady, considering, like a kindness. 'Maybe he's an insomniac,' she suggested.

'Maybe his wife snores.'

They walked back along the river, the idea of Mr Ardennes growing vague, fading in the porous dark. Robin tugged at her leggings, the wet cloth sullen, sticking in unaccustomed places. Her mohair jumper lay cold across her back. They left the park and entered the empty, stone-slabbed streets. Intermittent streetlamps. What might have been a dog, pulling its shadow around a corner. Outside her house, under the dud carriage lamp, they came to a stop.

'I'm in trouble now,' Jonah said.

'You're dead meat,' Robin agreed, and felt a queasy lurch in her stomach. 'And so am I.'

Jonah frowned and stepped back. He was looking at her shoes, which were the same as Tin's but with fake zips and more beaten up. Well, there was no point denying it. They had left the party together and everyone had seen them. And there was no fooling Tin, even if they wanted to. Whenever Robin tried to lie, Tin just laughed, or looked straight through her. They would both have to face her. And soon. Tomorrow. Because tomorrow was Monday, and it might already be tomorrow.

2

Under Old Light

3.17 a.m.

The heron stands in the water.

The river moves through clay, under stars. Silt and silver.

The whooping up of a fox.

Taillights, the retreat of a van.

The quarter-hour bell.

The heron spears the river.

A soft-limbed frog.

Pearls of water roll from its oiled neck.

The river pulls, rattling the willow leaves.

The small alarm of a coot.

3
Farm Kitchen
6.36 a.m.

'Davy!' a shout from the top of the stairs. His mum.

'I'm awake,' Davy says, which is true. He is even sitting up in the hollow of his bed, in its creaking metal sling, the curtain pushed half open. He lifts and drops a shoulder. The weight of the night on one side has numbed his arm.

A rumble from the boot room below, more than one pair of feet. From the tree outside, a spiral of birdsong.

'Davy! You asked to be woken up.' Already the other end of the landing.

He had been dreaming about Tin, but only vaguely. A face dark like Tin's. Her hair like an oil slick, something you shouldn't get on your hands. He stares towards his feet. His bedclothes are a dead weight, holding his legs down. He has asked for a duvet, but they still have sheets and bedspreads, eiderdowns in winter, cupboards full of them. 'Not Habitat, but adequate,' his mum says, because duvets are extravagant, in her opinion. And Swedish. She won't waste money on fads. More than adequate, Davy thinks, freeing his legs. He swings his feet down to the rug, taking in the smell of frying bread, the promise of bacon. His dad, already up and out for a couple of hours, will be back for breakfast, rubbing his skin red and adding salt to everything. Turning, Davy looks at the leaves, the branches in his window, the sky behind strong, a convincing blue, with fine shreds of gold and pink like a holiday postcard, the white clouds shiny and immaculate. It will be hot, he sees, and will all burn off before he gets outside, the high, strange colour of it.

He has homework to do, which is why he needs to be up. He has maths. Maths is easier in the morning, he told himself last night, but now he tells himself it is easier on the bus with someone else to help him. Miriam. He sits with the heels of his hands in his eyes. When he lets his arms drop, his legs look immense, a field of snow, his big thighs flat against the edge of the thin mattress. He lifts himself up, stretching out – to be upright, even, is a pleasure – and unhooks his dressing gown from the back of the door. It is not his dressing gown. Someone left it years ago, in his grandparents' time; he had pulled it out of a trunk last week looking for something else. It is silk and patterned, with a bit of a swing to the hem. Paul Weller in his belted coat. He goes along the landing and down the stairs. Activity in the bathroom. His sister. The escaping steam of the Timotei ritual.

'Ah, the vision of youth,' his dad says, as he walks into the kitchen. 'Eventually he rises.'

A table of heads look up, nod, and look back down. They smell of outside, and animal feed. A kiss to the side of his head – his mum in his dad's jacket with a bucket for the chickens. He says hello to Darren in the doorway, chewing; to Robert wiping the breadknife clean. Robert has a scar on his forearm, a deep pink trench. Even the baler didn't want him, the men joke. It had fascinated Davy as a small kid, the fact that the machine had caught him up and spat him out again.

Davy gets himself a plate, what's warm in the pan, crisp from under the grill, and looks around for the butter. And then in a moment he is completely alone, a kitchen of people exiting through three different doors, the clinking of mugs to the bottom of the sink like a thank you. He turns the radio from weather through static to where, after the talking – Greenham Common, strategic deployment, the staunch resolve of our American friends – there will be music, and sits down to his feast, the table a great slab of felled tree, sandy with other people's toast.

His maths is where he left it, the page of his textbook interleaved with the page of his exercise book, as if one might answer the other by lying together like this over-night. Through the window, in the lane, the dusty side of the Massey Ferguson, the deep rubber treads of the tractor tyre. Robert is shouting down from the cab to Davy's dad, who is holding one cup of his ear defenders out from the side of his head. Robert has another scar, on his forehead, where he was kicked last summer by Davy's sister's horse. Robert had been left in charge and they had gone on holiday, the only family holiday Davy can remember, to a Christian folk festival thirty miles away. The music was inexplicable, like punk had never happened. It had cost him effort just to stand there not laughing.

The tractor moves off and the morning enters in at the kitchen window, finding the milk rings on the table, the blonde in the hair of his arms. Without the idling engine, the radio sounds out. The end of Bananarama, the start of something else he doesn't know, drum machine and bass. The back door bangs open and shut. The tap explodes into a metal bucket and hisses off again. That is his job, the water for the chickens. But he is happy in the kitchen, in the warmth of his skin, and finally some sort of music. Synths and reverb, sliding strings. New Thomas Dolby, maybe.

His parents don't like holidays, not really. They prefer to be here, where they can keep an eye on things or do them for themselves. He, though, prefers not to do things. Or not farm things. He prefers not to know how farm things are done. Rugby is for meatheads, as his sister likes to point out, but nothing in it seems to him to come close to what can happen on a farm. You have to be a particular kind of alert to survive it. You have to be cut out like that.

His mum comes in one door and leaves by the other. 'Out of the bathroom,' she shouts up the stairs at his sister. 'And you – in,' she says, passing back the other way. 'Teeth, face, hair. The bus will be here and you're not even dressed.' She disappears, carrying a pile of folded blankets.

Davy nods but stays where he is. He looks slow, but he understands pace. He can be dressed and out on the Green in time, even if he stays here another ten minutes. Even if he stands up out of this bath of sunshine and helps himself to a second breakfast.

The dream of Tin moves close again, then evaporates like petrol, leaving a feeling that he has understood something, maybe urgent, but can't now remember what it is. He didn't go to the party last night. If it was a party. He hadn't been able to think up an excuse good enough to get him out on a Sunday, and at such short notice. But Miriam went, and Miriam, he knows, will fill him in on the bus.

4
Full-Length Mirror

7.27 a.m.

'*Oh Miranda, thou art fair, with golden, flowing locks of hair . . .*' Miriam stands in front of the dressing-table mirror in her parents' room, mostly dressed. She turns her shirt collar down over her tie and picks up a comb. She will not comb out her hair, she decides, reversing her hand. She will backcomb it. The long fringe, then the length at the back, taking off the yellow shine and suppleness. When she is satisfied, she puts the comb down and picks up a metal nail file, inserting the sharp end just above her kneecap and ripping the tights sideways slightly, a small hole. She bends her knee and watches the ladder run itself up her leg.

Miriam: How do I look?

Miranda: Gorgeous.

Her mum is not here to deny it. She is on the graveyard shift and God knows what bloodbath she's attending. Babies everywhere cascading down, to listen to her. Haemorrhage and shit, screaming and swearing, and the men out cold in faints. Her father takes the early train to the City. Miriam is supposed to get Toby up. She won't get Toby up. He can sleep. Or he can get himself up. He's not a baby. He can set an alarm on his birthday watch in several different time zones. And after all, to have the house empty to herself, as if the whole annoying conspiracy of them have been swept away overnight, leaving her alone in glory – it is just too juicy to resist.

Let's experiment with the expensive coffee, she thinks, walking across the cold stone floor of the kitchen. And that old packet of pancake batter. She keeps going, straight through to the dining room.

The dining-room table carries the remains of last night, many standing bottles. Not her last night, her parents' last night, or her dad's, getting the new neighbours over. The neighbours are actors, both of them, and she is interested in meeting actors, but she had left the house before they arrived, hitching a lift to the party of a boy in the year above she doesn't really know. His parents had gone out last minute, a family emergency in Bedford, and almost everyone had been there.

But not Tin. And not Davy.

Miriam surveys the table. Cutlery elbowed sideways and spent black matches. The staggered footprints of wine glasses. There is satisfaction in a table the morning after, its oblong devastation, in the thought of unknown adults sitting here declaiming things. Her dad had given her a bottle, reddish, leafy at the bottom, a label washed thin; wine made by their summer neighbours, the old men and women who somehow extract liquid from the dust and rubble of the hill. 'Don't give her that,' Miriam's mum had said. 'We're on skeleton staff, the whole hospital. We can't be pumping stomachs.' But Miriam had taken the suspect wine to the party and had opened it, pushing the cork in with the pointy handle of the downstairs loo, there not being a bottle opener handy. She had taken a swig – the ghost taste of storage drums, battered blue plastic, the inside soil of barns – then lost track of the bottle. And she had come home early, before midnight, it being a Sunday. But now she wishes she had stayed, given what was happening. Without Tin. Robin and Jonah, falling through an upstairs doorway, necking vermouth. Robin in her fishing-net jumper. Mud, a grass stain on one knee of her leggings.

Everyone had been roaming around, up- and downstairs, climbing in and out of windows, of cupboards, raking through drawers. Someone naked in the shower, two people. A radiator hanging off and water overflowing. Mostly dub in the kitchen. *Porky's* in the sitting room, on repeat on the video. She should have stayed longer. At least long enough to see the parents come home to another, their own, domestic crisis.

Miriam swipes a finger sideways, lifting a smudge of something from the table to her mouth. Lemon meringue. She is not allowed another party. For exactly this reason, for what goes missing from cupboards. 'If it all goes tits up, we can sell the wine cellar or remortgage the house. Whichever brings in more.' Her dad likes to repeat this as if it is true, a shrewd grip on his eyebrows. As if, like a château, they've got a cave stuffed full of wine under the kitchen floor. But the cellar is not a cellar. The cellar is a small cupboard in the cold part of the house, some garage shelves standing on flagstones. And it is less well-stocked than it used to be. Which she feels bad about. But not that bad.

Stretching over – spread candles, bread bloated in water – she lifts the coffee pot up out of yesterday night and carries it back to the kitchen.

Miriam likes to clatter the pots and pans. She likes to scoop coffee and pour milk with a twist of her wrist that decorates the marble counter. This is how chefs work. She has watched Artaud, pissed as a lord, conducting his ingredients inexactly. She smashes an egg, lifting the halves high for the strings of spit to stretch and drizzle. She finds a whisk and whips the dust from the pancake packet into a puddle of milk. Cutting a slab of butter, she aims from a distance at the cast-iron pan on the hob. It's hard to get good butter, the type worth eating by itself, which she does now, straight from the blade of the knife, clicking the gas ring on.

Her coffee coughs through. The batter spits and splatters. The smell is good, like a Carcassonne morning. She turns the pancake over, a flick of the palette knife to cauterise the bottom, then shimmies it onto her plate. There is nothing that can't be improved by squirty cream, she believes, and adds a blast, one for the plate, one for her mouth, dropping the can back into its slot in the fridge door.

The smoke alarm starts up – short, high stabs of sound. She stands on a chair, prodding with the end of a wooden spoon. That at least should wake Toby up, its panic exploding right beneath his room. Smoke rolls against the kitchen windows, browned sugar and butter, the molecules in somersault. She piles the bowls and spoons and whisk into the sink and turns the coffee off.

It's not that she likes coffee, exactly. It's that she likes to have it in her hand, strong and scalding, and then, after a while, the grains cool and thick in the bottom of the cup like the shallows of a river stirred up. No milk, she decides. Let's try it black like the farmers have it, those mute, tanned Frenchmen, crooked on their barstools.

Strange how she never really feels entirely where she is, even standing here in her uniform like any English kid. She is almost always half in France, doing nothing in the marketplace, pinball in Artaud's bar, cats yawning, rolling over in the dust and motorbikes whining past. And when she is in France, she mostly lies around annoyed, wondering what everyone else is doing without her. What Tin is doing. Davy. She stands in the payphone, slippery with sweat, the black slot gulping down her francs.

She would prefer to go to school in France, the lycée, but her mum says they moved here precisely so she isn't stuck in a classroom with thick kids three years older. The secondary modern is for tractor mechanics, or whatever the English equivalent is. Bikers. Meaning common kids. The grammar school is for Latin and going on to law school, without getting pregnant first or developing a glue addiction. They have bankrupted themselves to get her and her brother into the grammar school, her mum says. Her mum has no idea.

Miriam opens the cupboard. It's a good cup she reaches for: small, straight-sided, the fine gold rim ruined by the dishwasher. Because it should never ever have gone in the dishwasher. Because dishwasher salt scours the delicate best of things away. She sets it down and pours the coffee in. These are the cups they get out when they're trying to impress people, but not, for some reason, last night. She knows they are good because when her mum broke one, when the handle just came off in her hand, her dad went white and quiet. But then, he doesn't like odd numbers. 'In some ways,' her mum says, 'I thank God that there are only two of you. If there had been three, your dad would've made me have a fourth to even things out and my pelvic floor would have given way completely.' Her mum has many efficient ways to remove her dad from a room. Almost any internal organ will do it.

> Miriam: Did you hear what she said, the brute of a woman? Two children!
> Miranda: I don't listen to her, darling. I try not to listen to a single thing she says. Any of them, in fact. I block them all out.

Miriam nods and checks the time on the cooker. A slurp of coffee, a crammed mouthful of pancake. Another mouthful, cheek-stretching. Marching upstairs, she knocks open Toby's door, stands at the foot of his bed and pulls his duvet off.

'Schooltime!' she shouts, slamming out. 'Bus in seven and a half minutes.'

Coming back down, she stops at her desk and consults the timetable stuck to the wall. Art, maths, chemistry . . . Beside it, a photo from last summer. She is wearing her mum's swimsuit, the pricey one, a deep V at the neck, which looks better on Miriam than it does on her mum. Blonde sand, her blonde hair sandy, and a necklace she had haggled for on the beach, geometric and weighty. *Mad Max* tat, her brother called it, pointing out the green it left on her neck. Moroccan, in fact, according to the man who sold it, and lost somewhere in transit between then and now.

She unscrews the lid of her Quink, the barrel of her pen, and sucks the black ink up, blotting the nib into a tissue she keeps stuffed down the side of her desk just for that. It pleases her, this ritual replenishment. Ink filling the reservoir, petrol in the car. She has other photographs here, postcards, pages from *Tatler*, *Melody Maker*, all jigsawed together. *Just Seventeen*. She looks at Davy, torn from the local paper, in the front row of the rugby team. Thick arms, spread legs, wide necks, a stack of bulk and muscle; someone holding a ball like an Easter egg, and Mr Ward in the middle, his face mostly skull. Reaching over, she gives Davy cheekbones, more eyebrow, the ink branching into the softness of the newsprint, making him handsome and something else he isn't – calculating. And a bolt through Mr Ward's capon neck. She caps her pen, her eyes jumping along the wall.

Miranda: I don't like it, that old postcard.

Miriam pulls it off, leaving a neat, rectangular blank. She had nicked it from the junk shop, their shoebox of lost photos. On the front, a woman with a serious face and two small babies, one in the crook of each arm, wrapped up stiff like boards and out at angles, their eyes bright black. A mirror image, broken by the woman's dark plait, thick on her shoulder, fine by her waist like a whisper. *Come to Canada*, the caption reads, in faded brown script. And nothing ever written on the back. She doesn't like it anymore either.

Miranda: Rip it up, then. Halves, yes. And halves again.
Miriam: There. And into the bin.
Miranda: Don't ever have babies, Me-Mi.
Miriam: Angel, you know I never will.

Miriam walks the downstairs rooms gathering what she needs. Books, books, heavy books, pen, ruler, Tampax. Gum. Hubba Bubba. *Big Bubbles, No Troubles.* But this is an empty packet and anyway Davy will have some. KitKat, hankies. And everything stuffed in her bag. She stops in the hall at the full-length mirror and does her eyeliner, almost without looking. A cat's flick to each lid. And there's the sound of the bus, belching on the Green. Miriam smiles at herself, framed in the glass. All the DNA, cascading down from the very beginning, making her this. Complete. In two halves. Full of pancake and cream.

A revving engine, the impatient driver.

'Toby!' she yells.

The stick and slam of the front door. And there is Davy, jogging to the bus and already pink. Miriam hops over the crack in the path. She likes Mondays, the start of a new week. And particularly after a weekend of complications. A Sunday night of bonus shock and betrayal.

5
Kitchenette

7.54 a.m.

Kelly doesn't hear it coming.

'Twat,' his brother says and flicks his other ear. Stereo hot sting. Kelly punches up and out and misses.

They are supposed to be at work, Kelly's brother and his dad, but his dad is making them late, eating every last baked bean, putting his socks on and peeling them off again and turning them the other way out. Kelly's brother, Jason, showered and gelled, is twenty-six. Kelly has another brother, Dale, who is twenty-four, but he lives in his own flat with his own girlfriend.

'Kelly, take the dog before you go to school,' his mum says, tearing the corner off something from Manda's bowl and feeding it down towards the floor. His mum isn't dressed. She is in her dressing gown and will be until much later. She likes her mornings, is what she says, and doesn't see why she should rush herself stupid.

'I took her last night,' Kelly says.

'Did you?'

He did. He remembers because he'd walked right through the middle of a party, people all over Chandos Road. His year and the year above.

'And I can't take her now,' he says. 'I'll be late.'

'No, you won't. Will you? How late?' his mum asks.

'Let the kid go to school,' his dad tells her, forking ketchup sideways.

'Yeah, go to school,' says Jason, lifting a triangle of toast up from Kelly's plate.

'Don't eat all his breakfast,' his mum says.

'I'm not.' Jason's voice is wadded.

'You are. And look at him.'

Jason looks at him. 'He's a thin chip,' he concludes, and folds the other half of Kelly's toast into his mouth. Jason has chest expanders, which Kelly is not supposed to take out of his room, and a *Rocky III* mirror stuck to the side of his wardrobe.

His mum lays an arm across the table, the tips of her fingers to the edge of Kelly's plate. 'You take the dog today,' she bargains. 'And tomorrow, I'll take her.'

'Why can't you take her today?' Kelly asks.

'Because I'm watching Manda.'

'Not very closely,' his dad says.

They all turn to find her. Manda has a bare, plump foot in the dog's water. The water wobbles in the metal bowl, overflowing in splashes. She shuffles forward on her bum, tipping the rim to the floor. Her small hand hits the puddle. Slap, slap, splat.

'Leave it,' Jason says, but not to Manda. He is talking to their dad, who is turning the TV over.

'I'm looking for the snooker,' his dad says.

'I was looking at footballs,' says Jason. 'Wasn't we, Kelly?' It was Sam Fox, no sound, all over the breakfast sofa. Now it is Ceefax. A black hole of numbers.

'Go away, the both of you,' his mum says, running Manda's hands under the tap. She dries them on the soft of her dressing gown. 'I thought you were starting down the Old Mill. Demolishing.'

'We're supposed to be stripping out electrics. If we ever leave the house.' Jason throws himself into their mum's chair. There is only space for three of them at this table. When someone stands up, someone else sits down. Sometimes his dad eats in the lounge with a tray tipping on his knee.

Jason is wearing his stonewashed jeans, the ones with elastic round the ankles that Kelly wants, and a very white t-shirt. He has folded a checked shirt on the side, which will be way too hot for later. Him and Kelly dress the same, which you wouldn't really know from Kelly's school uniform, except for maybe his hair. Kelly keeps his sideburns short and neat.

'There you go, Uncle Kelly,' his mum says, dropping Manda on him. Manda is round and warm, weighty with nappy. She twists around to see who he is and then turns back to the table. She begins to slap his plate, throwing the knife high. Her hand is like a starfish, all the short, blunt fingers spread.

'Does Manda want some nice potato waffle?' His mum points to his plate, the heel of a yellow lighter. 'Cut it up for her,' she tells Kelly. 'Smaller bits.'

'Mum, she don't want it. She don't like potato,' Jason says.

Manda keeps banging down her hand. It is making her laugh, the jumping plate.

'You want me to cut it up?' Kelly asks her. 'Shall we cut it all up into tiny bits and pieces?'

He retrieves his knife. She bangs her hand down on his, onto the plate, down on the table. He cuts and she bangs, and the potato waffle jumps about.

'Don't play with your food,' his mum says.

'You're always telling me to play with her.' Kelly sets his knife down, at a distance, and continues chopping with the blade of one finger. 'We're playing hoppy potato. Hop-hoppy potato frogger.'

'Well, stop playing. That's teaching her bad habits.'

'I need to go,' Kelly says.

'Yeah, you better get going,' nods Jason, getting to his feet, swinging up the van keys. 'Or you'll be late calling on Nessa.'

'Are you calling on Vanessa?' his mum asks, sitting down.

'No.'

'He is,' says Jason. 'Yes you are. Look at you! Look at your face! Red like that ketchup!'

'Leave him alone,' his mum says. 'It's all right, Kez, you call on who you want. Why shouldn't he call on Nessa?'

'I'm not calling on her.'

'Yes you are, my boy,' Jason says, rotating his hips.

'She goes early,' Kelly tells them. 'To call for Claire. She'll have left ages ago.'

'And so should you of,' his dad says.

'Claire's is miles out of Nessa's way,' his mum points out.

'Well, I'm going, Dad,' Kelly's brother says. 'Whether you're ready or not.'

His dad stands up, wipes his hands on the tea-towel and then throws it over his head. 'Manda!' he whistles, whipping it off.

A baby shriek. The throwing about of all her legs and arms.

'Give Daddy a kiss,' Jason says, crouching down. He taps the side of his face. Manda makes a wet smack on his cheek. Her hand pats his jaw, leaving something, potato mush, behind. Jason goes for her neck, a raspberry in the soft pleat of her skin. Her stout feet hammer the table, kicking up underneath.

'Be a good girl for Nani.'

Kelly lowers Manda back to the floor. 'She needs changing,' he tells his mum.

His mum waves her fag at her teacup, meaning: Will no one let me have my breakfast in peace? 'Take the dog,' she says out loud.

'Go to school,' his dad growls. He pulls out his wallet, looks inside and shuts it again, pushing it back into his trouser pocket, its worn, square slot.

'Yeah, get them brains to school,' says Jason, and lunges for Kelly's head, grinding his hair around.

Kelly fights him off, ducking away for his school bag.

'Maybe he's brainy because maybe he ain't yours,' his mum says to his dad.

'Woman,' his dad says, and waves a bent finger. Then, 'His brains don't come from your side. I know that much.'

Kelly repairs his hair in the back-door glass. The gel has held, mostly. Jason comes at him again, but only to push something, a packet, into his top blazer pocket.

'Don't give him fags,' his mum says. 'I told you that.'

'It ain't fags.'

'Give it him back, whatever it is,' his mum tells Kelly. 'You don't want it.' But Jason holds his hand over Kelly's pocket like he's trying to arrest his heart.

'It ain't nothing for you to worry about,' Jason says. 'Men's business.' He drops his hand. 'Share them out,' he tells Kelly. 'Share them with Nessa.'

His mum eyes them, Jason and then Kelly. 'Bugger off, all of you,' she says. 'Leave us women in peace.'

Kelly opens the door, only enough to fit himself and his bag through, but the dog slips in the other way, around his legs and into the kitchen.

'Bye, sorry,' he says, pushing the door shut.

He walks the short length of the back yard. Hard standing, and not a green thing growing. His dad worked twenty-five years in Parks and never wants to see another flowering annual. He laid the concrete himself and there are pawprints in it. Kelly would lift it. He would get rid of the dog and have a lawn for football and a picnic blanket. He opens the gate, swinging the soft wood behind him. A padded thump.

Two houses down, he stops to see what Jason has given him. Durex, a brand-new packet. He frowns and grins, a hot wring of embarrassment, and gives the box a rattle. And then he pushes it into his bag and slings the strap over his shoulder. If he gets going, he might even overtake Nessa. Otherwise there's no one, really. No one who he likes who will walk to school with him.

All his cousins, his old friends go to the other school and say he talks like a nob. He hadn't meant to pass the entrance exam. When he did, his mum said he could go to school where he liked, but his dad had put his foot down. 'It's them and us in this town,' he'd said. 'Like how it is this entire country. Why make it any easier for them to push you down?' 'Who voted you shop steward?' his mum had asked. Even so, she had made Kelly fill in the grammar-school forms and his dad cough up for the blazer.

He would like to walk with someone, though. Because something had been going on last night, the party spilling out all over the road. He had seen Miriam leaving, in work boots like his dad wears but smaller, and messed-up hair, and he had stopped with the dog, who threw herself down flat to the tarmac as if he'd made her walk all night. Then he'd seen Robin and Jonah come out, and Robin had said hello, even though she looked like she didn't want to, and Jonah hadn't, because he looked like he was off his face. Jonah never talks to Kelly anyway. Kelly had glanced around for Tin, but he hadn't seen her. And Robin asking what his dog was called was only pretending to be casual.

Kelly comes out of the alley at the main road and stops to cross. Tractor and top-heavy trailer. Backed-up commuters, driving straight over the new mini-roundabout. Now that his mum has suggested it, he could nip to the old graveyard for a fag. Only he's a bit late already, and the last time he went, the vicar had spooked up out of nowhere and told him to move. 'How would you like it if someone sat on your grave?' he'd said. 'Smoking and whistling badly.' Which was rude, but Kelly had got down anyway because he'd started on a coughing fit and didn't want to cark it right there and then, on actual dead bones. The vicar had pointed: *Alexander Something Somebody Claydon, Beloved of—* But he hadn't meant Kelly to read aloud. He had meant the lighter, an old one on the ground, not even Kelly's, sighing down to snatch it up and stalking off again, weaving through the tombs. The sliding, crumbling stones. Kelly's dad won't step foot in the place. 'There's not one angle true,' is what he says. Which is why Kelly goes there to smoke, but only during the day.

He sees a break in the traffic and darts through, coming out on the opposite pavement in front of Vanessa's house. Her new house, shiny white door. They could've painted it any colour they wanted, and they still chose white. Has she already left? The house doesn't tell him much, all the curtains net so he can't even see which room is hers. He's not going to knock, he decides. He doesn't want to get caught up chatting to her dad when he needs to get going sharpish. Her dad used to do hair for TV. Now he does cut 'n' perm at home. Ladies'. Kelly turns and begins to walk, fast, against the flow of the traffic.

The thing about parties is that he never gets to go. But school is different. They all have to be there, locked up together, trailing around as a class. And when something happens on the weekend, and he would bet on his life that something definitely has, it always comes out in the wash. Because what else is there to talk about at school? On a Monday morning. And he'll be right there when it does. Because he's going to make sure that he is.

6
Porch

8.07 a.m.

Warmth, Robin's own, and she does not want to relinquish it. The clock radio is talking to her about strikes and traffic, people made redundant, but what day it is she isn't sure.

Last night something went wrong. Or did it go right?

The disorder of the sheets holds her down, close in and weighty like something damp. She cracks an eye. Square red digits. 08:08. Kiss the clock. A school day. And not actually late.

Her uniform is under her bed. It probably is. She could put it on without standing up. Could she? She reaches an arm out and down and under. She is a robot crane. What is this she has? Her mohair jumper, still heavy from the river last night. And what else? She hauls it up. A shirt. Last week's and damp. Stained greeny-black from lying underneath her jumper. She will have to get up if this is her shirt. Her only option. She shifts onto one elbow and looks out over her bedroom floor, its rubbish heap of clothing. Things have gone to the laundry, but no one has been to pick them up.

She feels both wrong and right, and a vermouth vacancy in her stomach.

Robin considers the opposite wall. The collapse on the floor. She had heard it, she knows, seeing it now, somewhere in the half-sleep of last night; a poster detaching itself, one corner, and then a second, taking its time, the Blu Tack unanchored becoming a pulling weight and the whole thing folding itself down to the floor, slowly and then faster, a thick paper clatter.

Red lips, a tilted hat, the slatted shade of a blind. Once a poster has been crumpled like this it never looks as good.

And now, a rude green hole. And oversized leaves spreading out, fleshy. The triffid wallpaper was here when they moved in. With almost matching paint. There was talk of having it all stripped down, but her parents bought this house, she knows, because it didn't need a single thing doing to it. 'It feels like an office,' she had said when they first looked around. 'It's used as a conference centre,' the excited man had replied, as if that was a selling point.

She can wear this shirt, she decides, making herself get up out of bed. She just has to blow-dry it. Rub off the mud. Because she does want to go to school. The days she doesn't bother, she always regrets. She can't, in fact, sleep all day, and if she does get up to meet everyone afterwards, it's as if she's missed a year and no longer speaks the same language.

She casts around the swamp of clothes. Her skirt. Something dried to the hem which she starts to scratch off but stops, the radio changing to Blondie and making her think: Fuck it. A search for tights. She would prefer tights, even at this time of year. She doesn't like her legs exposed. And there are bites – the back of her knees – from midges drifting up and in from the bottom of the garden. She retrieves her blazer and threads an arm. Pain, thin like a wire, runs around the inside of her skull. She touches the spot, cautious, just beneath the crown. But here's her bag and she swings it up – there has to be something inside but the weight is not reassuring – and then, tugging on a heavy shoe, still damp, she knows. No one will call for her this morning. The thought itself is a physical stop. How had she not seen it coming? And the life, the drive of the day, already drifting, deserts her completely, draining thinly away.

No one will call for her. What she has done. What she has actually done. The fact of it abrupt. Because Tin will already know. The girls who don't like Robin, who call for Tin first, before Tin calls for her, they will already have told her. She can't then go to school. And yet she can't stay here. Today, she senses, is a bed day. Another one. Her parents are not getting up and the cats are scratching her door down. It isn't really a choice. Even going to school is better than staying. Or is it? She thinks that it probably is.

She crumples up the hem of her skirt, pulls out the waist of her tights, her pants just to see – nothing, clean, or at least not bloody – and drops her hand.

Slowly, she lets herself out of her room, pushing the door back against the claws and mewing. The cats follow her along the landing, spreading out over the two wings of the staircase. Ridiculous, this entrance hall, the set of all her parents' melodrama, and why they need a house this big she has no idea. Because the cats can throw up inside without anyone noticing for days? Because it reminds them of the hotels they like to stay in? If she could, she would check them in full-time. If anywhere would have them.

Through the lounge, the hanging fug of Embassys, and into the kitchen. She opens the fridge and shuts it again. From the bench, a mouthful of Dr Pepper, the liquid warm and flat. Swallowing, she lifts the can to her ear.

'Room service? Breakfast for one and make it snappy.'

But last night comes for her like a dream, half-submerged, half-forgotten, slowly piecing itself together, even against her will. It keeps coming, and with it, a grim acceptance. She is not someone to deny what she has done, to defend herself. If Tin condemns her, there is no point fighting. Only they won't call for her this morning. Tin won't. In fact, she won't. The wall of it is blank and absolute. A grief. And what she has done attaches to her back for everyone to stare at.

Robin feeds the cats. Plunging a hand into the Rice Krispies, she leaves the house. She could go the short way, but if questioned, what will she say? Better, then, to go the usual, the longer way around and over the bridge. Better that way, she decides, brushing her Rice-Krispie hand off on her blazer, and somehow feels relieved. Even so, she will wait a bit longer, where she usually sits, on the top step between two columns of the porch. She drops her bag to the stone and shivers, once, under the bright sun.

In front stands the old graveyard, an ancient, rubbed-brick boundary, banked high, and the tree roots grown down into the soft angles of the mortar. She doesn't look this way, the sun like a concussion; instead, she looks sideways, along the road, at Nicolas nosing around the curve on his bike.

'You've missed them. They've already gone the other way around,' he informs her. He slows down a bit and then speeds up, looking pleased. A loose, metal rattle.

'Yea-ah,' Robin answers, watching his pedalling legs, his trousers wrapped and clipped. He turns into St Rumbold's Lane, his briefcase, something else, wobbling over the back wheel.

She pulls her legs in and under. Not quite yet. She is flattening the crust of lichen from the base of the railing, the sulphur yellow, the pale blue-green. And when she is finished, she will stand up. And then she will walk to school.

Bicycle clips, she thinks, rolling the dry flakes sideways and off the edge of the stone. That level of equipment is unnecessary, surely, like being in the Scouts.

She looks at her empty bag, plucks her tights from her shins, a dusty snap, and pulls herself up to her feet. The mess on the back of her shirt, the sore of her head, the stir in her guts. Her river-water mouth. And not even Nicolas is stopping. Is she really going to school? On her own? She turns, and takes in the big, blank front of the house. She will go, and she steps down onto the path to prove it. She can face Tin. It might even be a relief to face her. Tin is cruel, but never more than she has to be.

7
Staffroom

8.43 a.m.

Miss Harper looks at the clock. She looks at the low table in front of her, at the still, cold skin of coffee. She feels untethered, like a balloon let go.

She would like to see Colin, Mr Austen, even just for a moment before she goes down.

She should go down. The children don't know. And things grow restive in the cloakrooms without her. The children don't know. But Mr Gomme will tell them. Soon, in assembly, with everyone standing together.

Matron comes in and stares around. She stops just behind Miss Harper's chair and controls a sigh, as if what has happened has been designed to complicate her morning. Miss Harper leans forward, her elbows to her knees.

Matron has a locker here, which she doesn't need, having a whole room downstairs with cupboards to herself, but she visits every morning to keep a stake in the staffroom. Mr Dalton, sitting opposite, pegs his nostrils shut with a finger and thumb. He is prone to sneezing in the morning. He stares down at his marking – geometry, it looks like – without turning the pages.

The door bangs. Miss Harper looks up, but it is Dr Cole coming in and Matron bumping out again. Mr Austen is never in early. Which is not the same as being in late. Or being unreliable. Not exactly. Mr Austen drives most mornings, a shaky orange Escort, and sometimes Dr Cole accepts a lift. But not today. Dr Cole stands alone, his back to the sink, his big head down. He looks unmade; more, even, than usual. Like he hasn't been home. Like he hasn't even got one.

She will wait two more minutes and then she will go. She is usually down ten minutes before now, walking the corridor. The clock ticks noisily around. The staffroom is never this silent. Almost everyone is here, standing about or moving quietly. Mr Betts leans with his head to his locker, his shoulders shaking. Miss Wright comes to the table for sugar, and then comes back for the spoon. She wears a tent of fabric, its tiny flowers a summer meadow, pinks and browns and greens. Her round calves move past, the teeth of the tights rasping together, and something on her dress tinkles like little silver bells.

Miss Harper is wearing the pleated skirt and woodland-green jacket. She had felt the need to match together. The jacket has removeable shoulder pads, which she had indeed removed this morning, then poppered back in, before taking them out a second time and putting them in her tights drawer. 'You want to feel in fashion, but you still want to walk facing forwards through a door.' That was the joke the fitting-room lady had made, which Miss Harper had repeated to herself this morning, trying to buck herself up and out of the house. The woman had picked up Miss Harper's hair, moving it one way and then the other, looking at her over her shoulder in the mirror. 'You could make something of it, actually,' she had told her. 'And a bit of frosted lipstick.' But Miss Harper has done expensive hair and cheap makeup. She prefers to wash her face and grow her hair down her back, like it is now. A dark waterfall of comfort.

The door bangs again. Sue Sharpe, a bag full on each shoulder, pushes in and stamps across to the lockers. The delayed entrance of cigarettes, their flat, singed taint. A rummaging around: things in her locker in rustling packets.

'What's this? Who put this in here?' Miss Sharpe barks, pulling something out and thrusting it sideways.

It is a small picture, a postcard maybe, in a frame. From here, Miss Harper sees only a blur of bright colour, blue and orange. A sunset? It might be anything.

Miss Sharpe slams the locker door shut and Miss Harper jumps. A palpable violence, but she is grateful for it. The definite noise, the solidity of force is something to fix herself to.

'I'm not doing assembly,' Miss Sharpe announces, eyeballing around. 'I'm not standing through it. The whole performance.'

'A fair decision,' says Mr Betts, lifting his head. 'The right one, probably.' He turns into the room. His face is pale and his corduroy trousers are rubbed in the wrong direction. In lots of wrong directions. A field of grass, pushed every which way by the wind, all down the front of his legs.

Miss Sharpe eyes him. 'I'll be where I usually am,' she says. 'If anyone wants me.' Which means around the side of the art block, Miss Harper knows, chin out, artist's squint and her feet in a litter of fag butts. The door bangs shut.

'What does she want?' Mr Dalton asks, zipping up his PE jacket and unzipping it again. 'A detention?'

The clock ticks on.

Miss Harper gets to her feet. Dr Cole comes over and stands square in front and looks her in the face. His big body, his hands and arms, his beautiful dark suit hang crumpled from the girdle of his shoulders.

'Okay to go?' he asks.

She wasn't, but she is now. She picks up her lab coat and protective glasses, her unwritten list from the floor. 'I am,' she affirms, but it comes out like a question.

8

The Hall

8.50 a.m., assembly

Miriam feels a sense of arrival, clattering down from the bus, stepping into the Lane. An entrance. Here we come, she thinks, shaking back her hair. Here we come, streaming up Springfield Lane. The kids from the other school, at the concrete blocks, split abruptly off. Left turn. She feels them go like a gown dropped to the floor. They are not supposed to speak to the other school. Not on the bus, not in the Lane. Not anywhere in town with their uniforms on. Gomme's rule. But he is not, today, in the Lane to enforce it. They continue – she and Davy, the remaining half of the bus – under the shade of the trees. Leaner, Miriam thinks, fronting the cool air. Revealed for what we are.

They turn in at the back gates, absorbing a knot of boarders from the girls' house, passing the gym, the swimming pool, the art block, and funnel into the cloakrooms, girls to one side, boys to the other, where they exchange their outdoor shoes for indoor ones and hang up their bags.

Tin is already here on a slatted bench, her head tilted back and her eyes uncommitted. Does she know? It's hard to tell. And Miriam is not about to ask. Sometimes Tin is just like this, dark and contained, distilled, before she ignites like a bonfire. A football hooligan. Other times she remains unconcerned, a queen in a play, a bored Cleopatra, as if whatever has happened has nothing to do with her. Miriam checks the cloakroom, behind the stands of pegs, but Robin is nowhere to be seen. And there is no one here this morning. No one to confiscate their earrings, their luminous socks, or tell them to tie their ties the other way. Miriam hops around, a black AirWair in her hand. She grows celebratory, bumping into Tin's leg, someone else's shoulder, Vanessa's, who jolts away, protecting her hair – new perm, rigid with hairspray – until the tiny fuss of Miss Harper arrives with a clipboard and harries them all out into the corridor.

They push so they are tightly packed, chest to back, along the narrow dark.

'Robin's here.' Hot breath on Miriam's neck. Miriam turns. Robin is watching from the shadow of the stairwell.

She waits for the last of the boys to pass and joins the end of the queue, moving in the provisional way she has. I am not someone you should look too closely at, Robin's slide and retreat says. I am someone not entirely ready to be here.

'Robin's at the back,' Miriam relays to Tin.

Tin, reaching behind, lifts Miriam's wrist and wipes it across her own forehead. Miriam lets the borrowed hand go limp. What a drag, Tin's mime says. Tin drops the lifeless arm and Miriam reclaims it, shaking it out. They all shunt down. Tin is going to let Robin sweat it out, Miriam sees. Which is not at all the same as letting her off.

They pass portraits of headmasters, old men lost in gowns and varnish. They pass Chloe, atheist, year above, and Lisa, Jewish, two years below, standing where they do each morning to wait assembly out, their backs against the opposite wall, Gomme's wall, so the women in the office can keep a watch. We're all atheists really, Miriam thinks, and crosses eyes at Lisa, her sister attendant from the school play, Iras to her Charmian, who crosses them back. With the exception of James. But then who can be bothered with taking a stance? And assembly is getting to stare around, as well as hymns, and prefects dying on stage over and over, the tasty fuck-up of making them read out Latin.

She considers James, two in front, his shoulders square to the wall and everyone else turned sideways. It is James all over to find a Church of England school, then insist on being Catholic. His colour is high, his long face downcast. He looks like a saint in a niche, a carving stuck to the French cathedral she is always being taken to stand in front of and can't care about at all. She suspects him of praying, of getting his word in with his God first, like a shield, before he gets shoved the way of everyone else, all the C of E heathens, along the glossy darkness of the corridor.

They pass the board painted with the names of entrants to Oxford and Cambridge. In some years, three or four successes, in other years, only one. Tin unfolds an arm. She has scratched most of the gold leaf from her mother's name, leaving only the red underpainting. In the dark, Miss Harper close, Tin's quick, daily vandalism electrifies Miriam. She'll finish on the next pass, Miriam notes, and feels the satisfaction. Tin sticks out her tongue and licks the end of her finger. Left-handed, Tin. Which always, somehow, comes as a surprise.

They nudge past the prefects' room, rounding the corner of the canteen, push through the folding doors and emerge into the length and breadth and height of the hall, where they assemble in rows, a neat division down the centre like an aisle in a church, a line mown through long grass.

It is spring, but the order for Shirtsleeves has not been given and they are still in their woollen blazers. The sun pushes in and the hall sweats. Sweat and spray deodorant. We like Impulse, Miriam thinks, drawing it in, the exotic one with black flowers on the canister. We like the disco-reek of Brut. She stands in close to Tin and feels the pull. Wherever Tin is, eyes turn her way, seeking her out. Even sixth formers. Miriam moves her leg sideways, measuring their feet, lining up for a three-legged race. The heat comes off Tin's side, her thigh and arm and shoulder. They are mismatched. Tin is tall, long-limbed; Miriam has barely grown since primary school and still wears shoes in children's sizes.

The bell rings. He is late. Pushing erupts in fourth form and one of the twins, the blonde ones who specialise in breakdance and graffiti, is sent out, smirking backwards. A hymnbook drops, a dead thud to the polished wood.

'Get lost, Kelly,' Miriam says, kicking, as he gropes for it between her ankles. By her feet, the small, definite impressions of stiletto heels, breaking the varnish. They are not allowed stilettos. That will be from parents' evening, or the school play, a precise but wandering trail. She pulls her own hymnbook out from her inside pocket, fanning the pages, cracking the spine, the paper membrane-thin.

And then, finally, in waddles Gomme.

'Settle down now,' Miss Harper warns from the back.

Gomme stands in the centre of the stage, swaying slightly. His stomach, the white shirtfront, pushes through the black of his gown. He lifts a hand, smoothing down his old-man hair. They wait for him to announce the hymn.

'It is with deep regret –' he begins, in his Founder's Day voice, and opens his eyes unnaturally wide, as if surprised. 'It is with the very –' His white hands paddle the air, then make a grab at his lapels. 'It falls to –' It is his mouth, now, that stretches wide, as if someone is forcing his jaw bones in different directions. 'Mr Ardennes. That Mr Ardennes. Passed from us. Pronounced dead last night. Cold. That is, very early in the morning –'

A giggle, a single silver bubble, rises up from them to the surface. On stage, where the deputy heads stand, a vacancy. Mr Ardennes appears to Miriam then: his slight frame bent; his head to one side as if listening. Miss Wright in her flowery dress, almost on the edge of the platform, pulls a tissue from her pocket and blows her nose. But who will listen to us now? Who will stand, as Mr Ardennes stood, between us and the Mad Penguin? Miss Wright shakes her head. She doesn't seem to know. The slim emptiness asserts itself. He is not here. Mr Ardennes is not standing where he is supposed to be.

A soft hissing begins. Who can say where exactly it starts? It rises from them as a body, single and continuous.

Miriam watches Gomme go loose and a shudder pass through him. A body of water shaken.

Miriam turns to Tin, who is always distinct, even in confusion, but Tin has gone.

'Proceed to your first lesson,' Miss Harper tells the hall. 'Go on. Walking quietly now.'

9
Bike Sheds

9.07 a.m.

Nicolas lifts his briefcase higher and scoots around the gym. It is tight, but he forgot to pick up his viola after assembly and has to have it with him for later. And he doesn't want to leave it in the cloakrooms any longer than he has to, just in case. If he's quick, he will get to first lesson with everybody else, or not too far behind, because they all go the slow way round. And anyway, they're not even trying to be on time.

He circumnavigates Derek from Maintenance, who is shaking a ladder at the wall with more vigour than seems usual, and steps up onto the main path. All in all, even with Gomme being late to assembly and then the announcement – no hymns and no prayers, not one, which is odd, now he thinks about it. Even so, Nicolas is fairly confident that he has, in fact, a little time in hand.

'Where are you running off to?'

It is Tin, idling in the bike sheds. Where she shouldn't be. She is on the saddle of a bike, her face in the sun, her elbows resting on the handlebars. His handlebars, in fact, he sees, as he approaches. His bike. The bike his cousin has grown out of.

'I forgot my viola.'

'Your viola? Why even bother with the viola?'

He stops, arrested by her question. She is looking directly at him, dark eyebrows high, waiting for an answer. She has mistaken him, it occurs to Nicolas, for someone she takes an interest in.

'Why not take up the harpsichord if you want to be unusual? Or the harp?'

Her tone is unhurried, discursive almost, but Nicolas is more than aware of the time. He starts to explain, in brief, the practical difficulties of the pedal harp, not least the expense—

'Or,' she continues, 'the fretless bass. That's an instrument for the player who wants to stand out.'

'I'll think about it,' he promises, and then, with a little lunging rush in his chest: 'I would rather you didn't sit on my bike.'

'Would you? Why?'

He hasn't got a reason, he would just rather she didn't. He checks on his laces, a downward glance, and swaps his briefcase to the other hand. 'The air might leak out of the tyres again, and I didn't bring my bicycle pump. I don't always bring it.'

She stands. 'Better?'

It's not, really. She has only raised her seat. Her legs still straddle his crossbar. Standing upright, she is half taken in by the slanting shade of the roof. Her hair shines blacker.

Hadn't there been something in primary school? About Tin's father. Or quite possibly her mother. Something they were all supposed to remember but without talking about it. In any case, Tin had always been – Nicolas has always found her reasonably difficult to—

She swings a foot back and over and steps away from his bike completely. He smiles, by mistake. It is the relief, essentially, at not being attacked.

'Enjoy your lesson,' she says from deeper in, the shade of a rafter crossing the bridge of her nose.

'You too,' he says, and hurries away. You too? He didn't mean to say that. He meant to say that viola is not now, it's a bit later. And that he is going to first lesson directly, after he goes to the cloakrooms, and that she should probably be going there too.

He might also have taken the opportunity to remind Tin that she had forgotten to call on Robin this morning, something he knows because he had cycled past Robin's front steps. But Tin might very well be waiting for Robin now, he sees, in the bike sheds. Although, admittedly, Tin generally doesn't wait around for anybody.

Nicolas passes a sixth former, a tall one with a narrow suit and flat-top hair. He hears him behind, his low mumble, saying something to Tin, and her saying something in reply and making him laugh. Ringing metal, a strike to a bike frame. It's not at me, he thinks, the laughter, drawing the door back. Or maybe it is. He starts along the corridor, spurred on by the thought of his unattended viola.

It is not, in point of fact, actually his viola. He rents it from Steeple's, his parents do. If they keep paying every month for a few more years, it will be his, but he's not sure that he wants to own it. The bridge slips and the body has a crack in it that he can hear but can't see. He can't find. He has informed Steeple's, but the plum-faced assistant with the dandruff shoulders says he can neither hear nor see it, this 'putative' crack. Which tells you everything you need to know about why the man shouldn't be left in charge of a music shop. Or not the instruments section, anyway. Perhaps the score and books, the silent—

A jolt of alarm. A dark shape blocking the corridor. Gomme. Then the voice booms out and he sees that it is Dr Cole, the big-shouldered shadow, the swinging head, standing at the top where the three steps go up to the school office. Nicolas, having stopped in fright, starts again to hurry.

'No,' Dr Cole is saying, 'we're not doing that anymore. Not today. Maybe not again.' The two ladies from the office look at him, their hips pressed together. One of them, the younger lady, pushes her big butterfly glasses up her nose. The other one, Mrs Poole, has the sort of fringe that goes all the way around her head like gas swirling about itself in space. The Princess Di, that style is called, Nicolas knows, because he has an older sister. Her name is also Diana, as it happens, but very different hair.

It is useless to reason with the ladies from the office. They only take orders from Gomme and if they don't want to give you something, for example a second home-work diary, they won't, as he has found out to his own cost. But Dr Cole is new, and a deputy headmaster, so he probably hasn't learnt about that yet. Nevertheless, it is lucky for Nicolas that it is Dr Cole rather than Gomme standing here blocking the corridor, because Dr Cole won't punish him for being late, especially if Nicolas explains, as he now starts to do – Dr Cole doesn't even look down at him. He merely waves him along with an arm, stirring the dark corridor air. Nicolas edges around and then speeds past the office, past Gomme's wall – which more accurately is only part of a wall, essentially a partition, so Gomme can leap out on anyone he spies misbehaving – and turns into the cloakrooms, boys' side, with some relief.

Where he left his case, on the far benches, had been relatively clear this morning but is now a cascade of PE bags, of tossed-about shoes and cagoules, lost and abandoned property. Mr Ward does this to things not on pegs, Nicolas knows. He sweeps them all up together and throws them into a corner. Which can be more disorderly, in actual fact, than when things are all spread out, especially if you have purposely left something on a bench to come back for later, not to mention the potential damage that might result, especially to a musical instrument. It is lucky that his is a hard case, even if it is a ludicrously old one, taped together but still falling to pieces.

He sets his briefcase down and begins to push stuff to the sides. Battered, greasy sports-bags with graffiti all over. *THE CLASH*, fading, *Two-Tone* with checks, like a truncated chess board, and zip flaps gaping. As he picks them up, lumping them out of the way, something flies out and lands with a rattle on the tiles. A packet. He reaches a hand and turns the box over. An attractive man and woman in matching denim bottoms, but subjected, in his opinion, to an unnaturally yellow photographic filter. He knows what these are. And he knows what they're called, the slang name, although he can't quite at this moment remember what it is. What he doesn't know is where they jumped out from, which of these bags. *Smash It Up! Smash It UP!* This one seems likely, being on top of the rest. He pushes the packet of contraceptives down firmly and pulls the zip around as best he can, closing in an awkwardly sized lunchbox. Then he opens *Smash It Up!* again and retrieves the packet. Springing the locks of his briefcase, he transfers the box to an inside pocket and presses the briefcase shut. What on earth for? he asks himself, beginning once again to excavate the heaped coats and bags. What does he need them for? He doesn't need them! But the good-looking woman and man in matching jeans . . . they just look happy, carefree and glowing yellow under the unbroken cellophane. He locates his viola case, tugging it out by the corner, does a swift about-turn and takes off down the corridor.

The corridor is empty. Dr Cole has finished his meeting, it appears. The phone in the office is ringing and the ladies are letting it ring. But halfway along Nicolas is suddenly unsure. He hesitates, right at the exit to the art block, and stares down the long darkness, back in the direction of the bike sheds. Could Tin not have done something worse, more damage, standing up and showing off to the sixth-form boy? And especially if Nicolas annoyed her by not answering her musical enquiries properly. The clang of a bike frame. The oily slump of a disengaged chain. There are many quick ways to interfere with a bike and inconvenience its rider. Well, there's nothing he can do about it now. He is already late. And Tin has started whatever it is she might be doing. Finished it, even. He can go back at playtime, that is, breaktime to check. He'll do that, he nods, and sets off again, fast but not running, his briefcase knocking one shin, his viola the other.

Why even bother with the viola? How is that in any way a question worthy of serious consideration? And anyway, he has pretty much memorised the Brahms, should he ever be called upon to play it. And he does understand it, whatever Mr Prendergast said last time. It's just that he can't play it any less like a metronome. What Mr Prendergast has failed to appreciate is that music is mathematical. That's what it is. You have to count and be on time, otherwise you're not playing what is written.

He shoulders open the art-block door and heads for the stairs. Ground-level boys' toilets, a swimming-pool smell. And Whipsnade Zoo. Higher up, warm dust and spray fixative, to stop things smudging. He is not by any means the last. There are others still coming in behind him or hanging about on the stairs. The bell has gone! What on earth is everybody thinking?

'Cancer,' he hears. Someone sitting with their legs stretched out over the half landing.

'You think that or you know that?'

'That's it?' Miriam asks, a flight above. 'He's dead. Now off you go to your next lesson.'

'What did you expect?' James replies. Miriam shakes her hair out, directly in Nicolas's path, then flings it back over her shoulders. Nicolas turns sideways to overtake.

Well, he can see Miriam's point. Mr Prendergast might have played something solemn on the piano. Or at least asked Nicolas to. Because Nicolas's sight-reading is really quite good now, as it has to be, naturally, if he's going to take Grade 8.

But yes, Mr Ardennes died last night. That certainly is shocking news. Or very early this morning. In truth, he would rather people were precise about the time, which actually can be very exactly measured. Mr Ardennes has died. Only Nicolas can't quite – All the rushing about to get his instrument and so forth, and nobody taking the time to explain. It is terribly sad, he can see, and will have all sorts of ramifications, knock-on delays in the timetable and so on, particularly for sixth-form students, who are, properly speaking, Mr Ardennes' especial area of concern. But then a death, an actual living – It can't be helped, he decides, taking the stairs two at a time and creasing up his trousers. He for one has done what he can to get to first lesson on time.

He stops on the threshold, the gloomy back of the room. Miss Sharpe is not even talking yet, which is good news, and the air inside smells of fresh cigarettes, as if she's only just arrived herself. And there is Robin, standing by the far window, looking a bit forgotten-about even now. Of course, he can still remind Tin about this morning and she can apologise to Robin if she needs to. He will find a quiet art-room moment, he thinks, stepping in, looking about for Tin. If, that is, Tin turns up at all.

10

The Art Room

9.15 a.m., lesson 1

Miss Sharpe waits for them to deliver themselves from the shady half of the room, under the arch and into the front. They look lost, she sees. Some of them do. They wander in like they've come by mistake and stand about in the shifting, filtered sunlight. The windows need a clean, but she has put Derek from Maintenance off for a month, preferring this mobile, delicate light to outright radiance and clarity.

'Pebbles,' she says, after a while, indicating the low tables. At the centre of each, a small gathering of stones. 'Get a piece of paper,' pointing at the guillotine. 'One chalk, one charcoal each.' She comes around and begins opening boxes.

Sue Sharpe is two years from retirement. This morning, crossing some kids as she came out of the newsagents, three packets of Benson & Hedges and three Mars bars, she had felt ashamed. Her body seems to need more and more. One of the boys had asked for a fag and the girl had switched her eyes away. But given how she had woken up this morning, the phone a detonation in her heart, it's a wonder she hadn't needed more, something considerably stronger, to get herself up the hill. Miss Harper had delivered her 'terrible news', and not un-gently, at the same time impressing on Miss Sharpe the importance of coming into school. And Miss Sharpe had come, almost on time, like a bought fool. She had even thanked Miss Harper for phoning. 'I suppose it comes with the job, doesn't it?' Emma Harper had said. 'No. It comes with being human,' she had replied. Which was pompous of her.

She slides the chalk out of the box and rolls it over the table. The class crowds around, greedy despite everything. It is always like this when she brings something new from the cupboard. And quite right, who wouldn't want them? Sheeny like pills, the sticks make a dry chink when they tap together. Their polished sides appeal like silk. She unwraps the charcoal and lays it down in its cradle of paper. Such blackness, absorbing even the air around it.

To get through this hour and then the next hour and the next one – She lifts her eyes from the table and summons herself into the room.

'Dearly beloved.' It is Thomasin, coming in late. Tin they call her, as if they can't resist the taste of the word. Tin. 'You've got cat hair on your arse,' she says, brushing past Robin.

Robin turns to the windows. Already, shouts from the playing fields.

'Robin!' A boy's voice. 'How was your weekend?'

Miss Sharpe regards Robin's back, the two sticks of chalk she holds to the side of her face. Dreamy, that child. And something different about her this morning. She has grown taller, perhaps. Wider and then taller, as they do at this age. As some of them do, a sudden shift to new proportions. But it is true that Robin is scruffy. Her fine hair lifts static from the back of her head and her uniform is something wrong that has happened to her. And yes, even from here, a tight circle of hair on her skirt where a cat has wound itself up to sleep. Though Robin is better now than she was. When she first came, no one could believe her parents were so wealthy. In the staffroom, malnutrition had been mentioned.

'Well, sit down,' she tells them. 'We're already fifteen minutes in.'

'That's not our fault, Miss,' somebody says.

'I didn't mention fault.'

'But aren't you sad?'

Miss Sharpe scans the class, looking for the voice. The small, pinched-face boy – him, Kelly – usually. They have every right to be shocked. Sad, even, the ones who knew him. Which some of them did. Thomasin did. What they don't have, what she will not grant them, is the licence to exploit what has happened for their own entertainment. She points at the tables. She pats the pocket of her jeans and eyes the clock. 'Millions of years for the sea to shape a pebble. You have half an hour. Sit down. Draw what you see.'

There isn't a seating plan. Just sit with your friends, she says, if pressed. While you have friends.

'Can we sit in the back room?'

'No, Kelly.'

'Why not?'

Because it's dark. Because the sixth-form tables are there. Because that's where I go to get away from you.

'Why not, Miss?'

'Because, evidently, the pebbles have been arranged in here,' says a boy with luggage – a briefcase and a violin – gulping his words down. Nicolas, his name is. Or something similar.

Kelly lifts the flat of his hand and jerks it around, a robot waiter with a tray. It's supposed to be her, perhaps, pointing out tables, or is it Nicolas he's mimicking?

The others ignore him, collecting paper, sticks of chalk, spreading out, then settle down in clusters. It might yet go the other way, she knows, and easily, to rioting and laughter. But maybe even they won't fight it, the strong pull into silence. Not her imposition: the day's own request, or so it seems to her. Only Kelly remains on his feet, knocking into chairs.

'Robin! Come over here, don't be shy. There's plenty of room beside Tin.'

There is never room beside Tin, it occurs to Miss Sharpe. Except today there is a definite push, a magnetic repulsion, keeping Robin on the opposite side of the room. Well, friends are more like enemies at certain times, in certain lives. In Thomasin's, she suspects.

'Robin!' The persistence of that boy. 'Come on! We all want to hear about your Sunday night.'

Back in her corner, Miss Sharpe opens the register. Robin stands by the window and then sits down alone on a table of maths boys.

They draw the sugar paper to them. They frown at the assembled pebbles. The stones are grey, round-backed, seamed with white; the type you pick up on an English beach. That she picked up. Their arms, right hands, left hands, begin to move. Softness enters the room on bare feet. The rasp of chalk, of charcoal against rough paper. Once in a while, the tinkle of charcoal snapping and falling, a hidden flaw, burnt away to lightness. And through the open windows, the smell of the earth rising. Ozone from a clear blue sky.

Miss Sharpe looks out from her desk. Her desk is a rampart, all her paints set out around the edges and her brushes, fine to broad, in pots. Until a year ago she still had some of the brushes her mum had used in the pottery. But brushes disappear one by one and sometimes whole fistfuls together. Which would have pleased her mum. She had been a great one for doling things out.

She looks out at the class and down at her register. Robin – yes, and Nicolas, for all the world an accountant in miniature, the inflated knot of his tie, the sharp-cornered briefcase. Claire, not perhaps so bad this morning, considering, and Vanessa beside her. It's the new perm, just to the fringe, giving Vanessa that look of alarm, or is it? And that thin irritant of a boy – 'Why not, why not?' – Kelly. She marks them down, one by one, in plump 2B pencil. Crossing the room – Miriam, blonde as straw, her face laid down almost horizonal, and Tin, Thomasin Carmichael, dark. And a peculiar dark. A dark in the eyes far beyond pigment.

She has seen Thomasin walking the school with Jonah, the lunchtime circuit, handsome together like twins and he a puppy, despite the fact he is – what? Two years above. He is one of the bad kids, no question, but the kind you can't help liking, and he has made a home for himself in the art room. He likes, she knows, to shut himself in the cupboard and give himself a headrush with fixative. And Thomasin – but Thomasin is staring straight at her. Such calculated arrogance. Obscene, almost, in a child. James – yes, on the end of the same table.

Miss Sharpe looks at James, his long, austere face, his skin pinked as if stung by the wind, and sees the whole parade of brothers and sisters, one every other year all the way up the school and into university. All clever, and he the youngest and the cleverest. What had it been last week? 'I'm going to retire to a bigger town,' she'd been saying, amusing herself, 'or else to the middle of nowhere.' 'What, all the way to Aylesbury?' he'd come back, sharp as a whip. But only in words. He can barely hold a crayon. Religious, of course, the Connells. Being Irish, the parents at least. And not in the way of ballooning altars and chubby angels. A bare, shelterless faith. A marooning in the North Sea. And this morning, James unusually silent, as well he might be, scratching away like he's trying to see through the table.

She continues, head by head, marking them in. The boys like boys; the girls already almost women. She feels for the boys – or does she? So quickly and comprehensively outgrown.

She finds, as she descends her list, stray parents, the ones she knows, looming forwards, anxious or grinning. She finds herself enumerating professions. Lawyers, both mother and father, and a civil servant. Bank person? Not sure, not sure. Military, probably, all the boarders' parents, or diplomatic service. Something to do with hotels. It's surprising how many men don't bother to come to parents' evening. Leave it to women, then, but don't complain if we tell your kids the truth. Policeman – unusual that – two teachers, primary school both, and a manufacturer of small engine parts employing half the town. Thomasin's parents? A blank. And Robin's? Something in South America. Pipelines and cables. Or logging. Something that doesn't bear any scrutiny. At parents' evening, she had sensed them approaching, the way one drinker and smoker finds out another. Two sets of watery blue eyes. And that boy, head and shoulders above every boy else – Davy. Voice like milk, hands like great gloves. The soft brown eyes of him. Could he look any more like a farmer's son? A rugby lad of course, his meaty arms and legs, but not a usual one. And a good artist. Or might be.

Something in front of the sun, a cruise ship of a cloud, and a sudden drop into shadow, the whole room going dark. Almost instantly, the cloud rides away and light returns, warm and granular through dusty glass. She closes the register, her forearms beached on top.

She has, in fact, no idea what Davy's parents do, but farming – it's not impossible, even now. A few farmers' kids still come in from the villages. Smallholders, not landowners, a distinction that her dad had impressed upon her. But here . . . She isn't sure there is much of a difference. And there are landowners too, in truth. And another sort of affluence pouring in from who knows where, the Stock Exchange, in all probability, the big cars and bored expressions, traders, yuppies, whatever those parents are, and even more in the sixth form. Flotations on the free market, buying things up. Where she is from, they are closing things down. Pits and pubs, half the high street.

She looks sideways at her small, square board. A beachscape. Rocks and a shoreline, the half-painted humps like cobbles. Gouache is a concentration of colour, and no allowance for second thoughts.

'Have you already done Light, Shade and Pebbles?' she asks.

'No,' they say, mostly.

Robin is back at the window. Davy gets up and goes to stand beside her. Despite his size, he moves, Miss Sharpe sees, with ease and almost without sound.

'She won't be there today,' he says.

An exaggerated sigh. 'Obviously,' says Kelly, craning around in his chair.

Across the playing fields, the other school where Mrs Ardennes teaches. She won't be there today, no. She'll be at home. And what sort of exile that is, Sue Sharpe can only imagine.

Grey stones on grey tables. Millions of years. Charred twigs bent a little this way, that way as the tree has grown. Fingers blackened and whitened.

'Use the dust to soften the shadows,' Miss Sharpe instructs.

At the far end of the room Claire is crying. They are used to Claire crying.

Vanessa stands up and makes for the front. 'She says she doesn't even know if her real dad's dead or—'

'Yes, okay. Walk her round to Matron's room,' Miss Sharpe says, and rummages up a pass.

Their feet sound down the stairs and out under the stilts of the art block. This room, a box of passing light and shadow, rubbing the backs of pebbles.

—

Sue Sharpe comes back in, lodging herself on the side of her desk, and holds up a stick of chalk.

'Limestone cliffs,' she says. 'Ground and compressed.' After a fag break, she likes a chat. And they do too, really, despite their sliding eyes. 'With a new stick of chalk, you can draw a line of great precision. Look at those edges.'

They look. She looks: a white cylinder between stout yellow fingers, its end a perfect circle, like something from a geometry book. She fumbles for charcoal.

'Willow makes the best charcoal. At least for drawing. Where I come from there are charcoal makers. Or were. Men and women living outside with the kilns.'

'We know all about where you come from, Miss,' Kelly says. 'Where you come from there are humpy hills, each with trees on top, sticking straight up into the sky like a shaving brush.'

'Yes,' she says, but as if she is saying no. She'd like to forget Kelly's performance, his hands running up and down a shapely trunk, his thin hips twitching and her walking in. She is passionate about trees, she admits it. But in any case, Trees, Hills and Mass was last term. 'When I was ill in Paris, years ago when I was a student, my landlady, Madame Sorrel, gave me charcoal to eat, little lumps of it.'

'My mum gave my brother's girlfriend charcoal,' Kelly says. 'When she got pregnant. To stop her chucking up.'

He grins at her, wet lips and little gappy teeth, but his eyes look washed out, as if by genuine grief after all. She turns away, leaning to the shelves behind her desk, one leg up as a cantilever, and dislodges a book. It is her own shock, perhaps, which makes her want to shut him down, to prise his fingers off. Off what? Her trees and hills?

Off whatever it is that happened last night, this morning, which she has yet to comprehend.

'Hans Holbein' – flicking through to find the drawings, turning the pages out. 'Look at his line. Every minute shift of light, of plane. Of temperature, even.' She pans the book slowly, taking them all in, then turns the page. Young men and young women in courtly uniform. Sober and present. Without defence. 'This is what it is to *see* another human being. The alertness, the sensitivity required. And he's only got what you've got. Black and coloured chalk. A bit of ink. Almost unfathomable, how he does what he does.'

She hands the book left and stands up, catching sight of the great blue glory of the sky. Today of all days, over the playing fields, the trees of the town, such blatant beauty. And barely a mile away . . . What to do? Take round a cake, some wine? Not cake. A stew? A woman to appreciate a practical gesture, Lyn Ardennes, for all her style. Her blunt hair, the fine intelligence of her face, the way she stands, both ready and relaxed. Miss Sharpe has seen her, at more school functions that she cares to count, turn and throw a look like a line across the room to her husband. Anchored, private, charged with irony. They seemed, if such a thing is possible, a happy couple. A couple who, in middle age, had remained alive to one another. Had.

Childless. And that now a small relief.

'Are you *enceinte*?' Madame Sorrel had asked, over-looking her bed. 'Because I can't have Madonna and Child here.' It was an art joke of sorts, and maybe not unkind.

Miss Sharpe begins to move between the tables, behind the bent backs. Blazers, even today. The smell of warm animal. They pause their hands as she passes or, sometimes, intensify their scribbling. Sometimes, feeling her watching, a blush flowers on the back of a neck. It always surprises her, this eloquence of skin. She slows at Robin. From above, she can see what she couldn't see before, her face marbled pink and white, a little too plump, too rounded, like something fished out of water. And natural enough. The wonder is we're not all weeping. And the back of her hair, a fine ginger blonde, an old-fashioned colour – Hans Holbein red-gold, in fact – but something dark in it this morning and matted.

'Give the stones at the front more definition,' she advises. 'More than the ones at the back. Don't be afraid to use pressure.'

The girl swallows. Maybe she nods. And wipes her chin on her sleeve. I'm a dead trunk, Sue Sharpe thinks, moving away. A dry-stone wall. She reaches the window, turns and rests the back of her sacrum against a cold radiator. She doesn't feel like weeping. She feels like having a fag, the dull, insistent tug. She has had one and wants another. Maybe she should take up bubble gum.

She watches Nicolas get to his feet and square his blazer, doing the buttons up and then undoing the bottom one. He passes in front of her, peering about, and around the corner of an adjacent table. He is a boy who likes to assess, it seems. Who likes to stretch his legs. Miriam, as if sensing an audience, lifts her drawing up and tilts it away.

'Not too bad,' Nicolas says, lodging his hands behind his back.

No, but in need of a grounding line, Miss Sharpe sees. Some sense of horizon.

'Tin?' Nicolas draws in closer.

'I already told him,' Thomasin is saying to Miriam. 'If I want to see other people, I will.'

'What did Jonah say?' Miriam asks.

'What could he say?'

'Tin, this morning, on my way—' Nicolas's voice twists down into a whisper. Tin sits upright, apparently indifferent.

'I don't think so!' hoots Kelly, who has somehow inserted himself at the table. 'If anything, it's Robin who should be explaining herself to Tin.' He claps Nicolas on the back and dances away towards the windows. 'Isn't that right, Robin? You have plenty of explaining to do, from what I saw last night!'

Nicolas frowns and takes a step back. Miss Sharpe pushes herself off the wall. She is going to Miriam but catches sight of the confusion James is making and spreads a palm to the table beside him. With the tip of her pencil, she points at the gap between the curve of a pebble and the beginning of a shadow.

'It's not attached. See?' She cranes around to gauge whether he has understood. He nods, but his hand hovers. He has no idea, she can tell, how to resume. 'Light and Shade,' she says, addressing the room in general. 'Look at the pebbles. Look also at the space *between* the pebbles. The shadows cast.'

'But would you really?' Miriam asks, dropping her charcoal, pushing her drawing away. 'See someone else.'

'I might ask Olly out,' Thomasin says.

'Olly in sixth form?'

'Yes, Oliver in sixth form.'

'Olly won't do that,' Miriam says. 'Not to Jonah.'

'He might. For me.'

'Be careful,' Miss Sharpe says. She has planted herself in the centre of the room and fists her hands to her hips.

'What?' says Thomasin and raises an eyebrow. A curt black arc. The attention of the class pulls in around her.

'You have lovely eyebrows,' Nicolas comments.

Thomasin is beautiful, yes, Miss Sharpe admits. Thomasin thinks herself beautiful. She has dark eyes, long limbs, liquid hair. But that won't, after all, be enough. 'I said be careful, Thomasin. Or you'll end up on your own. And you'll deserve to.'

'You have no idea what you're talking about,' Thomasin says.

Miss Sharpe registers a dull shock, a thump to the chest. The girl talks to everyone like this. Even so, it is with effort that she stretches all expression from her face. 'We'll see,' she replies.

Thomasin reaches a hand and draws a line, fast and exact, across Miriam's paper. A charcoal horizon, perfectly weighted.

The bell rings. No one moves.

'That wasn't very kind, Miss Sharpe,' Robin says.

'I'm not paid to be kind.' Miss Sharpe drops her hands from her hips but feels somehow stranded.

'Kindness is its own reward,' James sings.

'I don't need you to defend me.' Thomasin's voice is stony.

'I wasn't,' Robin says.

'Write your name on the back of your paper,' Miss Sharpe tells the room. 'Chalk to the front, work in the class drawer.'

Thomasin stands up, a block of light to her front, her eyes dark and out of the window. The rest of the class begins to shift, moving slowly through the murky sunshine, offering up knuckles of chalk, splinters of charcoal. Saints' bones.

'Shall I spray it, Miss?' Kelly, tree-humper, holds up his sheet. A single shaky pebble, an outpouring of shadow. Another triumph of inaccuracy, Miss Sharpe sees. What is weighty and indisputable rendered evasive; what is fine and insubstantial laid down heavy like a brick.

'Give it a really good spray,' she says. 'You don't want to lose all that hard work.'

She returns to her desk, standing behind its bulk, and waits for them to go. They drift to the shady half of the room, circle about, and then move towards the door, gradually funnelling through. Robin, grazing the walls, follows at the back. Only Thomasin walks in the opposite direction. As she passes, she extends an arm and hooks something up, a scrap of lost white, from under Claire's chair. Tucking it inside her blazer, zipping the pocket shut, she exits through the staff door. The hinges, thrown wide, sigh shut behind her.

Miss Sharpe rights her cushion, a nerve jumping her back. Those deep inside pockets, she thinks, sitting down. Dark as charcoal, full of other people's troubles. Her eyes drift to the blue outside and roam about the sky. The morning light, an infiltration, passes back the other way.

Her bags are on the floor, beside her feet. From one of them, the corner of a picture frame sticks out and into her calf. It will be like this, she knows. And for a long time. Loss, like a small child, kicking at her ankle. She shifts her leg away, then shifts it back again.

II

Cloister

10.15 a.m., break

Miriam follows the others down the stairs and out through the double doors. She has lost sight of Tin and stops where everyone else does, just beyond the art block, pooling in the shade. It is cool here, even cold, on the covered brick path between the low walls. In the centre, a stagey square of garden lit by the sun.

They have ten minutes, but they need to be at the t-huts after break. There's not time to go far. Davy splits off to the tuck shop. Miriam throws her bag down, swings her feet up and props herself against a damp brick pillar. She admires her legs, the ruined tights, the protest of her scuffed-up shoes. She hitches her skirt up and pulls it taut, stuffing its bulk underneath her thighs. It is a regulation skirt with the full complement of fabric, the one they are all supposed to wear but no one ever did, until Tin started wearing it in all its defiant ugliness but rolled up short.

Miriam squints her eyes and turns her head to the cloister garden. In the blazing light, she sees a flash of this morning's assembly, the gloom blown out, the proscenium arch held up by the cloister's columns. X-ray people, bushes standing on stage. She turns back around and spots Tin coming out of the door they're not supposed to use. Tin stands for a moment facing the sun, where Miss Sharpe drops fag butts and they pick them up, then walks around the side, steps over the parapet, and sits down beside Miriam on the cold wall.

'I'm sorry,' Robin says provisionally, detaching herself from the doorway and edging onto the path.

Miriam takes a KitKat out of her pocket, unwraps it and snaps it in two.

'Tin?' Robin tries again. 'I said—'

'I heard.'

'I shouldn't have done what I did.'

'Oh, really?'

'No.'

'And which bit are you apologising for, exactly?' Tin asks. 'Or just for all of yourself in general?'

'I shouldn't have got off with Jonah,' Robin says. 'Last night.'

They wait, uneasy. Miriam screws her foil into a tight ball and aims for the bin across the cloister.

'But you told me you'd finished with him,' Robin attempts.

'But I hadn't finished with you. You were still my friend. Supposed to be.'

'Yeah, Robin,' says Kelly.

'Shut up, Kelly.' This from Vanessa, who looks at her hands, turning her rings. Her fringe, the new perm, stands up from her forehead as if in fright.

'And you said you never really liked him,' Robin persists.

Miriam cackles. 'Because Tin doesn't really like anyone.'

Tin leans around and bites the end off the KitKat sticking out of Miriam's mouth. A fast, fierce kiss. Miriam still has the other half. She sticks it in her mouth.

'Does it matter?' Tin asks, chewing. 'He likes me.'

Two sixth formers come around the cloister on their side. Sophie Callaghan, her long, tiered skirt swinging; Simon Holliday, his blonde fringe brushing his cheekbone. Their voices, her laughter sound in the high curve of the cloister's wooden ceiling.

'Tinny,' Sophie says, touching a hand to Tin's shoulder. An old friend of Tin's brother, she moves, Miriam feels, on a rolling wave of admiration. A billow of Laura Ashley.

'The Beautifuls,' Miriam says, without waiting for their laughter to fade, and lays her cheek down where Tin has been anointed. From this angle she sees that the roses have opened. Orange, yellow, a queasy salmon pink, shaken loose by the sunshine.

'Do you remember when we were in Seville and your mum said you could have anything in that hotel boutique?' Tin starts, as if the air has cleared. 'And I had to choose for you?'

'Ye-es,' Robin says.

'Where we go in Dingle you can buy paraffin, and t-shirts with Saint Teresa of Avila on them,' says James. 'But I wouldn't call it a *boutique* exactly. More a shop in a petrol station. Or less a shop, more a shed, in truth.'

Robin shifts her bag from one shoulder to the other. Davy, coming though the swing doors, sits down opposite, a packet of crisps open in each pocket. Pointing, he offers them to Nicolas on one side, prawn cocktail, to Vanessa on the other, beef and onion. He has his Walkman on and nods a bit. His eyes, Miriam sees, are elsewhere.

'The thing is,' Tin continues, leaning her back to a pillar, 'this week it was Jonah. Two weeks ago you tried it on with me. At the sleepover.'

'Whooo!' Kelly cheers. 'Ohhhh Robiiiin!'

Robin pulls her chin back like a rebuttal. 'I didn't,' she says, but her eyes flood with uncertainty.

'You know you did. You got into my bed and put your arms around me. And one leg.'

'Robin's a lesbian, Robin's a lesbian,' the chant starts up.

'No,' says Robin.

'Fuck off, little boys,' says Tin.

Is that what happened? Miriam wonders. Tin had got dressed in the middle of the night and walked home. On her own. Miriam hadn't thought much about it at the time. She had been pleased to claim a couch to herself, and a pillow, but had felt the lack of a blanket.

'And then, the weekend before that,' Tin says, 'you lost your virginity. On a car roof.'

'That's not true,' Robin protests.

'It wasn't her virginity, perhaps,' James suggests.

But there is no denying this. This they had all seen, from Jessica's mum's bedroom window. Turner, or rather Turner's arse, moving shiny white on the roof of the car, lit by the streetlamp.

'Is it true he charged you a packet of Marlboro Reds?' Kelly asks.

'Robin the lesbian, Robin the—' A pantomime of boys.

'So you see,' Tin resumes, 'how it's all looking a bit out of control? A little bit desperate? Can you see that? Because we can all see it. And I'm thinking – you ought to be more discriminating. About who you try to fuck.'

Robin stands pale, her thin arms limp. Just go, Miriam thinks. You're not actually caught. A breeze blows through, sweet and clean with shorn grass, and makes the garden shiver.

'No sitting on the cloister walls,' Karen the prefect says, skirting round the other side, but doesn't stop to test her authority.

'You think people like you, but they're just scared of you.' This is unexpected. And from Robin.

Miriam exhales, a long, thin whistle.

Tin shrugs. 'You don't think Jonah likes you, do you?' A twist like a grin has entered her voice, stretching it out. 'You can't be that deluded.' She swings away from the pillar and sits up, suddenly alert. 'But what do you think? Don't turn away. I'm interested. Honestly, why do you think he got off with you? Why, do you think?'

'Because – you won't – love him.'

'Oh! Only that?' It is often surprising what makes Tin laugh. The sound bowls down the tunnel of the cloister until it abruptly evaporates. 'Don't think he's ever going to go out with you. He will never go out with you. Not even to get at me.'

'*There are more things in heaven and earth —*' James begins.

Tin stands up and walks away, passing from the shadow of the cloister into the bleaching sunlight. A group of boys, their white vests flashing, cross behind her, heading in from the long-jump pits. They have missed their break.

'You got off pretty lightly,' Miriam says, but Robin has finally moved away, sideways, to the shelter of the art-block doors.

A sudden emptying out, and Miriam feels a mild disquiet, as she sometimes does, when Tin walks off like this. She should be pleased. That Robin has not been forgiven. That Robin, for once, won't be everywhere that Tin is. Instead she feels depleted, like half of her is gone.

The light blooms big in the sky. Miriam turns her head, squinting into the cloister. A flicker in her eyes, a stutter in the sun – and there he is, his head on one side, a listening tilt to his shoulders, Mr Ardennes. The middle of the garden. He holds his eyes to the earth. Miriam is not concerned. She sees that the cloister has been waiting for him. She will wait. She is ready to meet his eye. Something in his hand. A rag. A piece of paper, flaming white. Miriam stands up. The sun flares – and gone. A vacancy on stage where Mr Ardennes is not.

Death is close and sharp. Its blazing light. The thrill of climbing up too high, the tempting lure of a ledge. He is not here. The sun burns in the garden. He was here, and quickly gone. A wave of heat lifts her hair and lets it down again.

It must have been sudden, Miriam reflects, or she would have known. Her mum would have told her. And she is used to hospital talk, how wrong things go, how fast. Snapped cords and firing pus, veins clogged or giving way. Fluid – black, clear, lurid green – where fluid shouldn't be. The intricate tucks and pleats of the soft organs, their secret betrayals, packed in closely together. The body's full, surgical splendour. That they haven't been told anything is entirely like Gomme, who doesn't believe in passing on knowledge. And if he won't tell them, none of the teachers can. But Miriam's mum will, once she has clocked off and got her first glass down, and in more detail than Miriam's dad will stomach.

'If Mr Ardennes—' she begins, turning to Davy.

'Just tell me,' Davy is saying to Nicolas, his voice patient. 'Because I haven't got time to understand.'

Nicolas has hold of Davy's Walkman and is looking around in every direction. He is interested in circuits, Miriam knows, and she moves to sit on their side as if she is too, but nobody wants to get caught holding a Walkman. Walkmans get confiscated. They have all seen

Gomme unspool a cassette tape, his arm whipping about like starting a lawn mower, the brown ribbon scribbling and snapping in the air. Nicolas hands the machine back. He smooths his textbook over his sharp-crease lap and begins to recite, singsong, the answers to last night's maths homework.

And here comes Jonah, sleek and dark, approaching with long strides. He nods at Miriam, scanning the cloister, then swerves away again over the grass, towards the swing doors to the cloakrooms. If he's looking for Tin, he won't find her there. Miriam picks up her bag.

It is far from over between Tin and Robin, she knows. And Jonah. If they've had the prologue, anything can follow. Because Tin is an unsafe pair of hands. A difficult actor – razor-sharp or absent entirely. A pitiless director.

'Let's go,' she says to Davy, who looks up, then back down. His maths homework, the start of it. His neat biro numbers.

Stretching an arm, Miriam tries the bounce of Vanessa's new fringe. Surprisingly firm, she finds. Reassuring. Like the head of a cauliflower. Vanessa bats her hand away but her face is pleased. She glances towards the main school.

'The bell's about to go,' Miriam tells her. 'It's too late to go back for her now.'

12

Matron's Room

10.29 a.m., break

Claire lies on the bed. More of a table than a bed, high and hard. She looks down at herself, the symmetrical shape of her tented by the blanket. It is one of the things she likes best, the blanket tucked in tight, holding her down. Even so, the blanket is an uncertainty, its coarse, felted mix of murky green, of inky blue. There is red in it, she sees, this morning; in certain lights it is flat-out grey. On other days – any other shifty colour.

Each time, the same procedure: two spoons of Milk of Magnesia, thick like poster paint, pasty and metallic, and into bed. 'Stay there until the end of break,' Matron had said, shutting the door. But Claire is ready now. She has slept a kind sleep, without dreams, and feels better.

She shuts her eyes, a soft sting, the residue of crying, and opens them again.

It is not Mr Ardennes. Even if everybody thinks that it is. The tears come anyway all the time, more and more. But the fact that on Friday he was here and now on Monday morning – Why can't people just stay where they are? At least long enough to talk them through their A-level options, like he had started to do, pretending that Youth Training Schemes are not just for the other school. But she's fine now, shut in this room, held down close to by this blanket.

Sometimes, lying here, she tries out new names for herself. She used to like Angela. Now she prefers Colette. Because Claire feels like something she doesn't want to answer for. Something she is, in fact, less able to answer for every time someone says it. 'Not feeling yourself?' Matron asks, each time Claire knocks. 'Claire?'

All the questions they are asked. Every day at school, at home, in church, for homework and exams. Hundreds of questions, week after week. And she is expected to look them up, work them out, consider them carefully and write down the answers grammatically or concisely or logically or accurately and then submit them for correction. But what about her questions? She has questions. The question of herself. Why does nobody feel obliged to answer that?

'You're not yourself today,' Matron had said, shaking the thermometer out. 'It's the heat. And all the excitement.' No, she's not. And when she's with Vanessa, Vanessa speaking on and on, on her behalf, she's not herself either. Herself or anyone.

Claire shifts onto her side. The walls of the room are putty-white and vaguely reflective. There is a small, deep sink, a cupboard underneath, and a single framed poster. The town, with its medieval walls. The chimneys that twist up from the vicarage roof, the sharp edges of their bricks spiralling around like a staircase. The avenue of beech trees, dipping up and down, but the road straight between for three undeviating miles, all the way to the Corinthian arch. *The Ancient Town*, it says below, in gothic type. *More Than One Thousand Years of History*. She knows these photos now and sometimes, when she goes out into the real town, the old houses, the actual walls come into view and take her by surprise, asserting themselves against this sepia fade.

Beneath the poster, her shoes, one neatly beside the other under the canvas chair. *Faith*, written in gold inside, the shop she bought them from. Will Nessa come and pick her up? Sometimes she does, but it seems quieter than it should be. Maybe there has been a fight between Tin and Robin, like Nessa said there would be. But what does Vanessa actually know? Or Kelly, for that matter. She begins to wrestle against the blanket's hold, freeing her arms, and sits up, so high above the tiled floor.

She opens the cupboard for Disprins, drops one into a chalky glass and drinks the effervescence down. It's okay. This is what Matron does. A handle creak, and the door opens through the base of the glass. Not Matron but Jonah, she sees, lowering her hand, his dark hair swinging over his eyes.

'Chuck us a packet.' His green eyes on her friendly. Or not unfriendly. 'Please, Mitch's sister.'

She turns to the shelf and passes a card of foil over the small span of the room. He presses the pills out and knocks them into his mouth. A stride in, a sideways swig from the tap. The fall of his shirt is slim and soft, a washed deep blue.

'Hangover?' he asks. She half nods. 'Me too. And when will we ever learn?' A slide of hair, a stride out, pulling the door softly behind him.

Jonah is in her sister Mitch's class. He is actually nice, Mitch says, despite being the boy that everybody wants. Claire closes the cupboard but leaves the empty foil by the sink. He doesn't ever know her name. And although it shouldn't, that makes her like him more.

'Are you with Tin next lesson?' His dark head is back around the door.

'No.' She considers changing her answer, but he is already gone.

Claire buttons up her blazer and straightens her socks. Tin has Jonah zipped into her pocket, that's another thing that Mitch says. Pushing on her shoes, she slips out of the room, past the bank of new cupboards, all locked, one identical to the next, around the sharp elbow of the corridor and out through the cloakroom doors. She hurries a bit, feeling the emptiness of the school. Gomme won't, perhaps, punish her, but the bell has surely gone. She is swallowed by the hollow cloister, emerges into sunlight, passes the art block and then the high wooden fence. Behind the palisade: chlorine and shouting. The sound of water. It is unheated, the pool, and uncomfortably clamped by the high, blank fence as if a miscalculation has been made. A cold green pull, they have all been forced to it.

Mr Ward, roaring on the other side.

But who, now, will mark her geography project? Because Mr Ardennes was supposed to do it and Mr Ardennes was fair. Which Mr Ward is not. She had written it with Mr Ardennes in mind: retail development around the ring road. She had imagined him checking her maps, making his careful assessment. He was supposed to be interested in road building and floodplains, or so she thought. He was always walking off there after school, past her house, and coming back in the dark.

A blast of anger rolls in, hot dust blowing into her eyes, making them prick and fill. Why bother with their questions? Why bother, when there's no one here to bother with her answers?

She slips a searching hand into her pocket – a flash of bright panic. She stops, her mind jumping around the morning, where she's been. Not in Matron's room, but she had it before. She turns around and runs back towards the art block.

13
The T-huts
10.30 a.m., lesson 2

Robin approaches the t-huts. There is something of camping about them, she feels, turning off the Lane, slipping in with the boys at the back. Film-set army sheds. Temporary classrooms, they sit on the waist of the hill, propped up on blocks, surrounded by grass and connected by concrete-slab paths. When you run in, the hollow floor booms. In one corner, a caged oil heater with a shimmering rattle. Beneath – nothing. Dusty soil and hollows. You can crawl right under and sometimes she does.

She walks up the steps, through the outer door and the inner, and halts. Tin is in her usual place halfway back. Pushed forward by whoever is behind, not knowing what else to do, Robin continues up the aisle and sits down beside her without looking around. After all the avoidance, it is unexpected, Tin's proximity, and causes Robin's brain to empty out like a floor giving way.

When she can, she opens her bag to see what books she has. There are maths books; she doesn't have to borrow one. She is relieved to find a pencil. Beside her, Tin is sitting straight and still, her arms wide on the desk as if she is relaxed. But it is not that things are normal. It is just that they are not supposed to move from their allocated seats. And the fact that Tin often does move, and hasn't, even though Robin expected that she would, doesn't mean that Tin has forgiven her. Only that she doesn't care enough to bother.

Or is it a punishment? It feels like it is. Robin sits with her hands under her legs, the wrists turned in. Even in the boxed heat of the t-hut, her fingertips are cold.

The sore of her head. The mess of last night.

She apologised and Tin pushed her away.

Mr Dalton arrives red-faced, at a jog, old acne scars flaring. He teaches PE as well as maths, and his hair, long on top, razored at the ears, is damp and frizzy. They all stand up. Then Tin stands up, an unhurried indifference.

'Why do we stand at the start of a lesson?' Mr Dalton asks, no preliminaries. 'Thomasin?'

'It's supposed to show respect.'

'Correct. Now go back to main school and take your nail varnish off.'

Robin allows herself a look down at Tin's hands, the red strips of her nails, the debris of gold at the tip of her left index finger.

'I'll miss the start of the lesson,' Tin says.

Mr Dalton's tongue moves behind his lips. And retreats. 'You will.'

'Is it really more important? My nails. More than my education?'

'Neither are of much importance to me.'

Tin is silent, allowing this to resonate around the hut.

Robin holds herself still but feels her heart accelerate. She is not in trouble. Tin is making trouble. Robin feels its cold thrill rising all around.

'If it wasn't the varnish, I'd be sending you up for something else,' Mr Dalton says. He scans her, Tin's body, his eyes drawing down and then moving up again. 'The length of your skirt. The number of earrings you're wearing. The fact that everyone in the entire school, all six hundred and eighteen of you, minus one, is wearing a regulation white shirt and yours alone is white with faint blue lines on.'

'A subset of one,' James says from across the aisle. 'Or,' – stabbing his calculator – '0.162 per cent, rounded up to the third decimal place. If I've calculated correctly.'

Nicolas, a desk away, tilts his face back, checking the maths.

'I'm predisposed to inaccuracies,' James cautions, showing his calculator. 'I've leaking batteries.'

'Go to Matron, Thomasin, now,' Mr Dalton says. 'Everyone else sit down, open your books. Page ninety-one.'

They all sit down.

'Get up, Thomasin,' Mr Dalton says, holding his voice steady.

Robin waits, her eyes on her exercise book, the scatter of oil over the cover. Cloudy chip papers most nights last week.

'Look. There are school rules,' Mr Dalton continues. 'We all know what they are. It's my job to enforce them, your job to follow them.'

'Is that what your job is?' Tin asks. A lazy interest.

Mr Dalton stands in front of the whiteboard. He unfists his hands and stretches the fingers wide, then hangs his arms in the pockets of his tracksuit top, the fabric rustling like a crushed packet of crisps. He steps his legs apart.

'There is no one to exempt you now, Thomasin. No one. You're on your own.'

A confrontation of eyes. Tin has pushed and pushed Mr Dalton. He has sent her to Mr Ardennes lesson after lesson. And now? She will suffer without him, Robin sees.

Tin hates everyone, that is what Miriam says, but sent to Mr Ardennes' office, she usually went, and sometimes came back different, as if starting the day again.

Mr Dalton blinks, one eye before the other, a twitch in each cheek. 'Understand this – you're going to have to live by the rules. Just like everybody else.'

'Fuck the rules.'

'Easily said.' Mr Dalton grips his wrist, the black band of his watch, and lets it go again. 'That's an after-school detention. Ten minutes.'

'Fuck the rules.'

'Fifteen.'

'Fuck the rules.'

Each time she repeats it, Tin's voice grows softer, like she's talking a child to sleep. Mr Dalton remains dispassionate, doing the addition, his face scrubbed pink:

'Twenty.'

'Fuck the rules.'

'Thirty.'

He wipes his forehead with his sleeve, glancing briefly at the cuff. His hair is wetter now than when he first came in. Robin hears a fine, high complaint of hunger, her own, followed by a low rumble like moving furniture. She presses an arm to her stomach. She usually has something at break. Monster Munch. Or does she just feel sick? But Mr Dalton has skipped one, a five-minute increment.

Or perhaps he meant to, to get things over quickly.

'Fuck the rules.' Tin's voice like anaesthetic.

'Thirty-five,' Mr Dalton responds. His eyes have grown small. And has he got a slight squint? Because Robin feels his stare drifting sideways, taking her in too.

'Fuck the rules.' Tin's gentle voice.

'Forty.' His eyes pull back to Tin.

He'll have to give way at some point, Robin sees, before his numbers become impractical.

'Forty-five.'

'Fuck the rules.'

Unless there are no limits.

'Fifty-five.'

To what will be enforced.

'Fuck—' Tin says in lullaby, and then, at volume: 'Oh never mind, I'm going, watch me jump,' and is buoyed to her feet, as if on the hydraulics of her resistance, knocking Robin's elbow sideways.

Mr Dalton stalls for an instant. His acne scars are raw, like new burns. 'Look. It's a sad day. We all feel it.' He bumps a fist to his chest. 'Let's not make it any harder for each other.'

'It's not your job to feel,' says Tin, and walks out of the classroom, leaving the door gaping. Mr Dalton produces his asthma pump, turns his head and inhales. Three quick blasts.

Robin watches Tin descend the steps and climb the path, ducking under the lime shade of the trees.

'You should at least have given her a pass,' Miriam says from the back.

Mr Dalton stares straight ahead, as if something unexpected has happened. But Miriam is right. The consequences of being caught by Gomme out of lessons have grown unpredictable, and if Gomme can punish Tin for something – setting off the fire alarms, whatever it is – he will, because Gomme will always blame the wrong person if he can, as far as Robin can see.

And Tin is entirely alone. A clear and immediate insight. Robin feels a lunge of sympathy, too short and late. What happened to Tin when she was small, before Robin even moved here – And now this, Mr Ardennes. Tin will feel the loss. She already is. But they have fallen out and there is nothing Robin can do.

Mr Dalton shifts his weight from one foot to the other, a bounce on each ankle. 'She'll have to cope,' he says, coming to.

The mood in the hut adjusts. Mr Dalton makes a circuit, opening windows. Robin brings her elbow experimentally to the surface of the desk, Tin's side. She looks out of the window and notes the veil of pollen, yellow and luminous, filtering down from the trees. Leaves shifting. The knock of a woodpecker.

Unless Tin has done this on purpose, being sent to main school. Because now she can go where she wants, Robin sees. Wherever Jonah is. And he can say what he likes about Robin, about last night. Whatever he thinks he has to. She feels a press of alarm, cold around her chest. Would Tin do that, go up to the sixth-form centre? No, Robin decides. It's not like her to seek him out. Or is it?

'Quadratic equations,' Mr Dalton says. 'Thirty of them. Let's have thirty right answers.' Passing, he brushes the cage of the oil heater, releasing its whispering cymbal. 'Off you go. On your own. And show your working out. I want to see how you got there.'

—

Robin sits with the space beside her. The space where Tin is not. If Tin is all-round clever, she is less clever at maths. She can do it, if she's told what to do, but she cannot, faced with any given problem, always work out which method to apply. But Robin can. Usually she can. Maths to her is a mind washed clean. She likes to help Tin. She likes to have Tin beside her, huffing through. But she prefers, she finds, not to have her. To have an empty space in which to work. But it is true. It is true. She did all those things Tin condemned her for. She doesn't know why. She looks at her textbook. She flattens her exercise book open, her fist smudging the margin, and copies the first question at the top of a new page.

'Hand down, Kelly,' Mr Dalton says. 'Down. You haven't even tried.'

Claire comes in, her shoes sounding softly on the hollow floor. Heads lift and turn, any small distraction, following her progress across the hut. By some oversight, Gomme has not yet banned slingbacks. Claire wears shiny patent leather ones, with pointed toes, and underneath, immaculate white ankle socks punctured by holes, like lace. Socks not tights, Robin reflects. She is not the kind of girl to suffer the disfigurement of midges. Claire stands by Mr Dalton's desk and gives her explanation, quietly, so none of them can hear.

Mr Dalton strains his ear sideways. 'I expect it will turn up,' he says, his face a grimace.

Claire mouths something. Her eyes hover on the space beside Robin and then she crosses the room and sits down beside Vanessa, joining heads.

Robin surveys her work, the numbers side by side, where they should be. She sees each one with a clarity in space as if against a white wall. Its potency and potential. Its flaws. They are connected by many tensioned wires, holding every other in place, taut and spacious. If one shifts, all do; a transformation that unfolds in intricate ways, sometimes predictable, sometimes not.

She lays her pencil down. The end is wet and shards of chewed wood, red paint adhering, fall to the desk. The desks in the t-huts are not like in the main school. They are flat tables with hard plastic tops. She had fucked Turner on the roof of a car. She picks her pencil up. *I got off with Jonah*, her smallest writing, the very corner of the page. *I got into bed and put my arms around Tin and said, I love you.* That is what she had done. And Tin had pushed her off. And looked at her ever since with a sort of disbelief. Robin reads what she has written, then rips it off and puts it in her mouth. A small slip of squared paper, I-love-you letters, drying the tip of her tongue. All these things. Things that happen. But not in her control. Tin hadn't told everyone that, at least. She hadn't told them that Robin had said those words. Perhaps she hadn't heard.

'Have you checked them through?' Mr Dalton asks.

Robin nods, swallowing. She hadn't heard him move behind.

'Go on to page a hundred and nineteen. Ask if you get stuck.'

Mr Dalton walks to the front. He picks up a whiteboard pen and begins to turn it between his hands, pressing one end and then the other into his palm, his fingers running the length of its barrel.

But Tin did the same to me, Robin protests. In Spain. When Robin's mum – on the tiles of the hotel bathroom, all the duty-free bottles, the smell of bleach and miscarriage. Tin put her arms around me then. She told me – differently. It had been different, Robin admits.

She flicks through, trying to remember what page. More quadratic equations, probably. Or maybe something else. It doesn't really matter; they will have to do them all, every single question, before they're given the next book up. The prospect leaves her weary, like she could drop into an instant, weighted sleep.

'Page one one nine, Robin,' Mr Dalton says from the front, the end of the whiteboard pen pushing his cheek hollow.

If she could undo it, she would.

Or maybe she wouldn't. Because why should Tin only ever have Jonah and not even want him at all? And anyway, it's done. The worst has happened. Or the best. And there's nothing now she can do to take it back.

The door bumps open and Mr Ward steps in.

'If I might interrupt . . .?' He addresses a half-bow towards Mr Dalton, his fellow PE master, the small folding at the waist, the cinching-in of his heels that he does and no one ever returns, then looks around as if none of them should be here. They all stand up – a rumble of chairs, a shuffled Good Morning – and all sit down again.

Whenever Mr Ward appears, his drag sister appears with him. Or so it is for Robin. His corded legs in fishnets, the whites of his eyes, between lengths of false lashes, rolling. At this year's talent show, a Tina Turner wig and a black vinyl miniskirt. Alarm-red lipstick bursting the narrow banks of his lips. There was something very wrong in it, she feels, or was there? The tacky brown foundation.

'Go ahead,' Mr Dalton says, and resigns the whiteboard pen to his pocket.

Mr Ward pulls his lipless smile. Only the top of his head shows any colour, Robin sees, a slight redness from the morning's sun. 'Where's our Chandos house year captain?' he asks. The pale eyes scout about.

'I sent her to take her nail varnish off.' Mr Dalton looks at his wrist. 'Twenty minutes ago.'

'She's supposed to be in a meeting about Scafell Pike,' Mr Ward says, dropping his introductory smile. He takes hold of his necklace whistle and looks directly at Davy.

Never again. Robin knows – they all know – what Davy thinks. From two desks behind, she watches him lift the flap of his blazer up and pull his shirt from the skin of his back. Even the thought of Scafell makes him sweat, it appears. And he's already said no, twice in Robin's hearing. Each year this short trip requires a month of interruptions to round up the hillwalkers required. Those new to the school make up the majority, unclear, as Robin once was, whether or not the trip is voluntary.

Mr Ward takes a couple of steps towards the front of the classroom. 'Why?' he asks them. 'Thomasin Carmichael is a monumentally unsatisfactory house captain. I said so at the time of the elections and so it has proved. Because she's not in any sense a Joiner.'

Joiners and Splitters, already they are here. For Mr Ward, the world divides between the two: those suitable to fill positions of responsibility in the school and those he would eject without hesitation, should he ever be given the chance. He stares around, switching his whistle from side to side on its cord, and suddenly he is glaring at Robin, as if assessing now which category she will fall into. She doesn't want to look at him but can't too obviously look away. It brings on a sort of vertigo, being pinned like this by his stare, until she feels herself slipping sideways, as she sometimes does, sliding towards the window, where she hovers, observing, leaving her body to brave it out alone on the plastic chair, whatever bad thing is happening.

'Scafell Pike was first climbed over a hundred and fifty years ago,' he informs them. From her place apart, Robin hears him trying for his field-trip voice, but not enough to smooth the irritation from it. 'It's a demanding ascent which requires the best of one, mentally and physically. Even if you don't think of yourself as the outdoor type, I urge you to sign up. The pupils who come to the Lakes return quite different for it.'

Quite different, Robin agrees.

He starts outlining something else, payment by cheque, core and optional equipment, and then falls silent, pitching forward on his toes, narrowing his nostrils as if to drive his point harder towards them. But he cannot reach them. Surely even he sees that. The world, Robin considers, at least as far it is assembled in this small temporary hut, divides not between Splitters and Joiners but between those like her who avoid PE in all its forms, even Trampolining Tuesdays, and those whose bodies need whatever it is they get from rugby, hockey, cross country, even, and who for that will endure Ward and all the trouble he brings. But not Scafell. They are all with Davy on that. A week of Scafell is going too far.

Mr Ward drops his whistle hand and steps to the door. 'If she deigns to return, tell her to come and see me. Immediately. Because it hasn't been cancelled, the meeting. We soldier on, doing what we can –'

Even Mr Dalton looks away. If Mr Ardennes had never contradicted Gomme's rules, Mr Ward's assault-course tactics, he had sometimes stepped around them.

Mr Ward can wince and square his ropey shoulders, but it is no secret, the hostility he had directed at Mr Ardennes as a result. Mr Ward turns. His eyes lock again on the top of Robin's head.

'*You* must sign up,' he says, his fingers searching sideways for the handle. 'It will do *you* the world of good.'

He opens the door, steps smartly through, and pulls it shut.

Robin swallows and begins to collect herself. Shifting on the hard seat, she draws her arms, presses her legs in close. She looks down at the dark lap of her skirt and then around the hut. Everyone on chairs, in rows. Everything as normal.

She is still an only child. But the non-siblings have come every so often all the length of her childhood, the parts that she remembers. A sort of accompaniment, in a way, their mess of other unmade futures. And Tin had seen it, in Seville, in the hotel, for herself. And Tin had put her arms around her.

All the small deaths, and now a man's life. Shouldn't we love each other? Isn't it right, actually, to put your arms around another living body, while you can, and tell them that you love them? She hadn't been wrong to say so.

'Can I move please, sir?' It is Davy, in full sun by the window.

'Yes,' Mr Dalton says. 'But no gossiping.'

Davy gathers his things, walks two rows back and sits down next to Robin. He sets out his textbook, his Tipp-Ex, his geometry tin, and pushes her a piece of torn graph paper.

Ward can't make us go, it reads.

Robin knows this, but seeing it in Davy's blue ink comforts her. *Unless he drugs us and locks us in the minivan*, she writes underneath and pushes it back.

Or— Davy doesn't have time to unfold his *Or*. The scrap of paper lifts away.

'Sorry, Mr Dalton.' Davy lays his hand down on the bank of numbers in front of him. Robin looks at his arm. Even here, the sun, finding the black wool of his blazer, sinks its heat in.

—

'Will we send a search party out? I mean for our missing house captain.'

Mr Dalton gives James a weary look. James is possible Oxbridge, which makes him to some extent untouchable. Like a trophy.

'In case she's had some form of mishap,' James continues. 'A neurological episode, for instance, and is lost in the Thicket or is wandering the outskirts of town, incapable of remembering where she's going or, indeed, who she is.'

'I expect Matron's just busy,' Mr Dalton says, taking a step sideways, the narrow space the desks allow. 'And Thomasin is having to wait.' He turns his head and sneezes into both hands, then pulls a tight ball of hand-kerchief out of his tracksuit pocket.

'Or in case a sinkhole has opened up and swallowed her whole,' James persists. 'You will understand it much better than I do, Mr Dalton, I have only an imperfect grasp of probability theory, and if you don't, Robin will, or perhaps Nicolas, or perhaps not Nicolas –'

Robin's skin pricks. She looks across to Nicolas, but he is frowning downwards, lips pressed shut, a ruler braced to his page. James has all the words. Claire is back by Mr Dalton's table, trying to communicate something in whispers. She is standing on tiptoes, the white heels of her socks up, the backstraps of her shoes straining.

'One minute.' Mr Dalton holds a stop-hand up against James and bends his head to Claire.

'In any case,' James continues, 'given the geology of our town and the exceptional volume of groundwater our floodplains are called upon to absorb, if a deep void has opened up on the headmaster's drive, say, or in the south playing fields—'

'Thomasin has no justification—' Mr Dalton begins. A forceful sneeze into his handkerchief, and two more in quick succession.

The jaws of the earth gaping open, Robin hears. An unfathomable hole, overnight, in County Cork. Mr Dalton is waving now. He would like to stop James talking, it seems, but has been overpowered by a run of small, explosive sneezes. Claire waits, her eyes on an empty corner of the hut; James ramps up his volume. Texan real estate. Nepalese traffic intersections. A double pram sucked down, merely passing over—

'Because if Thomasin is anywhere near the Head-master's Drive,' Mr Dalton manages, returning to upright, 'anywhere close, she'll be lucky to escape with only another detention.'

James leans forwards. He interlaces his fingers under his chin. The backs of his hands have hair on them, Robin notes, thick and black like a grown-up's. 'Stop me if I offer an unwanted opinion, but it strikes me that she couldn't care less what you punish her with. Even a detention of apparently limitless duration. In this respect, Tin is not unlike the unrepentant sinner who, facing a literal eternity in hell, elects to live the life of Riley above ground and let the consequences come. She's a newly privatised company – our own British Telecom – plucked from the field of public good and flung, in the name of individual freedom, for ever beyond the reach of our collective financial, judicial and moral influence. Or am I wrong?' He presents a look of bland enquiry, but a sort of heaving has overtaken Mr Dalton now, like his lungs are filling too fast or against his will. Claire takes a step back and then returns to her desk. Mr Dalton turns away, one hand to the edge of his table.

'Tin doesn't like missing lessons, though,' Davy offers. 'She likes, actually, to do well.'

Robin considers. He is right, she sees, and is struck, as she has been before, by what Davy sometimes knows about Tin.

'Maybe I misunderstand her,' James says, a light wave of his hand. 'The Lord Above knows, that's one thing easy enough to do. My point is, we ought perhaps to check. I would go, but frankly I'm a coward when faced with physical obstacles and, to my shame, with moral and intellectual ones too. I suggest sending Davy. He's strong and can haul her out, whatever trouble she's fallen into. And if he goes via the rugby pitch, he might intersect with Mr Ward, or whatever the apposite term is – tackle him to the ground – and Mr Ward might be kind enough to lend him his emergency whistle.'

'I'll go. I'm brave.' Kelly shoots to his feet, thin and straight as a javelin.

'No one is going anywhere.' Mr Dalton has turned back to face them. He lifts a hand and pinches his nose shut. 'Do your work, James,' he says, his voice contained in his palm. 'And stop talking rubbish.'

James opens his mouth but is silenced by a yawn.

'Five more minutes,' Mr Dalton says, dropping his hand and stepping forwards, putting James behind him. 'If you don't know, go on to the next one. Exam technique –' knocking his knuckles together. 'Boom, boom, boom, and then we're moving on.'

Robin reaches the bottom, turns the page and sees that she is at the end. And through the window, here Tin finally is, sauntering down the path, her non-regulation shirt flaring white in the sunshine. No blazer.

With a rush of confusion, Robin wonders where Tin will sit, what she will say finding Davy in her place. She wants Tin beside her, her usual place, like a comfort. Then she remembers, and the distance reasserts itself. Tin might never sit here again. Robin's eyes blur.

This morning, she had waited on the cold steps of the porch until the last possible moment, then, coming down Ford Street alone, seeing them all on the bridge, the river flowing high and muddy, how Tin, without looking, had pulled away, and everyone else had followed, Robin had broken down. She had walked up the hill in the opposite direction, a side street, until the crying stopped.

It's the lack of sleep, being up in the dark and wet last night that is shaking her out like this. Vermouth on an empty stomach. I will not break down again, Robin resolves, as Tin bangs through the door. I will take it. Whatever it is she comes with.

Tin stops at the front of the class and lifts her hands up. The red of her nails has gone, but not in the way of being dissolved. More like she has scraped it off with something sharp. The teeth of a front-door key. She drops her arms.

'Has Shirtsleeves been given?' Davy asks.

'That took too long,' Mr Dalton says.

Tin shrugs. 'It's mayhem. Up at the Big House.'

A moment of hesitation, in which everyone searches Tin's face for a trick, and then Davy begins, wrestling his arms, hot at Robin's side, and they all strip, casting their blazers off and over the backs of chairs, the wool weighty with heat.

But Robin won't. She is cold. And last week's shirt, she knows, is dirty on the back.

———

'Swap books,' Mr Dalton instructs. 'You're marking home-work, the person beside you.'

'I'll mark my own,' Tin says. She is at the front desk, Robin sees, where teachers stack things and nobody ever sits, and has driven it forwards, right up against Mr Dalton's table.

'No you won't, Thomasin.'

'Yes I will. Because you can trust me to be honest.'

'That at least is beyond dispute,' says James. 'And brutally so, the Lord God shelter and repair us.'

'Or just mark Robin's,' Tin suggests. 'Because I made her do mine, and she let everyone else copy. Except maybe Nicolas. And Davy, who was with you, losing the rugby.'

For a moment, Mr Dalton doesn't respond. Robin looks at the floor, her stomach folding over like liquid. And then he bends his leg up, the box of his knee sharp against the fabric of his tracksuit, and stamps his foot down, striking the hollow floor.

'What the hell do you think you're doing? Here, in this classroom? No, put your hand down Nicolas, I'm telling you the answer. Because it's not just colouring in pie charts now. You're preparing for an exam. Two exams. Calculator and non-calculator. And in an exam, there's no helping each other. No passing little love letters around. What you can do and what you can't. Who's good and who's better. Who outright fails. It's only right answers and wrong answers and one result at the end. For life.'

Robin follows the tread of his shoes across the front of the hut. *Squash-Tek*, the logo reads, a peeling amber flash.

'A. B, C.' His tongue searches the pockets of his gums. 'D. E,' his voice deflating like a tyre. 'U.'

He turns and walks back the other way, towards the corner of the hut. Mid-stride, he is pulled back by the oil heater, the zip of his jacket catching in its cage, setting off its high, intricate murmur.

'It's polyphonic,' Nicolas says, lifting his ruler. He keeps it raised, as if holding space out for the sound to expand. 'Most probably because the frame is three-dimensional.'

Tin stands up, flicks the snagged metal free, sits down. Mr Dalton examines his zip and does his jacket up. Spreading a hand to the cage, he stops the wire ringing. He looks around, his skin aflame, the rims of his eyes red, then turns to look outside.

'Question one,' he says, out of the window. 'Davy?'

Robin picks her pencil up. She looks at Tin's back, a blank white page. Anything can be written. Tin might easily have come across Jonah by mistake, it occurs to Robin, the way he wanders around main school. She looks at Tin's arm, bare on the desk. The gleam of Jonah on skin. And even if they haven't seen each other yet, they will, Robin knows. She can't stop Jonah coming for Tin. Although, in a way, she has tried.

14

Foyer

11.17 a.m.

Nicolas half walks, half runs up the hill, his briefcase in one hand, his viola case in the other. He turns into the Lane and scoots under the trees. He hasn't forgotten, but he has left it until the last possible moment. Because he really likes maths and he doesn't want to miss it. Not even the last ten minutes. And he is also very good at chemistry. Which is why having viola at a time that straddles both lessons is simply irritating. And could very easily be avoided if they would just let him come at lunchtime.

He passes the bike sheds. Orchestras do need viola players, he reflects. He is, in actual fact, a valuable commodity. He might have explained it better. Although there is, he admits, a lot of waiting around between when you play and when you play again, when you don't. He glances towards his bike, but he can't see much from the path and can't just at this moment stop and check. He had forgotten at playtime. Breaktime. Later, he reminds himself. After lunch.

He enters the lunch hall through a side door and briskly walks its circumference. A clang of roasting trays. Disinfectant rising from the tables. He goes up the back stairs, stealing across the stage, and enters the passage on the other side. Badminton nets, rolled around their posts, and looming towers of chairs. The upright Chappell piano that nobody ever plays, because nobody ever tunes it, under its faded green jacket. He is, in fact, a little late, which he does not like to be. And Mr Prendergast is quite capable of telling his parents. Because Mr Prendergast likes to have a quiet word after orchestra, or even over the phone. Missed rehearsals and unpaid bills. Disruptive behaviour in second violins. Not that he ever—

But here Nicolas now is, at the door of the music room, pushing the handle down with his elbow. He tries again with more force. And a shoulder. The door is locked. It is definitely locked. He looks around for someone to report it to, because this has never happened before, and then he puts his viola down and begins to knock. He is allowed to go into the music room whenever he likes, and fairly often he—

Someone, Mr Ward, is charging up the stairs, raised from the changing rooms below and startling white in the dimness. Something embalmed. Nicolas stops knocking.

'Just go the other way around,' Mr Ward snaps, seizing hold of his whistle. 'Through the foyer and around the front of the school.' He turns, flinging his hand down, descends the stairs and disappears through the tennis-court doors.

Nicolas considers. He looks down at his case, at the battered brown cloth, the board showing though. They are not allowed in the foyer. The foyer is for guests and trophies. The foyer is where parents come in their best clothes and stand with their backs to the artwork display.

He picks up his case, but with a small weighting of reluctance, with the sense that he has been allocated an unreasonable quantity of luggage. He is hot and would like to take his blazer off, and Tin has said they can, but then he would have to carry it, and that, given everything else, is hardly practical. He turns his back on the door and begins to retrace his steps.

The corridor is empty now, quiet and dark and resinous with polish, as it should be. And he doesn't even have to go the whole length this time, he tells himself, hurrying between its narrow walls. Just the first bit. Something in the shiny darkness restores his efficiency. He feels well-oiled; it was only a hiccup with the locked door. He wraps around the corner and into a flood of sunshine. A step into brightness – and an electric flash of panic like the floor is unearthed. Because this time it is him, Gomme, unmistakeably. Gomme on the far side of the foyer, staring straight ahead across the empty stretch of space.

Held to the edge, unable to go forwards and unable to retreat, exposed to the foyer's wide, irradiating light, it occurs to him that he might very well get searched, even though he has a pass, a weekly one, to go to viola. Because Gomme shakes bags out upside down, looking for whatever it is. He holds them high and empties them all over the floor. And Nicolas sees that he is defenceless, quite unable to account for the contents of his briefcase. Not to Gomme. Not to his father, who, if Nicolas is punished now, will not in any case have time for explanations.

What on earth was he thinking? Contraceptives. A whole box of them, unmistakeably in his possession. He offers his briefcase forward, a heart-swallowing terror, ready to confess.

But Gomme remains stock-still, not saying anything. He doesn't appear, in fact, to have registered Nicolas at all. He is standing on his shoelace. His left foot. And he is not usually like some teachers who don't bother with an iron. Usually his shirt is tidy, his suit clean. Usually he doesn't wear the rabbit-fur hood on his gown except on ceremonial occasions. Founders' Day. The time last summer when the lady mayoress opened the computer lab and Nicolas had to hold the flowers, despite the wasp sting. And even then, on special days, the hood is not like this, not halfway off and dangling. Gomme lifts a big, flat hand and takes the sweat of his forehead backwards, wiping his standing hair down. Yes, it could very easily be the temperature, Nicolas sees, that has made him unshoulder the fur.

Gomme is looking across the foyer, about a foot above Nicolas's head, his eyes unfocused. It is almost as if Nicolas could pass underneath his notice. Could he? Perhaps he can. He takes a step to see. Nothing. And another. It is What's the Time, Mr Wolf? but without the turning about, without the shouting. He creeps across the floor, the sun on the polish blazing, one foot following the other now, his heart stumbling behind. What if Gomme waits until he's really close and then shouts? Or grabs hold of him like a hostage-taker? But he is gaining on the entrance doors; he has made it to them and is stepping through, down onto the hot slabs outside.

'Chatter, chatter, chatter!' Nicolas jumps. That is Gomme, a Gomme saying or something like one, but Nicolas is already on the side path and moving rapidly along beside the front flower beds, roses catching at his blazer. And anyway, it couldn't have been addressed to him, whatever it was Gomme meant, because Nicolas hadn't been chattering. He hadn't said a single word at all. Gomme claps his hands, or slaps something together, two books, a baggy thud. Nicolas shoots around the corner and sees that the glass doors, by great good luck, indeed stand open. There the music room is, resting like an insect on the grass, a giant balsa-wood model, octagonal and all its wings spread out in the sun to cure. He runs openly now, and takes a big, upward, heaving step straight in at the nearest gap.

It takes him a moment to recover his breath. As his eyes adjust, he sees that it is not Mr Prendergast waiting for him, but Mr Betts, the woodwork teacher, sitting the wrong way around on the piano stool.

'I'm supposed to have viola,' Nicolas tells him and looks around. There is handheld percussion all over the tables. Sheets of staff paper litter the floor.

'Not today, I think,' Mr Betts says. He sits with one knee over the other, a hand lost in his beard. His back, Nicolas notes, is in clear contact with the keyboard of the baby grand.

Nicolas eyes the guitars. The amps standing by, the waiting coils of leads. The fretless bass? Tin suggested that. Truthfully, he cannot see it. He has no interest in learning the chords to ZZ Top, or in pretending to be

Sting – who is also a teacher, he understands – even if, as Nicolas suspects, Mr Prendergast does.

He backs away, climbing down and out of the window. Really, if they are going to cancel viola like this, on the actual day, they should at least announce it in assembly. As he steps onto the path, he hears the bell go. A comprehensive waste of time and effort. At least he won't be late for next lesson. He skirts the music room and then the gym, coming out by the art block and into a counterflood of pushing third years. He turns sideways, protecting his case from their knees, but keeps walking more or less forwards. He can't understand what Mr Betts is doing, sitting in the dark, surrounded by piles of unmarked score and the marimba pushed to the door like a barricade. And if Mr Betts is in the music room, who is in technology? All the soldering and hammering and bending bits of Perspex that goes on there? From the outside, the grammar school sounds like one thing – old-fashioned facilities and only clever children and, given all the trouble he took to get in, past papers every evening with a stopwatch, learning the odd man out, three words in a row, one a false friend and so forth – but on the inside, ostensibly, it's . . .

'Nicolas?' Someone is calling him. Having squeezed past Jonah, and then all the other sixth formers who go around with him, Nicolas stops and turns back to face the way he came. 'Can you do a small favour for me?' Jonah asks. 'Please.'

Nicolas looks at his watch, and not without some difficulty, given what he is carrying. 'Yes, I can.'

'A quick one. Can you tell Tin . . . Actually, do you have any paper?'

Nicolas puts his cases down and produces his homework diary from his inside blazer pocket. For the sake of convenience, he allows Jonah one page from the front that he has already used. There is something calming about Jonah, Nicolas finds, watching him think, then write. For an athlete, Jonah's timetable permits a great deal of wandering slowly about, in slim-fitting trousers, and lying on the grass with Tin at lunchtime, although some A-level work must get done in between, presumably. And it doesn't escape him that Jonah does say please.

'Thank you,' Jonah says, handing Nicolas his piece of paper back, but folded into a square. The note has Tin's name written on it, beside one of Nicolas's own lists, last term's physics topics. Nicolas nods, businesslike, pockets the note, then pushes on and out the other side of the rush. His briefcase bangs one leg, his viola case the other.

He would, in fact, quite like to give up playing the viola. All the running around it has caused him. But he wouldn't, he knows, be allowed. It's just that now the possibility has been raised, he has to admit that he can see himself playing the harp, because he's the sort of musician, he suspects, who could make a reasonable fist of it. At least he'd like to try.

He stops for a moment. Because it might help him to remember. About Tin. Her mummy. Mother. They had all been told in primary school. Something uncomfortable. Like running away with a man. Of course – Nicolas begins to walk again – primary school is a very long time ago now. One can't be expected to remember everything. And taking into account how much they have changed since then . . . They have all learnt a great deal and come a long way. Chemistry! he thinks, picking up pace, taking the path to the labs. He is already a chapter and two pages ahead in the textbook, which will please Miss Harper, if and when he gets the chance to inform her of his progress.

But so much casual mayhem and wastage. Papers all over the music-room floor. Is this what it means, entropy? Death. All the atoms drifting apart?

15

Sink

11.26 a.m.

Mr Dalton appreciates the open windows, but the air in the staffroom is congested with pollen. With dust from the armchairs. Foam and hessian. He sits down and tries a blast of inhaler. And another.

He handled it badly. Maybe. He handled Thomasin badly. But better to hold fast to the rules. Especially today. Or that's what he had felt.

He hears the passage of feet above, tilting from one end of the corridor to the other. Through the windows the seagull cries of fourth years, spreading out over the playing fields. He'd rather be outside – the wide blue span of the morning – but he has paperwork to do, and only one free period before lunch, before an afternoon of lessons. He has two little boys and a wife in a box of a house by the ring road. He has an elderly father in High Wycombe. He feels like a thing in a cage. The sweat, under his tracksuit jacket, flows down the length of his back.

Yesterday, he was nineteen and necking pints with his rugby mates in a student bar in Loughborough. The Plough. He had been free to do anything, and without any sense of it.

Mr Austen lopes in and sits down opposite. Biology. Or physics. Mr Dalton nods but has no idea what to say to the man. He lifts his stack of marking up, trigonometry, a second-year black hole, sweeps a crust of sugar aside, and squares the edge of the papers down to the flat of the table. He barely knows Mr Austen. He has spoken to him once, maybe twice, since he joined. Which means they are probably on firm ground. No tears and no confessions.

Not that he had anything against Mr Ardennes himself. Far from it. Only Mr Dalton has always stood with Gomme and Ward, who are, in any case, the ones in charge. Who believe in rules, in the setting of clear boundaries. Because God alone knows what Mr Ardennes believed in. French communes and pupils voting on everything. Mothers' meetings all over the grass. And not just him, his friends. Half the staffroom. It can only ever lead to disaster. Bongo lessons and sociology CSE, whatever it is, instead of replacing the old tennis nets. Kids wearing whatever they feel like to school, sandals made from rope, and dropping out of college. No, you have to pick a side. You are either with Gomme or against him, and there's no point floating around in the middle, pretending you can talk across the line. You'll get nothing by it, except more work than you're paid to do and being passed over for promotion. And people like Emma Harper will find that out for herself soon enough. Or eventually. It is still unclear, however, where Mr Austen stands.

'I like it hot,' Mr Dalton says, setting his marking and then his red pen down, 'but this is too much even for me.'

Mr Austen looks at him and frowns. He shifts a big foot further onto someone's fallen biscuit, most of a digestive, probably not today's, and flaps the cover of his folder open and shut. Mr Dalton watches the crumbs work their way down into the carpet tile. But the man could cut his hair, hanging wet like a dishcloth. And buy a suit that fits. It's not the 1970s. Plain shirts are available. And sensible collars. Mr Dalton gets up, crosses to the sink and runs the tap for cold.

'That clock needs a new battery,' Mr Austen says, behind his back.

'It's wired in at the wall,' Mr Dalton points out, taking a gulp from his mug. Tepid chlorine.

'That wall needs a new clock,' the man says, and giggles like a girl.

But this is not his mug. The grey-green clay, the wash of minerals vitrified in glaze. Some bird, a swan, pressed into the front. Hand-thrown, and the touch of the maker visible, fluid in the surface. He had picked it up blindly.

He tips the water out and hangs the dead man's mug back up on the hook, stilling its rocking with one finger. Looking down into the sink, the tea-splashed metal, the burping plughole, he braces his arms to its sides. The heat. It always makes him nauseous.

'Football tonight,' Mr Austen states behind him.

'Not for me,' Mr Dalton says. 'Not on a Monday.' On Monday nights he drives to High Wycombe. It's been six months and his dad still can't get a grip. Tears.

Winter rain streaming down the hillside.

16

The Labs

11.30 a.m., lesson 3

'It's not Shirtsleeves,' Miss Harper insists. 'It doesn't matter what Thomasin says. Blazers on. It hasn't been announced.'

Miriam pulls on the heavy wool, the scratchy heat, and sits down on a stool. She has Tin firm on one side, the aisle open on the other. James, on Tin's left, pronounces a curse or a prayer, with saints, and draws himself tall. In the semi-darkness, they are wedged together. The breath of the bench is sharp. Decades of chemical spill has soaked the wood black, its surface, here and there, blowtorched by Bunsen burners.

Robin comes in and stops, her back to the heavy door.

'Sit with me,' Kelly shouts out. 'If you don't want to sit with her.'

Robin slides sideways through the dimness and into the nearest empty seat at the front. And then Nicolas trots in, pink-cheeked, and finding Robin in his place, claims the stool beside Miriam. He makes a show of managing his baggage under the bench, away from where she can kick it, and arranges himself to face forwards. Tie, blazer, textbook. Ruler, pen.

'Jonah told me to give this to you.' Nicolas produces a small, folded piece paper and holds it out towards Tin.

Tin looks at it and away. 'Give it to Robin.' Robin half glances around, her face blurred by the dark, and turns back to the front.

'No, Jonah definitely said—' Nicolas tries again to give her the paper, and not without a certain flourish, Miriam notes. Like he's serving legal documents.

'I don't need it,' Tin says. Nicolas looks uncertain.

'Burn it, if she won't take it,' James suggests. 'Or dissolve it in sulphuric acid.'

'Hydrochloric—' Nicolas begins.

'I'll have it,' Kelly says, passing behind them, swiping and missing.

From the bench in front, Davy turns and holds his hand out. Nicolas passes the slip of paper across. Davy can be trusted with other people's things. Even Nicolas can see that. Miriam tips her stool sideways, onto two feet, leaning closer into Tin's side.

'Jonah was looking for you. At breaktime.' She totters and crashes the feet of the stool back to the floor. Tin stares forwards at the fuzzy back of Robin's head.

'I don't much feel like teaching today,' Miss Harper begins. 'I don't much feel like doing anything.' She looks around, her bright eyes darting. 'Shall we play a game? Why don't we play a game of Who Am I? I'll think of someone, you ask me questions, then you see if you can guess. Yes or no questions.'

There is something hopeful about Miss Harper. Raised by the demonstration platform, swamped by her lab coat, she seems to Miriam like a child whose whims they must tolerate, whose innocence they must wearily protect. Miss Harper turns to wipe the board. *Living* and *Non-living*, two columns of suggestions made by second years, blur sideways in white arcs.

'Okay, who's going to start us off?'

'I will,' says James, perky. 'Are you alive?'

'No,' she admits. 'No.'

A silence.

'Are you a virus? Because contrary to what you've just erased, viruses are not strictly alive like, say, a fish, but neither are they absolutely lifeless like, for example, a roofing slate.'

'I'm not a virus, James.'

'A microbe?' he persists. 'What about a microbe?'

'Not a microbe. We're not dealing with viruses or microbes today.'

'Are you, then, a figment of God's imagination?'

'You can't keep asking. You got a no. Somebody else.'

They establish that she's a woman, an Englishwoman. And famous.

'Maggie?' 'Out!' Two bored voices.

'Floella Benjamin?'

'Both very much alive,' Nicolas informs them. 'Although I'm not entirely confident –'

Miriam shifts herself slightly, enough to angle her arm, and slides her hand into Tin's skirt pocket. She stretches her fingers around, investigating the seams. There is grit in there and something moist . . . Flakes of tissue or tobacco. And little bits of paper cut small. Tin doesn't react. She doesn't feel it, Miriam suspects, or perhaps she is indifferent. Miriam stays her hand inside, in the close dark, a small thing in its burrow.

'Are you the girl brought back to life by St Rumbold the child saint, whose fingerbones performed miracles of revivification, after she drowned in the ford of the River Ouse?'

'No, James. I am not.'

'Are you Hamlet's father's mother?'

'No.'

'Are you—'

'That's your guesses over – you've had another three nos in a row.'

'Two,' he corrects. 'And I'm a Roman Catholic. The premise of my existence is no following no following no, without limitation.'

Miss Harper regards him, unsure, it seems, whether he has said something clever. 'Yes,' she replies, 'but you're not the only one here who can speak.'

'Have you had sex?' It is Kelly, inevitably, grinning round.

'Yes,' Miss Harper says. 'No. I don't know. I am married, I think.'

'You should know,' Tin says. 'Unless you were unconscious.'

Miriam sees Robin start, as if from sleep, and then narrow herself on her stool.

'We're not back in last week's lesson, thank goodness,' Miss Harper says, rolling her eyes. But they are close. They are edging in towards the scarlet straitjacket of her embarrassment, towards the lesson on human reproduction she sprang on them, as it had been sprung on her, Miriam supposes, being the only young, female member of the science department. Of the school, almost. Her casual cynicism, assumed now like a costume, cannot convince.

'Shall I go next door and ask Mr Austen?' Kelly offers. 'He might remember.'

Miss Harper, they know, is seeing Mr Austen, the physics teacher, the new one with the greasy hair, the floppy legs, the ring binder.

'Has he proposed to you yet?' Miriam asks.

No response.

'We've done for one engagement,' Miriam reminds the room. Miss Arbroath and the blushing music teacher, Mr Prendergast. The teasing hadn't stopped, until Miss Arbroath had locked herself in her car, then disappeared on sick leave. 'We can do a second,' Miriam adds, because, if anything, Miss Harper and Mr Austen look like even softer targets. But today Miss Harper seems oddly impervious. She darts about behind the high bank of mahogany, dodging their rudeness. She makes little bundles of sticks on the board, four upright twigs and one crossing, to represent wrong guesses.

'And anyway, it's not a helpful line of questioning, sex,' Miss Harper insists. 'Ask me more about my profession. What I do.'

A fly blunders in and lands on a bench, on the white page of a book, on a bare wrist. It flies off again, directly into a window, the only closed one, and batters itself.

'Bother that fly.' Quick as a bird, Miss Harper speeds off the dais to flap it out. Returning, she dips down to pick something up off the floor. 'Bimetallic strips,' she announces, holding the slip of metal aloft. 'What occurs when they're heated? Hand down for the moment, Nicolas. Come on, you've all done this.'

It is true. They have all been through the brief excitement of feeding metal to blue fire and watching it bow, but cannot, at a year's distance, recapture the thrill. Except perhaps for Nicolas. He brings his arm down with a small thud, his frustration vibrating through Miriam and along the bench.

'They bend,' Davy says, eventually, from the stool in front. The back of his neck, between the point of his hairline and the rim of his collar, is broad and brown and matte, like silk. In the dimness, his collar stands up white.

'They do. And why do they bend? I know you know, Nicolas. I want to hear from someone else.'

The fly returns, or perhaps a different fly, visiting the bench, a gas tap, the top of Robin's head, and exits through a neighbouring window.

'Come on.'

'Two different metals, each with different expansion rates. Heated, one expands more and faster than the other, causing the strip to distort,' says Miriam, lifting her eyes from Davy's back. She can, she finds, absorb and retrieve facts like this, if she has to. And sometimes she has to. Because sometimes the day is something enormous and cumbersome that, together, they must roll through the morning, giving it a shove of information here, a tedious, shunting calculation there, in order to push it into the afternoon when, weary almost beyond protest, they can let it go, abandoning it wherever it has stalled. And especially today, when the effort required seems to Miriam excessive. Because the longer they pretend that nothing has happened, the more wrong everything feels.

'Correct,' Miss Harper says. 'And which metal expands the most? Which will be on the outside?' But she has exhausted their patience.

Miriam retrieves her hand from the press of Tin's pocket. She has hold of one of Tin's little pieces of paper and puts it in her blazer to examine later. Bending her elbow, she lays her head down sideways on the black wood. The vacancy on stage, the narrow place where Mr Ardennes is not. Miriam waits, expectant. A cracking-open in the dimness of the lab.

'The brass,' Miss Harper concludes, pointing at the scorched arc. 'The steel will be inside. But the steel still expands. Listening? Just not as much.' She drops the strip, with a short, bright ring, into a metal bucket. 'You'll have to know this. This will have to be on the tip of your tongues.'

'It's physics, really,' Nicolas says.

'That doesn't matter. You have to think across the boundaries.' Miss Harper gathers herself, patting her hipbones. She lifts up her clipboard and puts it down again. 'Oh yes, Who Am I? More questions. Come on. Look lively. You're not even close.'

A loud shaking-open of doors and, through the lifted windows, from the dark box of the lab, Miriam sees Gomme exit the main school and take to the path. His gown billows behind him, his beak cuts the air. The vacant slump of this morning has lifted, replaced by the busy fin of one hand, held in front as if parting water, and alert, upstanding hair. This is Gomme pursuing swearwords down corridors, Gomme propelled by suspicion that someone from the other school is hiding in the Thicket, that boarders are escaping or non-boarders trying to break in. This is, almost, Patrolling Gomme, and they are used to this. It is only as he draws level with the windows that Miriam senses something wayward about him, his body veering sideways as if carried by a strong current, a jelly glaze to his eyes. He comes to a swaying halt by a tree, one of the saplings that measure out the path between the science blocks and the new computer lab, and sits his hands on his waist.

Hymns, maybe, or lines from them.

'I think he's trying to serenade you, Miss,' Kelly suggests.

Miss Harper stands erect on the dais, her hands paused on the front of her pelvis.

Gomme pushes his shirtfront out and throws his head back. *'There was a young master from – There was a young fellow –'* he sings up to the tender leaves.

They watch, straining to catch the words, any clue to what he might be doing. His rabbit-fur hood dangles down behind, attached by one corner.

'Because there are ways!' he shouts. 'Means! A man must—'

And then he rights his head, but recklessly, with disproportionate force, and like a charade of slow motion, he loses his balance and staggers forwards, his hands held out, his wrists braced. He lands on one knee and stays down, head bowed, a man proposing to gravel. A sapling stands sentry by his side, its young limbs held up.

'Sit tight,' Miss Harper says, and shoots out of the door.

The weight of the class tips to the window, those of them who care. Miriam climbs onto the slide-projector trolley, Nicolas squeezing in beside her, Davy behind. Miss Harper approaches with caution, from the front, and then joins Gomme kneeling on the path. She is attempting to talk him up, but an odd composure holds him there, it seems. The midday sun pours down. Snatches of their duet blow in through the open windows.

Miriam draws herself tight into the windowsill, riding the trolley forwards. She looks straight down to the base of the outside wall, where small, battered plants – weeds and ferns – grow out from the stone, are sprayed now and then by Derek from Maintenance, and push through again. They have all seen Gomme wrenched loose by anger, as if rage itself can disorganise him, can place words beyond his reach until only spit comes out. The punishments he inflicts when he thinks that he's been disobeyed, by them or by a teacher, seem beyond all reason. Shameful, even. But this, Miriam considers, lifting her head, looks different. A different quality of incoherence.

'The question is,' she says, turning away from the window, 'is it enough? Has all this pushed him far enough over?'

'All what?' Nicolas asks, then, rocking back on the cushioned heels of his Clarks: 'You mean the disruption to the school timetable and so forth, following Mr Ardennes.'

'It looks promising,' Davy reflects.

'Agreed,' says Miriam. 'Although there's still the danger that this will only make him a small increment madder, and not mad enough that they actually have to retire him.'

Miriam feels an attempt on her bra strap and sharp-elbows backwards.

'Goony Gomme, Goony Gomme,' Kelly chants, jumping away. He is trying to raise a chorus, but the class has already begun to drift. Something has happened, but not something interesting to watch, Miriam decides.

Gomme might remain as he is, smiling and showing his teeth, disputing on his knees, all lesson long. The soft breeze lifts his hair. Beneath – his skull, shiny with sweat.

Miriam steps down from the trolley and picks up some safety goggles, a stray pair from the windowsill. The rubber strap has perished, but they stay on with a slight backward adjustment of her head. She turns and walks back to her place. James is standing at the front of the classroom. In noisy strokes he draws gallows and a noose on the cloudy board. Beside it, a hard line of dashes. Two words, five and five.

'You're supposed to do the noose after the guesses,' Nicolas points out.

'The Lord Save And Preserve Us, we've done with the guesses,' James says. He returns to his place, sits down and leaps immediately up, yelping.

'It's my leg,' Tin says. 'My womanly flesh. My thigh.'

She rounds the word – thigh – but her eyes sharpen.

'Keep your womanly flesh to yourself.'

'I can't. It spreads. Tits and thighs,' she leers.

James raises his forearms against her, and then repositions his stool and sits down.

'Sit next to me,' Miriam tells him. 'I don't have tits and thighs. More just nipples and knees.' She is wasting her effort. James has recovered his poise and sits square on the plinth of his stool as if nothing anyone says can now unseat him. But Tin's scrutiny continues.

'Have you never felt desire?' she asks. 'For another human body?'

'Not for a body.'

'For what, then? For a mind?'

'No.'

Tin waits. They all wait, the chatter of the classroom sucked smartly down into silence.

'For the purity of an idea,' he says.

There is jeering. 'My beautiful idea,' swoons Kelly, embracing himself and shuddering.

'I don't believe you,' Miriam says, eyeing him through scratched lenses.

'I do,' Tin asserts. 'I absolutely believe him. Tell me, have you considered the monastic life, my friend?' He raises his eyes to hers. 'Of course you have. Jesus Christ, you simpleton.'

There is a scuffling outside. Heads turn to the window. Miss Harper, her thin shins, her narrow feet scrabbling, succeeds in lifting Gomme up. They stand clinging to each other, a white triangle of lab coat, an inky cloud of gown, establishing a four-limbed balance; her hair swells, fine weed in moving water, and then she releases him, arms held broad, and watches his billowing form swing away in the direction of the Headmaster's Lodge.

'Is he okay on his own?' Davy calls through the window. Miss Harper flaps a hand, turns and runs towards the main school.

'There was a young bastard from Bedford,' Miriam starts. 'Who fell in a bathtub of custard –' She looks to Tin, who turns the other way.

'Which order?' Tin asks James.

'The Benedictines. Of Saint-Étienne.'

'After school?'

'After university.'

Tin nods.

Miriam drops her forehead to the bench, resting on the flat box frame of the goggles. An unholy alliance has grown between them, Tin and James. No one could have foreseen it. A greedy pleasure in speaking the truth, however savage. A rage for out-reading each other. For obsolete words and headaching ideas. But this – This at a stroke might make them strangers. Miriam raises her head. Tin is sitting upright, her eyes still and dark. In the half-light, James's long, bony face, his drenched grey eyes, already appear the mask of an ascetic. Or a fanatic.

'I imagine you'll be very happy,' Tin says. 'You can all recoil together, in silence.'

'It's not a silent order.'

'No? A sacrifice too far. For you.'

His eyes waver.

'Don't even think it. Don't even think of doing that to yourself,' Tin tells him.

It is too late, Miriam can see. His gaze bends away, the idea flushing his temples. He has seen himself new.

'It pains me to believe you're really that stupid,' Tin says.

'I intend to find out for myself,' he snaps, 'what I really am.'

'How – self-important of you.' Already a boredom, fine and dull as ash.

'I intend to live up to the highest version of myself,' James continues. 'However difficult that may prove.'

'We can all intend that.'

'No. That's my point. We don't all. You clearly intend to become your very worst, to see quite how depraved you can get until you're no longer recognisable. Even to yourself.'

'Do I?' One eyebrow, the warning lift. Her voice flat. Back down now, Miriam thinks, looking to James.

'You're thick with the years above,' James continues. 'Smoking, getting out of it, doing whatever you do. Even Robin's had enough.'

A long, straight look across the dark. Indecipherable. Extravagant, somehow. Robin, her side to the wall, lifts her head, her face struck pale, and fails to hold Tin's eye.

'What do you know about what we do?' Tin asks James.

'None of us escape your tales of glory, Thomasin. Unfortunately.'

She meets this, the punch of her name, with a mild smile. 'What would you have us do? Bread and milk. And lock ourselves up like anchorites?'

'Yes. Stay in. Use your mind.'

'I do use my mind.'

'You lack discipline. Your mind is – baggy.'

'And yours is brittle. But fuck off to your monastery,' she says, renouncing all interest. 'Inter yourself, why not, with all the other sexist fags?'

'Unfair.' It is Davy from the bench in front, not even turning.

'I'll pray for you,' says James.

'Don't you fucking dare.'

Miriam pulls the goggles off and lays the soft rubber down on the bench. Once, when she was small, she had walked up to a group of kids playing on the beach and started chatting, joining in, and they, being French, had simply walked away. She hadn't known until then that such a thing existed. A language barrier. Something they had no need, no desire to cross. Well, she knows now. Only she always imagined it would be Robin, sideways, uncertain Robin, who would slide in between Miriam and the fierce, cold closeness of Tin.

Miranda: But now you speak good French, *chérie*. Almost perfectly fluent.

Miriam: I do. I know.

Miranda: Better than Miss Wright.

Miriam: *Oui, peut-être*.

Miranda: *Et alors. Bon courage*. And Tin-tinsel get fucked.

—

Miss Harper pushes open the heavy door and takes the three wooden steps at a run, springing back up onto the dais.

'Settle down now,' she says, and feels a little breathless, brushing the skirt of her lab coat down. 'Where were we?' She straightens herself up and turns to look at the board. A hangman's noose. 'Oh, now that's—'

'Are you Janie Moore, the mother of Paddy Moore, C. S. Lewis's very closest friend – who was killed in what is commonly referred to as "the First World War", but what we might more accurately call yet another imperialist conflagration into which diverse and subjected peoples were mercilessly drawn – Janie Moore who C. S. Lewis subsequently adopted as his mother, not having his own, although the nature of their relationship still provokes speculation, despite the fact he was twenty-seven years her junior? Or are you the mother of the lame Israeli soldier who broke down on the outskirts of a Palestinian village and begged the Arabs for water and received it and asked their forgiveness and received that too?'

'No, James. No. You can be quiet, please, if you can't play properly.'

'That's just the problem, Miss Harper. I can't be quiet. My conscience doesn't –'

Miss Harper experiences a tilt, like the rolling of a boat, as all the eyes of the class slide together across the room and into a corner. She turns to find Mr Gomme at the end of her bench. She hadn't heard the door. He assumes his lectern stance, hands behind the tail of his gown, swaying.

He said he'd go home and rest. He gave his word. And she'd told Matron not to phone Dr Harrington. She glances over her class, a few of whom have risen and now sit down again, their eyes fixed to the corner.

'It falls to me,' Mr Gomme is saying. 'I – I am impelled to tell you –' Something of this morning's assembly, his stretched-mouth confusion, has returned, but then, with a spasm, appears to fall away. 'Hands,' he announces, releasing his own forwards. He shows both palms, pivoting them by his ears, the big white fingers loose knuckled. 'Not – Not – Flippers!'

'No. Not—' Miss Harper begins, but Mr Gomme's attention has locked elsewhere.

'Stand up. You, yes, you.'

In the silence, a weak scraping of a stool.

'Come here.'

It is Nicolas who walks the aisle.

'Let's see it,' Mr Gomme says. 'We all want to see it.'

Nicolas stands at the front, feet together, short arms straight. He glances back to his place as if for help. As if he'd like to bolt there.

'Come on! I've already caught you at it.' Mr Gomme scuffs a foot, impatient. 'The swimming gala,' he prompts. 'Legs gone blue. All the wet feet slapping!'

Nicolas looks bewildered. A fly, in agitation, buzzes from a corner. Mr Gomme swipes at Nicolas's shoulder, knocking him sideways a step, then swats the other shoulder, knocking him back again.

'Come on!' Another slap of frustration.

It's not that he's a big man, but he appears, at that moment, as a great deal of inexact flesh, and Nicolas so small a boy, shrinking into his blazer . . . Miss Harper takes a step forward. Mr Gomme frights away.

'Move!' he shouts at Nicolas, and tips from foot to foot as if to demonstrate. And Nicolas does move, a small seasick lean. A sneer of triumph breaks over Mr Gomme's face. He drops his hands and begins a slow beat to his sides, flapping the great black arms of his gown, then executes a scribbling half-circle in front of Miss Harper's bench. It is then that she sees what he is doing. What he has been trying to make Nicolas do. Under cover of the dark corridor, even just behind him sometimes, she has seen them do it, a slightly exaggerated gait. At Prize Day, a subtle rocking from foot to foot, a little slack around the bottom, a self-important waddle across the stage. On the rugby field, swinging their hips left and right, slapping their flippers to their sides, reeling in celebration. All of them do it, and not being able to stop them, they, the teaching staff, pretend not to see it. And Mr Gomme too, to Miss Harper's knowledge, has never once acknowledged it. But he is doing it now. The walk they all do. The Mad Penguin Walk. His parody of their parody of him, grotesque to watch, like someone eating themselves. She should make him stop. A plug of panic rises in her throat and she takes another step. He jumps again, taking refuge in the aisle, but he has taken hold of Nicolas's tie and is pulling him along. Surely, of all the children in the school, Nicolas is the last one likely to—

'Not – Not – Not!' Mr Gomme is shouting, banging his arm to his side, flapping one wing, bumping Nicolas around. And are there others now? Children off their stools, listing from side to side, waddling. 'Not – Not – Not!' they cry, turning tight-wired circles between the benches—

An explosion. Shocking and sharp. A tinkling fallout.

'Stop it.' It is Claire, her voice distinct, more than just a whisper. And they do stop, one and then another, the room falling still. It is the surprise, Miss Harper sees. They have never heard Claire speak out loud before. Little glass eyes wink up and down the bench and all over the floor – a flask, one of the expensive ones, most probably, against the blunt wooden edge – such a distance the smash has flung them. Mr Gomme, too, is quiet, his big arms hanging. Nicolas tucks his shirt in and adjusts the knot of his tie.

Miss Harper moves swiftly along the aisle, stepping over glass, a fallen stool. 'Mr Gomme,' she says, and takes a leading hold of his elbow. Loose fabric and flesh.

'He's – He's – Has he?' Mr Gomme's eyes roam around her face. 'Because a weak man will. Ask anyone. Ask a physics teacher! A flaw must fold.' His eyes slide over hers, shot pink. 'If he hadn't come to me then, on that particular day – Forever in the way, saying no, raising his objections. And now? A funeral on a summer's day, nothing less appropriate. Well, you won't find me weeping.' He looks out at the class, defiant. Or maybe only fearful. 'I didn't. I know that they say I did, but –' His voice, like a shred, rips in two. '"You can't impose your will", that's what he said, "on everyone".'

'It's over now,' she tells him.

'They hissed at me,' he says. 'Have you ever been hissed at?' Tears, a slippery fall, and no attempt at concealment. 'I didn't – Not – didn't I?'

'I know,' she says, and casts about for a tissue, a lab-rag of some sort.

Davy comes forward and holds the door ajar. They pass through. Not a waddle but a shuffle, Mr Gomme's shoulder heavy into hers. Matron, puffing out of the main school doors, intercepts on the path, the tarpaulin of her apron crackling.

'I'll take it from here,' Matron says. She nods and leads him away.

A wide-open sky, magnificent with sunshine. Miss Harper stands where earlier she had knelt. All around her feet the small, sharp stones, swept here and there, disturbed by their skirmish, show the earth bare and dry beneath. She plumbs the deep white pockets of her lab coat, her arms stick-straight. She cannot think, for a moment, what to do next, what she is doing here.

Death, with a strike, has stolen a man away, leaving them adrift, knocking Gomme to the ground. What it takes is never given back. It had been Mr Ardennes, when she first came here, new and untested. 'Whatever you need,' he had said. 'Without hesitation.' And she had asked him, often at the beginning and still now, even recently.

Last week, he had stood beside her when Gomme had shouted her down.

Miss Harper's eyes stare and her breath comes quickly. She sees the class though the dark windows of the lab. Something in a tank, shadowy and hidden. A vivarium. And then the bell rings and like a spring released all the shadows inside jump up, an explosion into life, and their clanging of pen tins and rulers and books slapped together into bags reaches her through the open windows. A full fifty minutes and not a thing to show.

'Don't you want to hear who I am?' she calls, racing back inside, her voice half-submerged by their clamour.

They don't. They just want to get themselves out, it seems. They have mouths to fill. They have bodies, legs and arms, in need of more moving about. They flood past her. She feels a little awed and a little disgusted. They are hungry for their lunch! Young people, fast and strong like a running tide. Nothing stops them. She had once been – not so long ago. She had never been like that. But what she had been, what she is now, she cannot easily say.

James, on his way out, picks up some chalk and dashes in the blanks on the board.

'Yes,' she calls, as he appears on the other side of the windows. 'That's right. And after all those silly guesses.'

'Marie Curie was Polish,' he informs her, disappearing.

'That's quite true,' Miss Harper reflects.

She watches the stream of heads move along the path in the direction of the lunch hall. Under the high sun, the black of their blazers appears red. That is something she could talk to Mr Austen, Colin, about at lunchtime, if she finds herself alone with him again. The phenomenon of colour. She turns back into the gloom. Only Claire remains, Vanessa hovering by her, the dustpan and brush hanging from her hand.

'You can go, Vanessa,' she says. 'Pop the dustpan back. The little nail on the wall.'

Miss Harper draws up a stool and perches on its height. Such a neat girl, Claire, and never until this morning a peep from her.

'Do you want to tell me –' she begins, crossing her wrists, but she can't seem to formulate a question.

17

Girls' Bogs

12.22 p.m., lunchtime

Vanessa walks into the cubicle and bolts the door. She stands facing a bent metal peg and feels a give, the fight in her shoulders, the lock of her jaw letting go. Slightly. Just to be in this small, close space and no one else around is a relief. And then, almost immediately, the main door sucks and bangs and three, maybe four others come in, sixth formers by the sound of them, their voices hard and smart with the polish of sinks and mirrors.

'That's what I'm talking about,' one is saying. 'She hasn't got much, but she makes the best of what she's got.'

'Yeah,' says somebody else. 'Actually, I don't see it. I don't even know how she got in. She's thick as shit, frankly.'

The blast of a nose, cascade of a cistern.

Vanessa hangs up her bag. She would prefer to wait, but maybe better not to. She manages her skirt, her knickers and sits down. She rips off two squares of shiny paper, folds them together and presses them to her skin, between the back and the front. Immediately the gush runs quiet. Do other people know about this, how to stop the sound of peeing? Or almost. Maybe not, because most people don't bother.

'But the problem with her,' the first sixth former continues, 'is if we're all sad, she has to be sadder. She has to be The Saddest.'

'The Very Saddest. Because she had him for economics.'

'I'd have had him.'

'Only a very sick person would say that.'

'Yes, and I am that person.'

'Actually, the problem with her,' a low voice says, 'the other problem, is that she's had sex and now she thinks she's Madonna.'

Someone snorts and runs the tap.

'One lace glove and cystitis. There's more to it than that.'

'More to what?' A different voice. The handle smash, the hinge bounce of a cubicle door.

'To pleasure. To being the cat with the cream.'

Vanessa is finished, but she doesn't want to come out. She is not one of the girls that sixth formers like. They hardly see her, in fact, if she's lucky. Because she doesn't belong. Because people like her don't come here. Her dad thinks differently. We're on the up, he says, meaning that they have moved across the road into their own house. A council house, but one they own. Meaning the kitchen, and all the new things. Appliances immaculate, as if they've never been used.

But she does have Claire. And Claire is pretty. And while she has Claire, no one really will touch her. The problem with Claire is that she is boring. She cries all the time and never wants to meet up outside school. Not the paint-factory disco, not even the open-air market on the airfield every other Sunday. Vanessa wants a different kind of friend. Someone better who likes C&A and shopping at the weekend. Shoplifting.

A sudden thumping, shaking the walls of the cubicle.

'Need help pushing that Tampax up?'

She flushes and creaks the door open. She knows she has been too long. There are only two of them now, standing at the mirror doing eyeliner. The taller one – it is Sophie Callaghan who everyone worships, who is just a Sloane, really, under it all – turns around and looks at her, like Vanessa has done something wrong that will never be forgiven.

'What happened to your hair?' Sophie asks.

Vanessa's hand rises to her fringe. They have sleek, dark hair, both of them, and cut the same, slant across the eyes, tight to the ears and into the high nape of the neck. Two shining, weighty helmets.

'It's called a front-lift spiral perm,' Vanessa manages, but feels her voice giving way. She doesn't describe the bendy rods, the new kind of roller.

'It's called a muff,' the other one says, 'but stuck to your head. An actual pubic bush.'

Vanessa isn't sure what they're saying but feels herself burn scarlet. She moves to the end sink and starts washing her hands. She tugs at the hanging towel, which is wet and refuses to rotate.

'Did your dad do that to you?' Sophie asks. She has turned back to the mirrors and is applying green to the inside rim of her eye, the top and then the bottom, pulling the eyelids back.

'Phone the NSPCC,' the other one says, uncapping a small glass bottle and spraying both wrists and the sides of her neck. 'No proper father should do that to a child.' And then, bending her legs, she sprays straight up between them.

They barrel out, scented, popular, laughing. Trampled flowers. Le Jardin, Vanessa knows, because she sprayed half a bottle out of the window so her stepmum would run short. Then told her dad to buy some more. She waits for the outside doors to clap and turns back to the mirror. Her face appears at a distance, a small red ball. Well, I like my hair, she insists. But she doesn't now. She looks ridiculous.

She opens her bag and pulls out a tube of hair gel, aqua blue, and a new card of Kirby grips. At least she has supplies. She can run her comb under the hot tap and plaster it down, the whole disgusting fuzz. She can drive pins into her scalp until her hair sticks flat like she's just been swimming. A drowned rat.

Instead, she unfolds a tissue and presses her eyes shut.

Justine, the other one is called, Sophie's friend, and short hair doesn't suit her at all. She has the wrong sort of face and only copies everything that Sophie does. Even the way she laughs, her chin to one shoulder, and the medallion belt too tight around her waist. Sophie has trumped her with a second belt, a thin silver chain slung low around her hips, which Justine will probably be wearing tomorrow, or something like it, and which should be confiscated, because none of it even counts as sixth-form business wear. Well, Justine's got about two weeks, in Vanessa's opinion, before everything starts to lose sharpness and look grown-out. And the same goes for all the other girls with Human League haircuts.

Vanessa is not like other girls. Other girls, when their perms fail and the roots go flat, have to make do with ponytails. But she will get hers done again just when she needs it. Just *before* she needs it, is what her dad says, and then she'll always look her best. Because Vanessa wants to look her best. She wants to look better than other people.

She balls her tissue up and drops it in the bin. Taking a fine-toothed comb, she detaches one section of fringe, inserts her finger and combs around, releasing the hair with a pat. The strands immediately spring apart. She tries another curl, the other side. Her whole fringe should sit high and shiny, each rolled tube in place around her forehead, but she can't quite get them to form. It's too hot and dry, the air, or it was all the messing about in the labs that's made the perm confused. And then there is always the static, the wool of everybody's blazers. Her fringe stands up. The more she combs, the bushier it becomes, sticking out. The wires of a used-up brush. It's how it's supposed to look, she tells herself. Big and up, like *Flashdance*. She pulls her hairspray out of her bag, a mini gold canister. Shielding her eyes, she sprays across the front of her head and back again, breathing it in. She feels it varnish her lips, its heady, tenacious grip.

That's better, she tells herself, returning her things to her bag, which is what her dad says. But is it? She angles her head this way, that way. It's the best that she can do, not having a headband or a scarf she can tie around to make a side bow.

She leaves, walking slowly to where she told Claire she would wait so they can go into lunch together. She holds her chin up but feels the scorch in her face, the prick of sweat under her arms. A scrum of boys from another year. Girls she doesn't know in tight pairs. Claire promised she would meet her here, outside the canteen, but all the benches are taken. What if Claire got bored of waiting and went in with somebody else? Without her. Claire does have other people she can go in with. Vanessa doesn't. Who would she sit with? People always go away. She stares through the window, but she can't see Claire. Only Miriam, and then Tin and Davy, sitting down on the other side of the glass. No Robin. She looks down, because that was her last tissue, the one she threw away.

Tin's mum died when they were in primary school. Vanessa always remembers that because later, when Vanessa's mum left home, Tin had been kind to her. It had only been them, in the whole school, left like that with their dads. They had been sort of friends for a while, before Robin came. But Tin had never really liked her.

She looks at her hands, at the lines chased into her gold ring that are supposed to twinkle like stars and do now with her eyes wet. Vanessa hasn't known anyone else die, but when her mum left, it felt like their old life had. Her new life, more lampshades and hoovering, had felt like a TV family.

She looks up. Claire is across the cloister, between the stilts of the art block, walking slowly up and down with her eyes fixed to the ground and her white socks wading the shadows like water. She looks weird, as if she's fallen into a trance. Miss Harper is circling nearby, head bowed, sweeping her gaze from side to side like a broom. They are looking for something maybe. Something hard to find. She feels embarrassed for Claire, whatever it is she is doing. Everybody is noticing and having to step around.

Vanessa turns and joins the crush by the canteen doors. She has no choice, really, she might already be late for her sitting. Not that there's anyone here to tell them which sitting it is. No teachers and not even prefects, like there usually are, to send them to the back. It's everyone all at once for themselves and pushing to get inside.

'Nesssaaaaa.' It is Kelly, a press of bodies ahead, jumping up to grin over somebody else's shoulder.

She keeps her face hard but allows herself to be carried inside with the push. She is hungry, suddenly, after all the upset of the morning. And it smells like chips. It's almost always chips now. Or ham fritters. She can save Claire a place. Or sit with Kelly if she has to. Last year, free-school-dinners had to sit on a separate table, all three of them, but then Dr Cole came and had a rant and now Kelly can sit anywhere he wants. Everywhere he isn't wanted.

They all press forwards, through the dark bit of corridor and into the canteen itself. There are people all over the place, shouting and standing up. She tries to keep an eye on the back of Kelly's head. She doesn't want to get too close. Or too far away. Kelly starts jumping up and down like he's doing the pogo. It feels like the end of a party, or the factory disco, how she imagines it, with all the lights switched on.

Vanessa comes level with where Tin, the others are sitting, taking up a whole table. She wouldn't want to be friends with Tin now anyway. Because look at Robin. Look where being best friends with Tin has got her.

18

Jubilee Close

12.31 p.m., lunchtime

Robin wanders vaguely along the Lane. She had seen Tin going into lunch and walked in the opposite direction. She isn't really hungry anymore but feels the need for sleep. She could crawl under the t-huts, she thinks, passing the path down, to where the boarders stash their bottles. She could go into town to where she went with Jonah, before the weir. The garage with the sofa.

And for that, all this exile.

Her heart's . . . She had never found out what Tin's heart is. Concrete? Delinquent? Stillborn probably gets closer. But then she has never known Tin any other way. She had moved here afterwards, when they were already nine or ten, and Tin then was exactly as she is now.

Inflammable. Unallied. Nothing like a child. And Robin not much of a tea-set, hair-slide sort of kid either. Bath cubes and stories.

James overtakes. 'Where are you going?' he asks, not stopping, half turning around.

'Nowhere really.'

'You can come home with me. There's always plenty. If you like boiled things.'

Beyond the shade of the Lane, the light is jaunty, yellow like sherbet. They walk down the hill into the basin of the town and up the other side. The streets smell of dust and tarmac. They sound like traffic and primary school, a long line of children hand in hand going somewhere, swimming, with rolled-up towels and earnest, fluttering voices – 'I've got electric powers, I've got . . .' – another long tail coming back, small, wet heads. They pass the Ship; men standing on the corner, beer and sun in dimpled glasses. They pass the police station, cul-de-sacs branching left and right, climbing the hill, and turn into Jubilee Close. The front door of the house is open and Robin follows James into the hall, where he lifts a chair and barges it into the front room.

'Shift round,' he says, dropping the chair down. His brothers and sister make room and Robin thanks them. She had agreed to come but is still mildly surprised to find herself here, sitting across the table from James, while Francis, the eldest brother home, races a few words in praise of God and food and clangs a spoon around the inside of a metal teapot.

It's an odd sort of room, both bare and cluttered. It has a hollowness, as if the lino is hosed down at night, and yet the walls are covered with photographs, with keepsakes. The Connells at various sizes, rowed against school-photo skies, the same patterned tank top busy under different grins. A tea towel with a lighthouse fading from it. Palm Sunday crosses, six of them in a ring, and an empty mushroom of Blu Tack. They are all sliding sideways, Robin notes. The rest might go at any time.

Mrs Connell swings in back first through the door and plonks a big glass bowl of steam down. The smell of metal pans and scalding water. For Robin, home lunch is the pound coin she takes from a bedside table to go along Nelson Street. A tuna-cucumber sandwich in clingfilm, warm from Mrs Widdins' glass counter, and a Creme Egg, which she eats sitting high on the kitchen benchtop with the telly on and the cats circling. But this – sweated, pink-boiled, in slabs. A panic like nausea rises. The Connells load their plates.

'Are you on the Ryvita diet too?' Mrs Connell asks. 'Like Róisín?'

'No, I –' Robin casts around for Róisín's plate. Two Ryvitas and a triangle of Dairylea cheese.

'Did you mean yes?' Francis asks. 'She means yes,' he shouts through to his mother.

'I should have known, looking at the skinny legs and arms of you,' Mrs Connell says, putting down a boat of white sauce, thick like custard.

Sergeant Connell's lunch keeps beneath a plate of orange glass, the underside beaded with condensation.

'Your father must have been delayed,' Mrs Connell says.

'Something going on at the station,' Colum, the quiet one, says.

'Have some respect,' his mother warns.

They are all going to be something. Doctors, Amnesty lawyers, political advisers. Even Róisín, who has applied for sports psychology, will get some sort of degree. None of them take their father's job seriously, police sergeant in a small town where nothing happens. Mrs Connell puts down a fist of mugs and begins to pour tea.

'Enough,' she says to James, who is loading his cup with sugar. 'Mother of God, you'll not have a tooth left in your head.'

Robin has never drunk tea. She has drunk more or less every spirit you can buy in duty-free, and a full range of SodaStream flavours, but not this. She adds three sugars and stirs them in. She helps herself to milk and immediately regrets it, the film of fat. Hers is a bone-white mug with a transfer of a blue cartoon dog on the side. *ESSO*, it says underneath. She takes an experimental sip, of hotness, of sweetness, and sets it shakily down.

'Mr Ardennes died,' Róisín says to the kitchen.

Mrs Connell appears around the door, a long cloth in one hand. 'What did you say?'

'It's true,' says Francis.

She sits down with a thump on Sergeant Connell's chair, draping one arm over his plate and flinching it up again. 'Oh, the poor woman. Oh, that poor, poor woman.' She closes her eyes, then blinks them open. 'And how did it happen?'

Robin looks at Francis, who usually knows things.

'They didn't tell us that,' Róisín says.

'Well, that's where – that's where your dad—' says Mrs Connell.

'I suppose it is actually.' Colum frowns down at his hands.

'Is it not odd that they didn't tell you more?'

'No odder than always,' says Colum.

'He was old and overworked,' Francis says.

'He was middle-aged,' Mrs Connell corrects. 'If anything, I'm five years older.'

There is a silence, in which they eat at speed; they have twenty fast minutes before they have to be back. A silence, in which it occurs to Robin that she had seen Mr Ardennes last night, in the murk and mess of the park, wearing his jacket like a shadow. Or had she? She had, and feels a wash of shame. Had she been so drunk that it only now returns to her? Soft and dim, lacking the edges of fact. She glances around at the bent heads. She tries to chew and swallow, to occupy her seat. There is something substantial about them, the Connells. Adult-like. They are all prefects, or will be, with the exception of James perhaps, and Róisín is deputy-head girl. And they are tall. All taller by a head than she is, than their own mother is, even sitting down. Mrs Connell stands up.

'He was a good man,' she concludes, and picks the cloth up from the floor.

'You know Thatcher's coming?' Francis says, laying his knife and fork crosswise.

Colum lifts his head. 'What? No. Coming where?'

'She's coming to open the Enterprise Centre.'

'Give the Falklands back,' James says, standing up with his empty plate. 'It's eight thousand miles away and has nothing to do with us.'

'Let's go,' Colum says. 'Let's protest.'

'Of course we'll go.'

'Let's lie down in the road.'

'No, you won't,' says Mrs Connell.

'Yes, we will,' Francis replies. 'And on the mini-roundabout.'

'Mum's a secret Thatcher supporter,' Colum confides to Robin.

'Not so secret,' Róisín says.

'No. I don't like the woman. But she's got a job to do. And when she comes here, your father's got a job to do too.'

'He won't get near,' says Francis, lifting Robin's plate. 'She'll have her own goons. Are your parents Tories?' he asks Robin.

'I'm not a Tory,' Mrs Connell insists.

'No-oo,' Robin says. Neither of her parents vote, as far as she knows, but they both curse the miners, which tells her more than she wants to admit.

'Gomme will be there. As a town nob.'

'Francis,' says Mrs Connell, walking out of the room.

'There in his dead-rabbit cape,' adds Colum.

'He should be there with the trades unions,' Francis continues. 'Standing for teachers' pay and conditions.'

'I'll be in the Lakes,' says Róisín.

'You're never going to Scafell.' Francis turns his chair to face her.

'I don't have a choice. All the team captains have to.'

'Don't be bullied by that man. Especially not after what happened last year.'

'What happened last year?' Robin ventures, picking up the salt shaker and setting it down again. White china with roses.

'A second year nearly died of exposure,' James tells her.

'He didn't nearly die,' Róisín says. 'He fell in a beck and went a bit numb. And then a bit quiet.'

It had been Róisín who had taken her coat off and tucked it in around Robin, three years ago when she couldn't stop shaking.

'That's exactly how hypothermia presents,' James says. 'A quiet torpor, and then you lose consciousness and the body shuts down. It's either that or the delirium, when you're near freezing to death but feel divinely warm. People strip their clothes off, if they've still got use of their hands. Or they attempt to burrow into something, like a bear into snow—'

'Bears hibernate in caves,' Francis says.

'Polar bears hibernate in snow caves,' James insists. 'Hide-and-die, it's called, the human burrowing urge. On Everest—'

'The Lakes are nothing like Everest, James.'

'I'm talking about Everest. On Everest, the path to the summit is paved with corpses. They leave them there all about, lying on top of the ice, because they can't spare the energy to carry them down. And they don't decay. They just get plundered. It's not the pristine environment you'd imagine.'

'It's a poorly organised freezer,' Colum says.

'For pity's sake!' Róisín pulls her hairband out and slaps it down on the table. 'He died only this morning.'

'And this morning, we're all in mourning,' sings James.

'Or will be. When Father Bernard gives us the nod and the wink,' Colum says, but quietly, as if to James alone. 'And then the Great Red Scowl.'

'Being crass is not the same as being clever,' says Róisín, pulling her hair tight back and wrapping the hairband around. 'Or brave.'

'Just refuse to go,' Francis advises his sister. 'Tell him we can't afford it.'

'We can't afford it.'

'What can't we afford?' asks Mrs Connell, coming back in.

'Scafell.'

'We can certainly afford it, or we certainly can't afford it,' she confirms, 'according to what best suits you, Róisín.'

They clear the table. Francis brings in a plate of Penguins and one of mini chocolate rolls.

'One of each,' he says. 'Take yours, Robin, before James gobbles them up.'

She takes a mini roll and unwraps it slowly, flattening the foil down to the tablecloth. Does this happen every lunchtime? she wonders. The sitting down like this. Placemats.

As one, the Connells stand up and leave the table. The sound of the TV news starts up from the next room.

'I'll be a minute,' James says, and leaves her standing.

She looks at the photo wall. The little Connells smile out in matching haircuts, a kick in the same place in each fringe. But not James. Even as a small boy he looks sceptical. He glowers and juts his chin, pulling at his hand-me-down jumper.

'You may well wonder where we got him,' Mrs Connell says, returning chairs to the table. She lifts a crumpled island of crochet and shakes it out. 'How are your mum and dad?'

'Fine, thanks for lunch,' Robin answers.

'Bye, Mum,' James says, coming back in.

'Bye, love.'

He takes a Penguin out of his pocket, a green one, and puts it down by Mrs Connell's hand.

They stride back through the lunchtime town. Colum walks with them, his shyness catching hold of Robin, spreading its silence, before he veers abruptly off and crosses the road.

'You don't have time!' James shouts at his brother's back. 'Banana fritters,' he explains to Robin. 'The new Chinese.'

'Any good?' And that, suddenly, is exactly what Robin wants. Chips and curry sauce.

James waves a hand. 'Yes. No. It's a merciless addiction.'

They pace up the long hill and into Springfield Lane.

'Slow down,' Robin tells James. The backs of her shoes slip off.

Other kids are coming back, pink in the cheeks and blazers flapping, streaming in under the trees. Even the shade is hot. In between the trees, the light hangs down in bars, swimming with dust and pollen. They pass the gate to the other school.

'Robin!' someone calls. It is Turner, standing by the concrete blocks, his bleached hair glinting.

'Daniel Turner,' Robin says, and Turner smiles like he can't help it.

They come to a stop in the same fall of sun, bright on Turner's head, warm on Robin's skirt. James draws his arm across it, his hand pale in the yellow light.

'I'll catch you up,' Robin tells him. 'Thanks for that.'

'My blessings.' James nods at her, at Turner, and continues back to school alone.

'What are you up to now?' Turner asks.

Robin smiles. She's game for anything, really. For chips and curry sauce and lying down. For getting away from school and out of the sun. Out of the glare of Tin.

19
Neither Inside Nor Outside
solar noon

Lyn Ardennes pulls open the balcony glass, blind with pain.

Men and women move around behind her, behind a sound barrier.

With tea. With plates of inedible stuff. Edging round the living room.

Sergeant Connell, flustered, tamps his radio down.

On the other side, soil shrinking away from the walls of a terracotta pot.

She has lost her husband.

In the middle of life, a place, she believed, of safety.

How easily we're fooled.

But not by him.
> Not only fooled by him.
> She had fooled herself.

She can neither look out of the window nor into the room.
> The future and the past, an iron jaw.
> She presses her eyes closed, fracturing the light.
> The sun, passing, rests a warm palm on top of her head.
> She is held, gently, between vicious teeth.
> Salt-bright, the middle of the day.

20

Out of Bounds

12.58 p.m., lunchtime

'Are you coming?' Tin stands up. She means Davy and inserts two fingers into his collar, the skin of his back hot like an engine, and pulls them out again.

'Yep,' Davy says, pocketing a Just Juice.

'*Bread of heaven, bread of heaven, feed me now and evermore, and evermore . . .*' Miriam sings, breaking her doughnut in two and pushing a wad into her mouth.

Tin turns to the windows, presses the bar of the fire door down and steps out of the canteen.

They cut through the shadow of the cloister, climbing the low wall, Tin first and then Davy, jumping down. A soft hollow of dust. They skirt the art block and walk out onto the wide green flat.

'Here,' Davy says, and holds out Jonah's note. 'You should at least read it.'

'You read it.'

'Please meet me —'

And there he is, at a distance – Jonah on the far rugby pitch, turning around as if to face her.

Half the day and not once crossing paths.

He is not the loudest, not the one who most throws his body around, but he is the pivot. All the others move around him.

'Why is he always like that?' she asks.

'Like what?'

'Surrounded.'

She veers sharply right, away from the sports fields. Anger to the surface like blood pushing back to frozen skin. All the nerve endings full, sharp and alive.

'He was completely out of it,' Davy says. 'Last night with Robin. He had no idea what was going on.'

'You weren't there.'

'No. But Miriam was.'

Beneath Tin's feet, the sweet, incidental spring of the cricket crease.

Davy persists. 'You shouldn't punish him.'

'Shouldn't I?'

'Do what you like. But I wouldn't.'

They go up a grass hump, over a rusting fence and push into the Dell. The light dims with chlorophyll and the smell rises, damp and rotten. Old woodland. Its own temperate climate. A sort of path through. Leaves have come out since she was last here, new green and downy, still crinkled from their buds. Others hang in pointed pink cases like insect wings. Prehistoric. And here, close to the edge, cow parsley has sprung up to knee height. Thigh height. Some of the flowers are open white, others green, their heads bent, unfurling like the croziers of ferns. She wades through its froth, its dampness gaining on her. Goosegrass pulls at her legs, leaving a strand like waterweed clinging to Davy's calf.

Towards the middle, the green flood gives out. It is darker. The insulation of dead leaves plush. A mushroom. A fallen trunk. A halo of midges. They step over the hurdles of brambles, around them, where they lash and tug. She stops abruptly and Davy collides with her back. She doesn't move. He puts his arms around her and kisses the back of her head, once. A bird calls from a nearby branch, a run of fine, bright notes. Further off, another responds.

'It's a shame you only go out with beautiful people,' he says, letting her go.

'It was a deer,' she replies.

They move on, the cow parsley beginning again as the light rises.

'*Anthriscus sylvestris*,' Tin states, emerging into the sunlight. Her mum taught her that, the Latin name. Davy follows, pushing through. They are out, but not quite where she expected to be. She surveys the lawn. There was a hunting lodge here even before the Tudors, or so they are always being told, somewhere in what is now the sixth-form garden. It is out of bounds, but it is empty, and anyway it's unlikely they'll be challenged. Not by sixth formers. She won't be challenged. Even so, they stay close to the Dell, where the earth lifts in a little embankment, and lie down on the rise.

The grass is warm. Davy folds his arms behind his head, crosses his legs and closes his eyes. Tin, lying on one side, pushing her shoes off, regards the expanse of him. A mod, he wears his tie with the slim end out and his trousers tapered to his rugby-player's legs. In winter, a parka with a target Tipp-Exed on the back. Looking at him, she remembers a painting Miss Sharpe showed them once, a giant Madonna, high and broad like a barn, her blue cloak sheltering many small, suffering humans. The same round face, the same ample home of a chest.

'You're getting fatter,' she says, laying her head against him.

'Don't just even,' he replies, sleepy. 'Five English minutes. Not attacking anyone.' He puts his arm out and strokes her hair. His big thumb rests on her forehead. 'Swifts or swallows?' he wonders.

'I don't know. You're the country boy.'

'And what? You grew up in Watford?'

She looks at the sky. Small round clouds cobble the blue. Birds cross over, a world above.

'How's your brother?'

'Livin',' she says, in Miss Harper's singsong.

'That's good.'

Davy, almost alone, remains loyal to the idea of her brother. But he must know that the athlete, the captain of the rugby team who picked him out, who brought him on, has long since disappeared.

'Anyway, I'm supposed to be a bulwark,' he says, quietly. 'That's my role. I need to bulk up.'

A stretch of soft time, a bath in warm air, losing the skin's boundaries. The full sun. From somewhere far away, drifts of unimportant shouting. Tin closes her eyes and her eyelids go molten. An alien slackness comes to her limbs, and then to her mind.

'You'll miss him,' Davy speculates.

'Who?'

'Jesus Christ, Tin.' She feels his head lift, his chest, his chin press to the hot top of her head. 'Seriously, he saved your arse more than once. Mr Ardennes.'

'Mr Ardennes,' she repeats, coming to. 'He preferred to keep people in school rather than kick them out.'

'He liked you.'

'Not much. He liked pissing Gomme off.'

'It wasn't that, but he was the only one who could' – Davy yawns – 'stem the madness.' His head drops back to the ground. His chest spreads and settles.

Tin pulls the scrap of fabric out of her inside pocket. Eyes closed, she inserts her index finger through its corner loop, as she has watched Claire do, and raises it to her cheek. To be adopted is an endless disinheritance, she can see that. A thin, daily erasure. But this rubbed and crumpled rag, its twist of shredded ribbon. It surprises her that Claire, so neat a person, would carry this about. An unclean thing. A threadbare reassurance. She flicks it off, and then retrieves it from the grass and zips it back into her pocket.

From another place, the first bell.

'Let's just stay here,' she says. Davy shifts and her head descends into the fat of his belly. 'But you're obese,' she protests.

He lifts her skull gently from his front, lays it down on the grass and stands up. 'Five minutes. You can't manage even that.'

'Apparently not,' she says, squinting up. He is a giant shadow against the burning sky. The Incredible Hulk. An alien landing. She presses her eyes shut and feels him walk away, the dry earth quaking. By her head, the sound of a bee working a patch of clover, humming down, revving itself along.

The sun bears down with its full weight. The anger has burnt off and she is lonely for Jonah now. The beauty of him. The length of his limbs, his clear taste. Sometimes she has to look away, the desire so sharp, forceful and impatient. Why, when she wants him, is he nowhere around? And when he wants her, it drives her somewhere alone. And now Robin and Jonah, Jonah and Robin. A fine, double-edged blade. It has entered somewhere, between her ribs, sliding in its pain and pleasure. What it opens up – It is hard to know the damage.

She rolls over, warm on the warm ground, her breasts, her pelvis, the fabric of her uniform everywhere touching. Desire, supple and expansive, rises all around, in the wide, dry reach of the earth, each thirsty pore, going unspecific. Her skin is live with heat, with the sharp pins of the grass. The high sun presses down; water moves deep below, clean and cool with time. Her pulse pushes to the ground. A collecting pull to her pelvis. In the skin across her back, under her eyelids, the leaves and branches of the Dell spread out, tattooing themselves dark and green and blue. The smell of the grass like tonic.

What else are gardens for?

But all the lust and fighting, and this is what it amounts to? A small tug from the root.

She turns onto her back and watches the swallows. Swifts. The curt black arcs scything the blue. Free. And if they were to see me? A weighted thing, fallen down.

Small blue sandals, unbuckled. Bare feet on a hot pavement.

A bearded man on the stairs and a record turning.

Sugar mice, all the string tails, all the pink noses lined up on a tray. A garden birthday party. Hers? One she had been taken to.

Snow in the mouth.

A black bear, jointed, small enough for the palm of her hand. And one day, unaccountably lost.

These fragments. Not many. She shrugs them away.

More a short-circuit, giving herself back to herself in broken toys. Not any ghost else.

Only what she thought was behind her has come around again.

She stands up, hooks on her shoes, hot inside where the sun has been, tucks her shirt in and pulls it half out again, the way she wears it. I could just leave, she thinks, over the stile and down the railway line. She looks across, the dip in the grass, the gap in the hedge, a solitary tree standing attentive. Instead she walks directly across the lawn to the sixth-form centre, pushes the glass doors and takes the forbidden way back.

Coming out into the car park, Tin sees James, standing on a small mound of hard sand. Derek from Maintenance, carrying buckets, a spade clamped under his armpit, rounds a bush, the back of the minibus, and steps onto the path beside her.

'What's he doing on there?' Derek asks. 'Hey!'

'Invading your desert island.'

James looks around. 'How do you know I'm not marooned? Or here as a tourist, admiring the view and sampling the local cuisine.' He waves a paper plate, then scoops something, yellow sponge, into his mouth. 'Anyway, I had no idea it belonged to anyone in particular, this – sandpit.'

Derek looks incredulous. 'What d'you think that's for then?' He lifts his bucket: a traffic bollard, battered, in red-and-white livery, stands by the kerb.

'Go-karting,' Tin suggests.

'That's for telling you to go round. Not stand on top.'

'And I'm perfectly happy to share,' James continues, brushing crumbs from his front. 'Beach and cake.' He tilts his plate.

'Builders' sand, not seaside,' Derek says, putting the buckets down. 'Big difference.' He steps forward to inspect James's offering. 'That's swimming in syrup.'

'Pineapple upside-down cake,' James tells him. 'Third-year home economics, and scant regard for weights and measures.'

'More than your cake's gone pineapple upside-down today,' says Derek. He looks about, a glance over both shoulders. 'Right, off you get. I need to dig that out.'

'He's going to undermine you,' Tin tells James.

'It's been done before.'

'Off,' Derek repeats. 'I've got sandbags to make up.'

'We should be safe on a hill,' Tin says, stepping up beside James.

'Two hills.' James folds his paper plate and indicates the heap of sand, the wider rise of the school grounds, dripping syrup.

'We are for *now*,' says Derek, inspecting the back of his spade.

'Now and until the next ice age,' James tells him. 'Still, we know where to flee next time there's a flood.'

'Derek's HQ,' Tin says. 'And stand on top of his sandbank.'

'You're not coming anywhere near my shed. Flood or drought.'

'*A cold coming they had of it . . .*' Tin drones the line.

'Because' – Derek takes a practice swing with the spade – 'you look like trouble. And not a practical survival skill to your name.'

'Did you write my school report?' Tin asks, stepping down.

She begins to walk, James beside her, towards the main school. Silence runs between them, a strong, smooth current. Behind, a rasping cut and a gritty slide: the metal blade skimming the stone paving slab.

21

The Divide

1.17 p.m., lunchtime

Nicolas follows. He is not usually friends with Kelly, but everyone else is in catch-up maths, going over what he knows already. He would rather be there, but Mr Dalton sent him away. To play, Mr Dalton said. As if he were five. Kelly's short legs plough through a circle of lounging second years, who protest, one boy grabbing at Kelly's ankle, and then march diagonally across the grass. Nicolas goes around and catches up with a little run.

There had been nowhere to sit at lunch, and no individual, foil-wrapped butters. People with loaded trays had been backed up all around the till, and those who had managed to pay were still in the aisles, standing about and swapping things. Nicolas's lunch was surprisingly heavy and when the twins had somehow upset the cutlery trolley, and quantities of silverware had shot across the floor like fish poured from a net, missing his feet by only a fraction of an inch, he had gone around counterclockwise and sat himself down on the first empty seat, which happened to be next to Kelly and opposite Vanessa. After a short interval, Claire had squeezed in too, on Vanessa's chair, at the very same table, because there was no one on duty to tell her she wasn't allowed to.

Kelly stops to cough and then speeds up. They are supposed to change their indoor shoes for outdoor ones if they want to play on the grass, and Kelly hasn't, Nicolas can see. And neither has Nicolas, he realises, which is an oversight due in part to the hurry Kelly seems to be in, if not entirely. They scuff over the running track, a hot, stony place, a place for Nicolas of nausea and humiliation, and approach the Divide. It is a long fence with unwelcoming greenery attached, which does an adequate job of separating the playgrounds of the two schools but little in the way of improving what is, objectively, an under-utilised section of the grounds largely taken up by a badger sett, at least on this side of the fence. Kelly stops, looks in both directions and then strides along to where the hedge thins. The other school has different breaktimes – precisely to keep them from doing this, Nicolas knows, attempting to meet – and won't be out for a number of minutes. Kelly settles in to wait, leaning his arms to the wooden fence and crossing one leg over the other. Nicolas stands beside him and pushes his hands into his pockets, casual. They don't have much time, but they do have some, and he will make it his job to keep an eye on his watch.

Nicolas is grateful to come to a stop. He hadn't exactly meant to have such a big cooked lunch, and with pudding, but the male dinner lady, who is new, who wears a white hairnet like all the other dinner ladies but has a hole in his nose where an earring should be, had kept on going with his ladle. 'You might as well have it,' he told Nicolas, throwing his wrist. 'Nobody else is wanting mashed potato.' And so now here he is, feeling fullish, in full sun, and no wonder. He looks at Kelly, who is investigating an ear and reviewing the results on the end of his finger. Not so much an in-public habit, in Nicolas's view, even when outside. Kelly finishes, lifts his hand to shade his eyes and turns them on Nicolas.

'Who do you like?' he asks. 'In class. If you had to pick just one girl out?'

Nicolas looks at his feet. The grass is dry like August, the toes of his shoes dusty. He is not prepared for this, and so early in their friendship. 'Vanessa is quite nice,' he suggests. He had noticed Kelly leaning across at lunch, lifting things from Vanessa's tray. He's not sure if that means he likes her or not.

'Don't waste your time, Nessa's stuck up,' Kelly says. 'A daddy's princess. And her mum's not her real mum either.'

Nicolas absorbs this information. He has only a vague idea of Vanessa's mum. Who he thinks of as Vanessa's mum. A level of shine, bangles and lip gloss, and not to be diverted by small talk, to judge from the night of the school play when he, as usher, had helped her hang up her coat.

'My dad and her dad went to school together,' Kelly adds, as if Nicolas's silence is casting doubt. But he doesn't doubt what Kelly says. The town is exactly like this. There are families who have lived here for generations and all know each other's business. They've got the town sewn up, is what Nicolas's dad says. Gypsies in all but name and what they don't own, they've stolen. Which is not quite right, because Kelly lives in a house, as far as Nicolas can—

'And,' Kelly continues, swapping his shading hand, 'my mum and her mum, her other mum, are cousins.'

Which makes Vanessa and Kelly cousins too, Nicolas sees, of some sort. Second cousins, or cousins once removed. It seems strange that he hadn't known it before. Maybe everyone else knew.

'Not actual cousins but like cousins,' Kelly clarifies. 'Their mums, my nan and her nan, were best friends like sisters, but weren't.'

Nicolas recalculates. So not related by blood at all, then. Close family friends, in essence, but over more than one generation. Kelly might have said so at the beginning and saved him all the trouble of misunderstanding.

'What about Miriam?' Kelly asks, getting back to the matter in hand. 'She's blonde.'

Nicolas smiles. He has never thought of Miriam as anything other than something to avoid getting tangled up in. All the hair. And singing.

'You do, you do! You fancy Miriam! Yes you do, you close bastard!'

Kelly's lips are wet. His grin shows all his small, spaced teeth. Nicolas converts his own smile to a frown.

'Don't look at me like that,' Kelly tells him. 'You never know, you might be in with a chance. She might be one of the ones that likes them clever. Did you ever think of that? You never even thought of that, did you?'

A bell rings, but different, long electronic pips. The other school emerges, pouring out over the concrete from multiple doors along the low façade, a wide, rolling push of sound. There is a uniform, but it's just grey bottoms really, with a jumper they don't have to wear and nobody is wearing, and a sort of Aertex shirt with an embroidered crest on one side. A crest made up in 1982 is not a crest, Nicolas's dad says. It's an advert. But a crest that's just a leaf is easier to draw, in Nicolas's opinion, on school projects and the like, whereas their own crest, the crown and the ball and chain, wrapped around the neck and ankle of the swan, can be said to cause considerable trouble.

The pupils spread out, but none of them approach the Divide, or not closely. There is a distance of concrete and scrubby grass on their side, where they walk around, and a number of rusty iron sheds that they all seem drawn to, despite the heat that the corrugated metal must conduct. Radiate. And the fact that the sheds can't contain anything more interesting than lawnmowers. Nicolas squints up at the sky. It is wide and blue.

'The thing about Ardennes,' Kelly reflects, 'is you'd think they'd have shut the school, at least for a day.'

'Yes,' says Nicolas, 'one would,' but actually he's doubtful. The last time they shut the school, not this school, the primary school, was for the Silver Jubilee. They'd each received a commemorative coin in a plastic presentation pouch, and there'd been sausages. And maypole dancing. This seems altogether different.

'Just one day off, they could have given us that, the mean buggers.' Kelly sighs and begins to rattle the fence forwards and backwards, vibrating neighbouring leaves and sticks. He stops and raises a foot to the bottom rung. 'I know I could do with a holiday.'

Well, perhaps a day off would be welcome, Nicolas concedes, although many people are, in principle, against disruption to the working week. By coalminers, for example, who are causing all sorts of problems above ground, standing about on roads and so forth, when there is work to do below. James's brothers are collecting toys for the miners' children, who are already going without birthdays and breakfast, apparently, and Nicolas has contributed two Famous Five books and a small Slinky in its box, which is supposed to walk down the stairs but won't because, he suspects, it has been manufactured carelessly and is undersized, and therefore needs proportionately smaller stairs, which are unusual in most houses but perhaps not in the North of England. In any case, he hasn't mentioned it to his father, who disapproves of people taking days off, although not, perhaps, of the miners' children in and of themselves. Nicolas is rather regretting the books, which naturally he has grown out of but still, on occasion, likes to refer to.

Nevertheless, it does perhaps seem improper that nothing has been announced to mark the occasion, given that Mr Ardennes was head of the sixth form and very well respected. No doubt something will be, at the appropriate time. Nicolas swallows, a lump like lunch in his throat. Mr Ardennes had once been kind to Nicolas when he had tripped over on only his second day here. Bigger boys who have left now. Mr Ardennes had helped him to his feet and sat on the wall beside him while he got his breath back. It's nice to have someone kind like a mum in a school. But perhaps Mr Gomme is keen to set a good example. Yes, because what would happen if the people in charge started shutting everything down, schools as well as heavy industry? Dinner ladies and nurses, even graveyards going on strike. That, clearly –

Kelly is worrying the fence again, shaking the post by Nicolas's feet in its loose and dusty foundations.

'What about you?' Nicolas asks. 'Is there someone – Do you like someone in our class?' He is unsure about this game, whether it can go the other way.

'Who do you think I like?' Kelly flashes back, eager as if he's been waiting. 'Who'd you put me together with?'

'Robin?' Nicolas tries. Really, he has no idea.

Kelly considers. 'It's not that she's ugly. It's just she's . . .'

'Unkempt?'

'Mucky. She doesn't take proper care to present herself right.'

'Claire?' Nicolas immediately feels sorry. He hadn't meant to offer Claire up for appraisal like this.

Kelly is silent for a moment. 'The thing about Claire is no one's really helping her much.'

Helping her?

'She's upset, right? So they send her to Matron, and then she comes back again, upset. It's pointless, because Matron never makes anyone feel any better.'

To some extent, Nicolas has to agree. Matron had given him a plaster for his blister last week and it had come more or less straight off, or mostly, just sticking to the raw skin by one corner, which only made the wound worse. In fairness, though, there's not a whole lot you can do about new shoes rubbing.

'Claire is well turned out, though,' Kelly decides. 'I'll give you that. Nobody can say that she doesn't make the full effort.'

Indubitably. Claire to Nicolas is a glass of milk. A book new with promise that hasn't even been creased. Especially the days when she hasn't been crying.

Kelly attends to the field, tracking his head from side to side. He has pulled a length of grass from the foot of the hedge and is chewing the juicy end like a shepherd. A football game has started up in front of them, just on the other side of the fence, bags thrown to the ground for goalposts. The boys from the other school run around in their shirts, calling each other out.

'There he is, there he is, there he is! – Good work, good work, in the box! – No no, Mike Mike Mikey! – Getting lazy, boys.'

'Above a certain temperature,' Nicolas says, 'twenty-eight degrees Celsius, say, eighty-two, eighty-three degrees Fahrenheit, we should have the legal right to not wear our blazers.'

'You already have the legal right not to wear a vest.'

Nicolas looks down at his front, the whiteness thickening where his vest begins beneath the polyester shirt. Cream in the milk. And a stain he hadn't seen. A pink skid. That will be the strawberry custard. In truth, he'd eaten a bit too quickly and now feels bilious. He moves the knot of his tie across, and with it the fat silk end, so its length lies a little to one side, over the custard, and does all his blazer buttons up.

Things had gone a bit far in chemistry, in his opinion. His tie and then his shirt collar – Everything disarranged.

The fence shakes. 'But where are all the decent girls hiding?' Kelly demands.

Nicolas looks up. There are girls, but they are keeping to the other side of the football, walking or sitting in twos and threes and fours.

'Sky it! Come on, come on!' the footballers shout. 'There it is! Argh-oooh. Unlucky. Corner. Mattie! Bottom corners. Get back get back get back.'

'None of the girls in our class have had actual sex you know,' Kelly announces. 'It's all just bragging.' He sounds angry all of a sudden, as if he's been lied to.

'No,' Nicolas agrees. He has no idea. He hears things, or half hears them, but he isn't invited to parties. 'Today, in the boys' cloakroom—'

'Their skirts are much shorter, see?' Kelly notes, pointing a finger about. 'With splits.'

'And tighter,' Nicolas agrees, and feels the reprieve. He knows about the skirts. His sister took hers in herself, at the sides, and now has trouble with stairs. Her knees won't lift up to the front, but she can just about manage if she crooks her legs sideways. Even so, the skirt twists, taking her shirt with it, and she is forever pulling it around to the front by the waistband. She doesn't leave the house like this though, in the new skirt. She wears the old one and changes halfway, at Shona's house. 'Pencil skirts,' he confides to Kelly.

'Tanya!' Kelly shouts, but the girl spins away, laughing, tight in her brood of friends.

'Piss off, creeps!' somebody yells.

Nicolas takes his hands out of his pockets and looks at his watch. 'We should really be getting back now.' He had forgotten about the time.

'Now? They've only just come out.'

'Actually, I need to check on my bike.'

'Candice!'

'The thing about my bike is that it's a Raleigh –'

'Yes, Candice! I'm talking to you!'

'– but it used to belong to my cousin, the one who lives in Stevenage, and it's pretty old now and needs almost constant maintenance.'

'See that one there,' Kelly says, pointing. 'I got off with her in youth club. Well, after. In the old adventure playground.'

Evidently, Kelly isn't too interested in bikes. Nicolas peers across the hedge. Mostly it's the hair he can see, long and crinkly, because the girl he thinks Kelly means has turned her back. Crimpers, that's what the appliance is called that does that pattern, wavy like crinkle-cut chips.

'What's her name?'

Kelly shrugs. 'Samantha,' he supplies, after a while.

The sun is certainly hot. Nicolas feels the slick of sweat around his neck, just above his collar, and in the crease of his eyelids, making his eyesight hazy. As a matter of fact, crinkle chips are significantly dearer than normal ones, which is why his dad told his mum to stop buying them.

'The thing is I don't really want another full-time girlfriend,' Kelly tells him, draping his arms over the Divide. 'I don't really have time for all that trouble at the moment. And if I start at the bakery, that's some very early mornings.'

'No. Yes, I see.' In point of fact, Nicolas doubts whether Kelly has ever had a proper girlfriend. Or perhaps he has. He did see him last summer, in the shallow end of the open-air swimming pool, his arm around the waist of a girl in the year below and their skin shiny where they'd both been dunked. Not this Samantha, though. Very different hair. Even plastered to her head by swimming. He doesn't really like swimming, but he likes that the kiosk there sells frozen things. Mars bars and sometimes Marathons. It's still advisable to wait for them to thaw out a bit though, because if you bite in straightaway, when they're very cold and hard, it makes your jaw hurt and the roots of your teeth wither. Even so, there is something odd about eating chocolate in swimming trunks, in Nicolas's opinion. It feels—

'What about your sister?' Kelly asks.

His sister? 'She's not in school today.'

'Her time of blood and shouting?'

'Dentist,' Nicolas confirms, and then sees what Kelly means. Either way it's a lie, which just popped out of his mouth. And Diana, his sister, could walk right out in front of them now, or at any moment, out from behind one of those rusty lawnmower sheds.

'She'll be a bit of all right,' Kelly comments, 'once the braces come off.'

'What about Tin?' asks Nicolas, glancing about. They have rather lost track of their game.

'The thing about Tin –'

Nicolas waits, looking at his feet. Dust from the running track lies in the pores of the leather, in the pie-crust stitching, pale like ash. 'She's a bit too tall for you?' he suggests. The fact is most of the girls are taller than Kelly. All of them, in truth.

'Tin's got very dark nipples,' Kelly states.

'Oh.' Nicolas lets this mystery diffuse. 'And then, of course, Tin's already got a long-term, serious boyfriend. She is – isn't – is – going out with Jonah.' Nicolas offers his knowing smile.

'More isn't now,' Kelly replies. 'Now Robin's fucked Jonah.'

Nicolas feels a strange shock on hearing this, as if a propriety he didn't even know existed has been breached. 'Robin?' he queries. 'But Robin and Tin are best friends.'

'Were. Were best friends.' Kelly turns his eyes on him. They are small eyes, Nicolas notes, under the sunshine, and yellow like some sort of flower. 'Although really, they only do all this to keep things interesting.'

'Who does? Do what?' Nicolas asks. He is entirely lost.

'The complications. Tin and Jonah. Underneath they're as boring as any old married couple.'

It doesn't strike Nicolas much like that. To him, Tin and Jonah seem altogether more unstable, volatile even, like the formation of a planet. If anything, it is Robin and

Tin who are like something fixed together. A roof above his head. He can't explain why.

'Are you going on the Planetarium trip?' Nicolas asks.

'What?'

'The physics trip to the Planetarium?'

'Oh. No. I'm not going.'

'I need a partner for the coach,' Nicolas explains. 'Of course, I've been before, but I want to go again. The temporary display changes, naturally, and then it's near impossible to see everything in one go, particularly if the coach driver decides to take all the most congested roads, including semi-constructed carriageways clearly marked as such on the map. We arrived two hours later than scheduled—'

'They agree the route before,' Kelly says. 'The coach company with the school.'

'Yes, even so –' Nicolas lapses into silence. He rests his hands on the rough wood of the fence and his chin on top. Because he likes Robin. Not like that. Not Kelly's game. He likes her even though she was put forward for the County Maths Challenge this year and he wasn't, although he had been chosen for the two previous competitions, and been awarded fifteenth and twenty-second place respectively, and would have been selected the year before that too, Mr Dalton said, except he'd been too young to qualify. But Robin never teases him or asks him questions that make him feel . . . that he can't answer, the way some people do, so he can't tell whether they're being nice or laughing at him. He feels disappointed. In Robin, maybe. In the thin ice of the world.

At primary school, with the maypole dancing, and weekly singing along to the radio programme on cassette, old folk songs from rural and industrial settings, which they don't do now, perhaps because they're supposed to be learning ballroom steps with Mr Ward, but nobody else really wants to, he can tell; at primary school it had all been very much less—

'Well, it's Jonah's fault too,' Nicolas decides. 'It's disloyal of him as well.'

'Robin's a slag, really,' says Kelly, summing up. 'Hey! Angela! Nicolas wants to finger you!'

Hot panic slams against Nicolas's palms. Shame runs all over his face in a rush. Girls, the nearest group of them, turn their heads and scoff.

'No, of course I don't,' he croaks, half-deafened, blood like timpani pounding in his ears.

'Yes, he does,' hoots Kelly. 'He just told me that he does. Angela! Will you do it with him? If he uses a rubber johnny?'

One of the girls lifts a middle finger and rotates it slowly over her shoulder. 'He'd be lucky,' she says. Angela shrinks and moves away. Nicolas knows her, sort of. His sister knows her.

Two footballers collide, shouting, and a weight of boys comes down on top.

'I think it's practically the end of lunchbreak,' Nicolas says.

'What? No. The bell went ages ago.'

Nicolas turns and sees that the playing field, their side of the Divide, is entirely empty. He is ambushed by an urgent need to get away, to put things straight.

'I've got French,' he says, alarm squeezing his voice. 'I can't be late for French.'

'I can,' Kelly says. *Je suis en retard.*' He grins, a gap-toothed smile.

'You do German,' Nicolas reminds him. He gives Kelly his cross look and gets himself going promptly across the grass.

Miss Wright is very kind, but sometimes she does shout. In French as well as English, which somehow makes it worse.

22

The New Block

1.30 p.m., lesson 4

Miss Wright is already in the classroom, high up in the New Block. Not so new now, sixties, in fact, but full of light, with windows over the grass and, beyond, the playing fields. She turns a catch and slides the warm glass up, the sun dropping like a blanket onto her shoulders. She has lived in Balham. Really, this is the countryside. There are hedges in plain sight.

She hiccups and gives a little hum. She had cried and talked all lunchtime and then taken a slug of the savage whisky Mr Betts was passing around. If he'd been careful to conceal the contents of his locker before, he wasn't today. He'd raised his Liverpool FC mug and shaken his head. She'd watched the sawdust fall from his beard to the staffroom floor.

She had cried and looks like she has, her eyes small and nose raw. It makes no sense to her to pretend otherwise. 'Do you have to be so loud?' Matron had asked. 'Everybody else is just trying to get through the day.' It had taken Miss Wright a moment to understand, fraught as she felt with liquid shock. How else to go on? To stand up and face a class? The loss is irredeemable; there is no such thing as polite grief. Did Miss Wright have to be so loud? Yes, she did. And louder. And she feels better for it. On the surface. Or at least what's on the surface now accords better with the mess inside. She looks out over the playing fields and takes a full, unsteady breath in.

The air through the window smells of the ground, the hot, packed earth of the sports pitches. Two boys late at the far fence. So small and dark from here and easy to pick off. And Mr Ward striding out towards them.

Half of everything that happens here she disagrees with.

Turning back into the room, she hears her class approaching. A difficult form, and she welcomes the brash life of them, preparing herself with a soft slap to each cheek. They rattle down the corridor and break through the door, smirking, throwing and hushing their voices, shoving. Spots, growth spurts, moustaches even, or the shadow of them, flesh burgeoning. A multi-headed monster. They stand as a body behind their chairs.

'*Bonjour, mes élèves.*'

'*Bonjour*, Miss Wright, Mrs Beatty.'

She is recently married and her old name sticks. She doesn't correct it. She prefers it, she finds, to her new one. She sits down and starts the register as they clatter into their chairs. This is their form room and they like to investigate the contents of their desks, overturned, as they often are, by the passage of the day. With exaggerated pronunciation she mangles their names, watching who will grin.

'Daar-viee,' she says. 'Cl-aairrrr.'

'*Oui*,' they answer. '*Oui*.'

'*Présente*, Madame Wright,' says Miriam, whose parents have a French farmhouse and have often told her that they do.

'*Présente, presentoni*,' they mock.

'*Pas de Robin?*' she enquires.

'I think she went home for lunch,' Davy offers. 'Maybe she wasn't feeling well.'

Miss Wright puts Robin down as absent, then makes her mark ambivalent. Thomasin, almost on time, walks to her place. As she passes, she tips the lid of Claire's desk and drops something crumpled inside. A hankie perhaps. Whatever it is, Claire remains looking forwards, a neat set to her face, her blouse, her hands. No tears, which is perhaps a surprise, but colour rising on her cheeks, which isn't, given the heat. They all look cooked. Sitting down, Thomasin retrieves her textbook from the depths of her desk. Her attention rests on the front cover: something written in black marker, big and dense like a slogan.

They are compelled at the start of each year to cover their books, in wallpaper, adhesive vinyl, brown paper, and Miss Wright is often surprised by the care that they take, even Thomasin, the corners turned and stuck. And then they do this, graffiti each other's books. A biro whisper on the flyleaf, indelible ink on the front; acts of communication both acutely personal and assertively public, amplified. She had come across something only this morning, a declaration of love or perhaps of mockery on the back of Davy's homework book. *Big Lovers for Life*, it read, and hasty, scribbled hearts in a row.

Miss Wright's eyesight is sharp, but not quite sharp enough. She pushes herself up and takes her little stroll while the class sorts itself out. Passing Miriam's elbow, she turns and glances down at Thomasin's desk. *NOT PRETTY – NOT CLEVER* inked across the front of her textbook in stark, standing letters. She watches Thomasin uncap Miriam's good pen – *NOT TRUE*, she writes underneath. Defiant black ink. Miriam hacks out a laugh. *Not pretty, not clever, not true*, Miss Wright repeats, moving herself forwards. Not, not, not.

She stands at the front. Catching two lengths of hair, she smooths them down over the front of her dress, assessing the split ends. Her dress is a field of flowers, high-season colours, and her hair has the same pinkish, greenish blonde running through. A creak of the door and Nicolas appears, rosy-cheeked.

'*Je suis très désolé,*' he says, and looks it.

She nods, tucking her hair behind her ears, and watches him to his place. It is not a day for interrogations.

'*Savoir,*' she says to begin.

'*Su,*' they respond. 'To know, knew.'

'*Avoir –*' she asks.

'*Eu,*' they answer. 'To have, had.'

'*Boire –*'

'*Bu*. To drink, drunk!'

She comes around to the front of the desk and hauls herself up. Her great thighs spread; her small, pointed feet dangle. She keeps going, calling out infinitives, the class shouting past participles back, some a little before time, a scatter of voices after, a rising, baggy clap of sound. We don't use our ears enough, she often says. Our voices. It's always eyes and hands, pens and smudged paper. But that's not how language works, not how it grows. This she has explained to Gomme on more than one occasion. He, nevertheless, will have his written homeworks. Back and forwards, round and round, soft and softer; loud and louder, her voice high, golden and buoyant and theirs following, ringing the loose locker doors.

'*Naître –*'

'*Né*. To be born, born.'

'*Être –*'

'*Été*. To be, been.'

'*Venir –*'

'*Venu*. To come, came!'

'*Vivre –*'

'*Vécu!* To live, lived!'

They sit. A whistle blows on the rugby pitch and Mr Ward's voice tears into the air. The tenacious ones, Miss Wright reflects. Hard as iron studs.

There is a knock at the door. A face wavers in the reinforced glass and Jonah comes in, greeting Miss Wright with a wrinkled smile, his dark hair sliding. An uncanny beauty. An electric shock that stops her mid-breath. His eyes are green, with a strange, vertiginous depth. She feels she has to hold his gaze to hold him upright.

'*Bonjour, Jonah, ça va?*'

'*Monsieur Lafayette est dans le jardin,*' he offers. And then: 'I'm very well, Miss Wright, how are you?'

He is a tall boy – taller still in those shoes, the stacked rubber soles, brothel creepers – and loosely jointed. The school's long-distance hope. On the track, his energy is sharp. Off it, he idles around, on perpetual lookout, it seems, for any diversion. His eyes roam. He finds Thomasin, but not before she removes all trace of herself from herself. Could a person be any less present, Miss Wright wonders, and still be in a room?

'Miss Spencer wants to know,' begins Jonah, 'have you got a spare board rubber?'

'I don't know. Have I?' Miss Wright half turns herself around, and she half sees Jonah put something down on the desk closest to him, setting it passing hand to hand towards the back.

'You've got three,' he says, approaching the black-board. And so she has. The wooden blocks nudge together on the ledge, a dusty toy train.

'That's greedy,' she says. '*Prends-en un*. Help yourself.'

He picks two up and claps them together. From the felt thud an ashy cloud expands, powdering the cuffs of his jacket. Miss Wright sneezes. A short snuff of a sneeze.

'Why did Miss Spencer have to send *you*?' She supresses a second sneeze with a tissue.

'I offered.' He spaces the two remaining rubbers symmetrically on the ledge, weights on a balance.

Miss Wright pushes the tissue back into her pocket. Something dark around his eyes, she thinks, turning herself back to the front. She has seen it before in other boys, other girls. A latent danger, a gathering infringement, as if when tested he'll lack all ability to protect himself. Against what, though? She is not sure.

At the door, he throws a last glance at Thomasin, who remains unreachable, a TDK tape in front of her that wasn't there before, and leaves.

Miriam swipes the cassette up. 'Side one, track one, "Boys Don't Cry",' she reads. 'Side two, track twelve, "Sexual Healing".'

Thomasin lifts her palm and holds it out, a flat request.

'Very neat handwriting,' Miriam says, extending her arm, holding the tape away from Thomasin. She screws up her eyes. 'Neat but illegible, due to a generous splatter of blood, now dry.' Miss Wright looks again. She had taken it for paint, rusty brown, on the cardboard inner of the case. Miriam relinquishes the mixtape. Thomasin opens her desk and spins it to the back. A brittle rattle of plastic.

'It's a shame I didn't bring my tape player in today,' Miss Wright says. '*Mon lecteur de cassette*. We could all have had a listen.' She cocks her head at Thomasin, receiving in return a vacant stare. Such cold and splendid indifference, all the petty gods. But love and music. At that age, really, is there anything better? At its strongest and its sharpest. And not to be tossed away, if only they knew it.

Miss Wright settles herself on the desktop. She looks at her hands, the dimples and the freckles, the new gold ring. She listens to the ambient shifts and whispers. They have been through something together since waking up this morning, even if most of them don't know it. An assault, a car crash. A violent storm at sea. They have been hammered and pushed under, then thrown by the wreck and hurt of the day onto the hard sand. Yet here they are, holding fast, on the very sill of life. The young and the lucky. If they can crawl a little further up, into the warm sunshine, into the sustaining charity of air – She looks at her class and feels a benevolence spreading out to take them all in.

'*J'ai déjà vous raconté l'histoire de ma chirurgie esthétique?*' she asks. 'The story of my plastic surgery.'

'*Non. Je crois que non,*' Miriam answers, the French elastic in her mouth, a Languedoc farmer's.

'In English, though,' requests Davy.

Miss Wright pulls the fabric of her dress out from her breast. The little silver bells, hanging from her collar on silk ties, jingle and fall quiet. 'I once had a boyfriend, a fiancé in fact, who had a car,' she begins.

'How old were you?' Miriam asks.

'Nineteen. *J'avais dix-neuf ans.*'

'How old was he?'

'*Il avait vingt-six, vingt-sept ans.*'

'*Trop vieux,*' Miriam decides.

'A lot too old,' Miss Wright agrees. 'It was night. Not

late but dark, and we were driving back from a pub in Reading. It was an old car—'

'What sort of car?'

'A crappy sort of car. A van, actually, because he was in a band, or he thought it was a band. They did Genesis covers.'

'It was probably just a Ford Transit,' Nicolas reflects.

'Possibly,' Miss Wright concedes.

'Did he have a ponytail?' This is Davy, who often wants to know how things look.

'He had it long at the back, short at the front. Already slightly going on top . . . I know, what a hunk! *Un beau mec!* So, we were driving home in his crappy van. Ford. The bodywork was rusty. The exhaust smoked. You could lift the rubber mats up and see the tarmac rushing under your feet. And we came to a bend in the road –'
She crooks one wrist.

'*Droit.*'

'*Non, pas à droit.*' She waits.

'*À gauche.*'

'*Oui.* But the van didn't go left. The van kept going straight. *Tout droit.* I was pinned to the passenger seat, watching a blank wall come closer and closer. "Turn the steering wheel!" I started shouting. "Turn the beeping wheel!" "I am beeping turning!" he yells. And he is turning it and I'm turning it, but the van keeps going straight on for what feels like for ever – a white-wall eternity – and then bam! We drive smack bang into the end of a building. A chemist's, in fact.'

'*Où est la pharmacie?*' Davy enquires gravely.

'I slammed forwards to the dashboard and was knocked unconscious.'

'What about seatbelts?'

'None. *Pas des ceintures de sécurité.*'

'*Quelle catastrophe,*' says Thomasin, languid.

Miss Wright runs the ties of her dress through her hands. She examines their ends, the little cluster of silvery bells, then turns her head and looks out at the high blue sky. The curving pitch of swallows. All the windows open, and still so close inside.

'I have no memory of what happened next,' she resumes. 'I woke up in hospital. I do remember my mum brought my nan in and when she came through the curtains, she turned bright green like –'

'Absinthe,' Miriam supplies.

'Or like an apple.'

'*Verte comme une pomme,*' Miriam agrees.

'My nan opened her handbag and was sick. Straight into her smart handbag. "Have you seen yourself?" she kept asking. So I got out of bed and went to the loos and stood in front of the mirrors and my whole face – I didn't really have a face – my whole head had blown up like a puffball. A bloated fish. Like the Michelin Man! I looked like the moon, with pokey holes for my eyes and mouth. According to the doctor, I'd broken every bone it was possible to break in a face.'

'Did it hurt?' Davy asks.

'Everything hurt. *Oui, je sais. Pauvre de moi.* Poor me. But then eventually I had my plastic surgery. Surgeries. Eye sockets, nose job, chin, jaw. They reconstructed my entire face from photos my mum had given the consultant. But –' Miss Wright raises a finger to the tip of her nose. She smiles and feels her cheeks dimple. 'You see, I used to have this long, pointy nose and pillar-box mouth. No lips. None. And the surgeon had given me this cute nose—'

'*Le nez!*'

'*Le nez en bouton!* And high cheekbones. *Les pommettes!* And this little pouty mouth, *toute petite.* "What photo did you give them?" my nan asked. "Shirley Temple?"' Miss Wright shakes her head. A spring of hair escapes her ear and she tucks it back in place.

'What about your fiancé?' Miriam asks.

'Stephen?' How to answer for that? Miss Wright unpeels the back of her legs from the desk one by one. She draws the elastic of her cuffs out until her sleeves billow. 'To tell you the truth, I was much prettier afterwards.'

'Ohhh . . .'

'I was. And I thought, I don't have to marry him. I can go out with someone much better looking!'

'Whhhooo . . .!' A rattling of desk lids.

'So, I had to tell him, I'm sorry—'

'You jilted Stephen?'

'I did. I jilted Stephen Jenks!' She begins to laugh, a long, bubbling laugh that goes inside with a shudder.

'That wasn't very loyal,' Miriam tells her.

'No,' agrees Miss Wright, which sets her laughing again. 'It wasn't!' She had been untrue. Pretty, clever, not true.

They wait. A tear travels her cheek and she brushes it sideways. She appreciates their forbearance. The way they sit, allowing her to laugh and cry.

'You know the strangest thing about it all? After the surgery, people I'd known all my life, my aunties, my old best friend, walked straight past me in the street. They couldn't see me, I just looked too different.'

'Like being a ghost,' Davy suggests.

'Maybe. But then I moved away to Southampton, to university, and nobody knew what I was supposed to look like –'

'Have you got photos?' Miriam asks. 'From before?'

'Yes, photos! We want to see you ugly!'

'I'll bring some in. Before and after. And you can all be sick into your desks. *Vous pouvez tous vomir dans votre pupitres!*'

Desk lids lift. A little waterfall of retching.

Miss Wright slides to the floor. She looks at her feet, at the tan points of her shoes pressing her toes together. Her dress makes a lampshade from which her two meaty calves stick down in tights. She turns and looks at the clock.

'What a long day today,' she says. And then: 'I know he was popular. With you all. How much you'll miss him.' Her voice feels wavy. She can't bring herself to say his name. She hadn't planned, in fact, to speak of him at all. 'I'm sorry you have to go through this.'

'Is it your fault?' asks Thomasin.

An unfamiliar sensation: Miss Wright has Thomasin's full attention.

'No,' she replies. 'But neither is it yours.' What is she trying to tell them? She has no idea. She is just trying to give them some words, in order not to leave them without any. 'It belongs to life, death. But it's not, in the end, the most important part.'

'James wouldn't agree with that,' Miriam says.

'No,' Miss Wright concedes. 'But what does he know? James, for some unaccountable reason, does German.'

She looks about the class. Stopping at Thomasin, she passes her a wink. A split second and a smile comes back, unguarded, and immediately disappears. Miss Wright feels a flush of relief. Finally, something like a human response from this child.

'*Ouvrez vos livres*,' she says, and lifts her battered text-book up. 'I suppose we could even do some work.'

23

Headmaster's Office

2.25 p.m.

Kelly follows at the back of the class on his own, the length of the middle-floor corridor, then spins around on one heel and starts back the other way. He feels a holiday kind of elation, bouncing away from the classroom door like this, back again between the narrow walls, clapping the loose notices with the flap of his hand.

The bell has gone, but Dr Cole won't turn up for a while. He is usually late, with deputy-head excuses.

Kelly half jumps down the flight of stairs, two, three steps together, and then the entire flight of the little landing. The slam of his feet ricochets up and down the stairwell. At the bottom he ducks the windows of the school office, under the gawp and knock of the women inside, and slides himself, back to Gomme's wall, into the corridor. Half a corridor really, open at both ends, so Gomme can swoop and grab. But there is nobody here now. Gomme has been marched away, loop-the-loop, and Kelly has the freedom of the corridors.

He takes a quick breath. Excitement elbows him on. The door to Gomme's office is even a slight crack open, which it never normally is. Kelly gives it a Monkey Magic kick and jumps back, expecting – he doesn't know what – but the office is empty. Empty of all Gomme! He glances back once and then goes in, feeling hot to the ears, tight in the chest and dangerous, and pulling the door almost shut behind him.

He has been inside before. He has been taken by the shoulders and shaken hard, right here by the window. For Insolence and Impropriety. Standards of Deportment We Expect You To Live Up To. And then, another time, for something else he hadn't done, lifted off his actual feet.

From here he can see the front lawn, a thick green carpet, and a slice of both cedar trees, the roots snaking in the grass, the giant trunks red and stout, planted down like dinosaur legs. He looks at Gomme's chair. It is not the sort of chair that he would have. Just an old chair with wooden arms and legs, stiff-backed, and a sort of woven seat, dry reeds or straw, stretched loose in the middle by Gomme's big arse, almost like it will break. A clapped-out throne.

He hasn't got a plan. If he had his bag with him, he could've left his brother's condoms on Gomme's desk. Why hadn't he thought of that? He could, though, take something of Gomme's, a trophy to prove he dared to come inside. It makes him grin, the anticipation of it. He casts around, but the room is a dud, empty of everything. Not a glass paperweight, not the swinging steel balls like he's seen at his brother's work. Not even a photograph of Gomme's ugly daughters. Just blank wooden walls and a wastepaper basket with ink stains inside, and two wire trays, side by side, empty on the desk. There are books, a stack of them on a side table, with the Prize Day labels ready on top. *A Spotter's Guide to Pond Life*, he reads from a spine. He doesn't want that. Nobody in their right mind is going to want that.

Kelly hesitates, then pulls open the desk drawer, the wide one in the middle under the blotter. There is nothing. A spilled box of paper clips and a handful of pencils, and not even good pencils, the same ones they all get from the stationery cupboard, but these ones still with their points. Something at the back, a small folder, with a belt of paper around the middle that, with a skip in his heart, he breaks open – a letter-writing set. A present someone gives you when they don't know what you're like. Or when they don't like you. Kelly slaps the folder shut and deals it to the back, shunting the drawer closed, and starts going down the side drawers. Nothing in the first, just lots of paper stuffed in to bursting and the top bits bent and ripped. He opens the second. Nothing. Papers, papers. Nothing in the third, a wedge of index cards stuffed up, gone yellow. He pulls some out. *Edward John Wood,* he reads, *5ft 11", Year of Entry: 1974.* Scribbly writing, fading brown. *Elizabeth Gillian Plover, 5ft 3", Year of Entry: 1961.* Something, something, *and down a peg or two.* Old pupils. Probably mostly dead by now. Not even in any order, chronological or alphabetical. *Paul Alastair Julian Rowan Christopher . . . Beloved of* – Paper tombstones! And more middle names than can be crammed onto the card. Get rid of Alastair for starters. And Rowan. Because who wants to be called that?

Kelly's middle name is Dart, which is a good name if you think about it, even though his brothers gave it to him because, really, they just wanted a dog. But he never gets to use it. He's down at school as Matthew, his brother Jason's middle name, in case he gets teased. And when they finally got a dog, it was a girl and they called it something else.

His baby niece Manda's middle name, one of them, is Penelope, which Kelly had thought of because of the cartoon, Penelope Pitstop, but he didn't mention that to his mum. Her other middle name is Louise, like her own mum. Kelly drops the cards and rams the drawer shut.

But what about all the things Gomme confiscates? Where does he lock those up? Kelly's Shark Island, for example. He has never got that back. He cranes around. There is nothing here, not even a mini-safe like his brother has, which Kelly has tried to open by listening to the clicks but can't. He stands, considering what next—

A crack like a gun.

'Fuck me!' He leaps backwards, hands clapping his heart.

A mousetrap. Strong hinge, fast-sprung. Steel bite snapped shut. There in the darkness under the desk where he hadn't even looked. No mouse. Only his heart going like the clappers.

Kelly is pleased to have sworn so loudly. Impropriety, right in Gomme's office! And not to have been shot.

A strange silence follows. Sound hoovered up, the air plugging his ears. Outside Gomme's window, the trees held still by the heat. It occurs to him that there is a smell. Stagnant like a standing pond. Old dog-piss puddle. The tell-tale clout of rising damp. He does his dad's checks: ceiling, pipes, leaking window. Proximate electrics. None of these. Dry rot, then? His dad would have this wood straight off, the panelling, then the plaster, where it's blown. The soft joists up. It gives him an uneasy feeling, something in the wrong place, water where it shouldn't be. Inaccessible rot. A long ice-cube shiver slides down his back. Someone walking on his grave. He turns away, his foot knocking the sprung trap.

It is not that he particularly likes mice. But if you close the cupboards and wipe the surfaces down, why would –? Something so small.

All the wrong of the day seems seated in this room. Its cruelty and confusion. Its horror. Things gone bad. Drawing back his hand, Kelly makes a hammer fist and punches through the seat of Gomme's chair. The dry cane gives easily, the strands snapping like the strings of a harp, like nerves, and his fist going right through. It is scratchy to pull his hand out again, even with his fist undone and fingers straight like a beak. But it is a good clean hole. And big enough that nobody is sitting down there again in a hurry.

Kelly rubs his knuckles, confirming himself to himself. Them and us, his dad says, and they will break the backs of the small if you let them. But not this mouse. They can't catch him! This mouse is small, but fast and brave. Mighty Mouse, master of escape!

He sticks his head into the corridor, turning his neck both ways to look and listen. There, right at the end, is Mr Ardennes' door. Which is shut. Which has his name on it, *J.-L. Ardennes.* That will be something French, the hyphen. Kelly has never stepped foot inside and now he never will.

He darts out of Gomme's corridor and races up the stairs.

'Hey now, now Kelly!' He skids to a halt and glances down: all the stair treads straight, descending, the angles sharp, and Miss Harper at the bottom near the school office, looking up, her black hair floating, the white of her lab coat sticking out around her like a starched nun's hat. 'No running,' she calls up.

'Sorry, Miss. Late for English!' He takes off again, tripping up on the final flight of stairs, swinging around the turn of the banister, putting a floor, two floors, between him and the busted chair, and feels a grin explode.

24

School Office

2.28 p.m.

Miss Harper stands in the centre of the school office, a glass box filled with heated air and Wendy's anxiety. Mrs Poole is not happy. Mrs Poole bangs things around and meets Miss Harper's photocopying requests with a front of silence. Wendy has offered to do it, but Mrs Poole silenced her with a pile of invoices.

'I can do it myself,' Miss Harper suggests. 'It's just one sheet, two copies.' She wonders whether to add that she has used Mrs Poole's photocopier before, out of hours.

'Just as normal, Mr Gomme says, everything as normal,' Mrs Poole repeats, half under her breath. 'And then Mr Cole comes along and says nothing is normal. We're not doing anything normal anymore. Never again.'

'It's challenging,' Miss Harper agrees, taking a step backwards. The air, spiked with Shake n' Vac, is thick to breathe. 'Don't worry about the photocopies if it's a bad time. I'll come back later.'

'You can have it this way or you can have it that way,' Mrs Poole tells her, or, more accurately, tells the glass wall. 'You just can't have it every which way. Or not under my supervision.'

'You're coping really well,' Miss Harper says. 'Keeping everything going.'

Mrs Poole looks at her, her face flat with incredulity.

Miss Harper turns but finds her path to the door is blocked. Wendy has come around behind her and is standing in close. Miss Harper sees a small version of herself swimming in the round pools of Wendy's glasses.

'It's just that the newspaper has been phoning,' Wendy hisses. 'A couple of times.'

'Which newspaper?'

'The *Town and Enterprise*. We don't know what to tell them.'

'We don't have to tell them anything, do we?' Miss Harper feels a prickle of panic. The back of her neck, her palms. 'We don't have to talk to them at all.'

'Mr Gomme has dealt with it,' interjects Mrs Poole. She stilts across, the flesh of her feet overflowing the rims of her court shoes, and pulls the sheet for photocopying out of Miss Harper's hand. 'Mr Gomme told them if they don't stop phoning, he'll send Derek from Maintenance down to cut the wires. With a ladder and his electric hedge trimmers.' She rounds on the photocopier and bangs the lid open.

'The thing is, Derek only has shears,' Wendy adds. 'Derek would like petrol hedge trimmers, but Mr Gomme won't sign the slip for Finance.'

'Perhaps best not put calls through to the headmaster,' Miss Harper suggests. 'Just for this afternoon.'

Mrs Poole jabs at some buttons. The machine wheezes into life, gathering its energies together. 'Wendy, up and get a new bottle of toner from the supply cupboard.'

'Oh, I meant to do that. First thing this morning before all this blew up.' Wendy smiles downwards and shakes her head, as if her ineptitude is a small, endearing child attached to her hip. She hurries out, clunking the door shut.

Mrs Poole turns to Miss Harper. 'And you'd be wise to check with Mr Cole before you bother filling all this lot in.' She points Miss Harper's sheet at her. 'There might not even be detention rotas now. That might be another normal thing we're not doing anymore. And mark me, you'll be the last one to hear.' She slaps the paper down to the bed of glass.

The phone rings. Mrs Poole picks it up an inch and drops it down. She is talking under her breath. About doing her job. About the office in the car-parts factory. The dole queue out of the Jobcentre door, around the corner and into Nelson Street.

Miss Harper waits. She looks at the wall beside her, at the great spread of faces photocopied from School Photo Day. Small, cut-out squares. Children in rows, in forms and years, but so reduced, so dark and grainy, as to be almost indistinguishable. And some ringed red with marker, which she hasn't seen before and doesn't like the look of. Next to them, on a brown hessian board, are all the staff photos arranged by department in a circle, Gomme and the deputy heads in the middle. *Who is Who?* it says on a strip of card at the top, Wendy's round cursive. Wendy likes making labels. She likes making wavy borders out of gold paper and fixing them up with the staple gun. But why, Miss Harper wonders, do we have this board in here, in the office? Surely it should be outside in the corridor where visitors can see it.

She turns away. She doesn't need to see herself. She knows what she looks like up there, nervous like a rabbit and her front teeth showing.

And she doesn't want to see the deputy heads.

She knows too that Mr Austen's photo isn't yet up, because she'd looked for him on Friday afternoon, when she'd come in for something that Mrs Poole couldn't give her or wouldn't, and Mr Plumstead, the old physics teacher, was still stuck fast where he'd always been, smiling thickly down between his nose and his chin. Mr Betts is supposed to take the staff photos. He just hasn't got around to doing Mr Austen yet, or so she assumes.

She looks out of the window, out over the back of the school, the terrace of stone slabs and the broad, flat playing fields beyond. She had been standing more or less here when the boy with epilepsy had landed. It had only been one floor, mercifully, a short flight out of the library window, and only concussion and a broken collarbone, but the thud on the stone had been sickening. What was his name? He hadn't stayed with them long. And they had never really got to the bottom of what had happened. It wasn't the epilepsy that had launched him out, according to Dr Harrington, but he couldn't say what it was. She had come across him once, the same boy, walking the lunchtime circuit on his own and backwards. 'How do you know it's me going backwards?' he'd said, his eyes locked to hers and his feet retreating step by step away, an odd, deliberate action. That was the sort of boy he was, for a term, and then he'd disappeared, moving school or country, leaving her with little

237

sense of his name. Dirk? Craig? Something abrupt like an order. No doubt his photo is still up on the board, if she really wants to know.

The door bangs and Wendy swings back in with two plastic bottles, one in each hand.

'I wasn't sure which was which in the dark,' she says, giving them both a shake. 'Derek needs to change that bulb. Supplies cupboard as well as downstairs pegs, girls' side.' She sends Miss Harper a quick smile, as if to say excuse the atmosphere, and don't worry, we're still friends for Friday morning coffee. Mrs Poole takes the bottles, bangs one down, unscrews the lid of the other and sees to the machine with emphatic efficiency.

'It will need to warm up,' she warns Miss Harper.

Miss Harper's eyes drift back to the board. In the middle, Dr Cole, his eyes firing, his shoulders in landslide. They had got him up there quickly enough.

Gomme had appointed Dr Cole in the second round, having advertised once but found the quality lacking. Word has got out, evidently, about how things are in the school. 'Why didn't you apply?' Dr Cole had asked, barely into his second week. 'You're already doing the job.' 'Yes, I am,' she had told him. Which was exactly what she'd said to Gomme when he'd told her she lacked the experience. 'I'd appoint you tomorrow,' Dr Cole had said. 'I'd appoint you today and backdate your salary.' Then, last week, he'd asked her why she stayed.

But Dr Cole might not be working out quite how Gomme had envisaged. He has his own ideas and draws his authority, it seems to her, from somewhere entirely outside Gomme.

And now, another vacancy. She lets her eyes flick up and along, searching out the familiar face. Because she wants to see him, in fact. All day dashing around, hardly thinking straight, as if she can outrun herself – She is ready now to see him. And suddenly she spins around, a leaping flame of anger.

'Where is Mr Ardennes?' she demands. 'His photo?'

A little pause. 'We took him down,' Wendy states, and turns the blank glare of her glasses to Mrs Poole.

'How is that possible? How can you take Mr Ardennes' photo down so fast, when Mr Plumstead has been up there for weeks? For months after he retired?' Miss Harper takes in their staring faces, but her throat is a flame-thrower, her voice searing the air. 'How can you remove Mr Ardennes today? What sort of mad-crack office efficiency is this?'

'We took Mr Plumstead down an' all,' Mrs Poole says, striking the photocopy button with a fist. 'And put up the handsome Mr Austen.' The machine's innards swipe and churn, delivering up twice into the tray, two printed pieces of paper.

Miss Harper looks at the board in spite of herself. And there Mr Austen is, tacked up beside her own face, grinning out from a tight white square.

'It has to be kept up to date,' Wendy tells her. 'It's part of the new job description.'

Miss Harper stands absolutely still. She considers demanding that they put the photograph back up. She could, in fact, demand it. And then she removes the hot sheets from the tray of the photocopier, nods a curt thank you and closes the two women and the chemical carpet firmly inside their box.

Outside the dark swell of the corridor meets the flush of her cheeks. A quietness and a coolness. She levers up the spring of her clipboard, inserts the photocopied rotas underneath and lets the metal jaw snap hard down. Strange how something like this can make your legs shake and throat burn. A scorching anger.

She was wrong to lose her temper even so, she reflects, crossing the corridor and starting up the stairs to the staffroom. And Wendy is easily offended, although it's sometimes hard to tell with the bounce-back of her glasses. But to take down his photograph today, so quickly. They were wrong to do it and she was right to tell them. As her anger revives, she starts running upwards, her quick ankles licked by rising flames. She reaches the middle landing, flying off the stairs and into the corridor.

'No runnin', Miss.'

She spins around. The thin cheek of that boy, Kelly, wagging a finger from all the way down the other end of middle corridor. She pushes backwards into the staffroom, looking stern but saying nothing, letting the door swing shut on his grin. Well, he must be used to being ignored by now. But what is he doing still in the corridor? And last lesson already started.

'Who's teaching English 1?' she asks.

Dr Cole lifts his head. He shoulders himself out of the corner. 'On my way. Via our friends in the office.'

Miss Harper lowers herself to a padded seat and sets her clipboard down. She still does what she has always done, which is more than she's paid to do. Perhaps it is time that she stopped.

25

English 1

2.30 p.m., lesson 5

'*Where is the beauteous Majesty of Denmark?*' Tin demands, striding in, her voice filling the room.

Miriam loves to hear these words aloud. In Tin's mouth, tasty in the air. But even more, she loves to speak them out herself.

'*The King is a thing – of nothing,*' she replies. A line like spitting, lightheaded with bitterness.

'*Alas, he's mad.*' Tin unhooks her bag and skids it across the floor. She unshoulders her blazer and sends it after.

'*How came he mad?*' asks James, sweeping in and stopping.

'*Very strangely, they say.*' Tin bows the word: straaaangely.

Claire appears.

'*How is it with you, lady?*' Miriam asks her. Claire circles them and slides in beside Vanessa. 'The fair Ophelia,' Miriam explains.

They contemplate Claire's back, Tin, Miriam and James, standing in the aisle, the classroom filling around them. Moving in across the front lawns, through the open windows, the warm air carries the smell of pine. Two dark cedars grown old together.

It is good to have Tin back to something like herself, throwing out lines, taking her stand in the room. She has spent the whole day turning away from Miriam, or at least that's how it's felt. Still, Tin's good mood can evaporate quickly. Like lighter fluid, Miriam thinks. Like her dad's gold-plated investments.

Nicolas arrives, sets his briefcase flat and explodes the catches.

'*Methinks it is very sultry and hot for my complexion*,' Miriam tells him, swiping his revision folder up and flapping it about.

'*'Tis like a camel indeed*,' says Tin. She is watching the door, Davy walking in.

'*The King's to blame*,' Davy says, inclining his head as he passes. Which is what he always says, the only quote he has learnt. Tin's eyes rest on his back. He pulls his chair out and lowers himself down. Something has happened between them, Tin and Davy. But what? Miriam doesn't know.

'*How now, a rat?*' Miriam shouts and lunges, one arm lanced to the floor, the other cheerleading behind with Nicolas's folder. '*Dead for a ducat, dead!*'

'*A hit, a very palpable hit!*' James claps his hands. And then, wringing them: '*Drown'd, drown'd. To muddy death!*'

'*One woe doth tread upon another's heel, so fast they follow.*' Tin from the height of a chair, her voice fine and measured.

Miriam folds herself onto Nicolas's desk, throwing her hair, his file over his rigid arms. '*I thought thy bride-bed to have deck'd, And not have strew'd thy grave.*'

'*Who was in life a foolish, prating knave.*' Tin jumps down.

Nicolas gives an inhospitable shake and Miriam gets up. Locking her hands around the legs of his chair, she begins to yank: '*I'll lug the guts—*'

'We're revising.' Kelly's voice, an unsteady alarm.

Miriam lets go of the chair and straightens up. Dr Cole is at the threshold, one shoulder against the door-jamb. He is a big man with a slab of a face and small dark eyes. His hair is grey and roughly shorn. He wrests his tie from his throat. Miriam sits down beside Tin and gets her *Hamlet* out.

'Hand these round,' he says, coming in and dropping a pile of paper on Claire's desk. His suit, a navy pinstripe, flaps around him like an irritant. Claire hurries up and passes out the photocopies. John Donne rinsed in ozone, fragrant from the Xerox machine.

English 1, its posters for Osborne plays and Kingsley Amis covers, has been stripped down. Dr Cole has had Derek from Maintenance clean the dust and ragged paper out and paint the walls white. It is stark now, a blank sheet, like anything can happen. Standing at the back, Dr Cole reads the photocopied poem aloud.

'*As virtuous men pass mildly away*,' he begins. In his voice, which is thick and Northern, the words stand distinct, until the tang of the rhyme comes back to gather them in close. '*Whilst some of their sad friends do say . . .*'

He rarely reads. Usually they stumble through whatever it is – soliloquies, Hardy's prose – while he chews his cheek or laughs outright. Today the words flow over and around them, odd lines catching here and there like sticks in a river. *So let us melt, and make no noise*, Miriam hears. *Like gold to airy thinness beat.* The mower starts up on the front lawns, under the arms of the cedar trees, a low, atonal accompaniment to the paced reading. *Thy firmness makes my circle just, And makes me end, where I begun.*

It is finished. The slap of his palm to the dryness of paper jolts them upright.

'*If they be two* – what's he talking about?' Dr Cole demands, and starts walking the aisles. 'Two what?'

'Souls?' Miriam suggests. They have had Dr Cole for two terms now, his abrupt call and response. It is better to volunteer early, the easier questions, than to wait and be asked the unanswerable later.

'Souls. That is, people,' Dr Cole confirms. 'Donne is writing about two living people. Who are they?'

'A poet-narrator,' Claire whispers, raising and lowering a trim hand. 'And an addressee. A woman.' If Dr Cole is surprised to hear her speak, he doesn't show it. But Miriam is. The unfamiliar voice is shocking, like Claire is shouting down the silence of a play.

'And what's the occasion of the poem? Surface level. What's happening between this man, this woman?'

'Donne is leaving for France on some sort of diplomatic effort,' James says. 'He's writing to comfort his wife, who he married secretly, by the by, and against the wishes of her family, causing them all sorts of financial misery for some years to come. Sixteen-something.' A flap of his hand. 'I forget which year precisely. Early seventeenth century. I say comfort, but in essence he's saying don't make a fuss. Planets spin, people die, accept what comes and don't complain.'

Dr Cole moves to the windows. He turns his back on the glass. 'A man is leaving on a journey, a woman is staying behind. The occasion of the poem is their coming separation. Clear?' They nod. 'And yes, the poem advocates stoical restraint. In the face of loss.'

'But should we be stoical in the face of loss?' asks James. 'Really?'

'I don't know how you should be,' Dr Cole replies, and resumes his pacing.

'*If they be two, they are two so, As stiff twin compasses are two; Thy soul, the fixed foot, makes no show To move, but doth, if the other do.* What's this? What's he describing?'

Dr Cole comes to a stop at Nicolas's desk. He picks up his Oxford tin, rattles it hard, removes the compass and holds it up. A small instrument, miniaturised by the mass of his hand. Flimsy, Miriam sees, against the white wall.

'*Thy soul, the fixed foot* – which leg? The stab leg, yep.' Dr Cole splits the compass, descends the spike to the blunt tip of one finger and starts it turning. The pencil leg twirls in the afternoon sun, drops out into shadow and takes the light again. A trinket pirouette. 'It looks like the fixed foot is motionless, but it – the person left behind – moves as the other moves because they're hinged together, yes?'

He completes the rotation with a snap of his wrist and walks to the front, dealing the compass onto a convenient desk. Miriam looks sideways, but Tin, in javelin sunlight, has closed her eyes. Miriam does the same and sees the compass puppet show, the afterimage, reversing out white against black on the lids of her eyes. Only that. She blinks them open.

'And the result?' Dr Cole demands, swinging his head about, the heavy way that he has. 'Where's our maths genius? Where's Robin?'

'We think she went home,' Davy says. He drops his hands to the flap of his blazer, lifting its heat from his back.

'The result is a curved and continuous line, joining a series of points equidistant from a given point,' says Nicolas, speaking as if affronted. 'On one plane. That is, it's two-dimensional.'

'In other words? In simple terms?' Dr Cole urges.

'A circle,' Tin says, opening her eyes.

'Hallelujah.' Dr Cole snatches the compass up, stabs it to the wall and inscribes a sharp lead circle into the clean plaster.

'That won't rub out,' Miriam comments. 'Derek will have to Polyfill that.'

They begin talking about maths, its exact, unnerving beauty; about circles and space, divine and cosmic geometry. The infinite perfection of God, Miriam hears. Round golden haloes. '*Ego sum Alpha et Omega principium et*' – James begins, stopping at Dr Cole's insistence and resuming in King James English – '*The beginning and the ending, which is, and which was, and which is to come . . .*'

Miriam tips her head. On the front face of the desk, beneath its lid and above her knees, Tin is writing.

Welcome to . . . Red felt-tip plush on freshly sanded wood. *The Bloodbath*. Miriam looks back up. Derek must surely sometimes question the point, the actual viability, of Maintenance.

'Well, it's not circular.' Nicolas is standing his ground. 'Time, most commonly, is conceived of as linear and sequential.'

'A day is a long, straight leash,' Dr Cole admits. 'In certain company. Even so, modern physics —'

Miriam looks back down. Around the red words, the outline of a sanitary pad unfolds. With wings. Always precise, Tin, if unreliable in every other thing.

'Well, yes, at certain points in the universe,' says Nicolas. 'Because of the relationship between time and space. At the edge of a black hole, for instance, time is liable to bend, there is a curvature both of . . .' Dr Cole allows the explanation to peter out.

Eternity classically defined. Spring and summer. The cycle of the agrarian year. 'Don't you all live out in villages?' Dr Cole shouts. 'Children of the soil. Round and round ploughing things. Endlessly baling hay?'

'Davy lives in some sort of cottage,' James says. 'But it's more of an ornamental tussock in front.'

'Farmhouse,' Miriam corrects. 'And pampas grass.'

Dr Cole moves to the back and leans against the wall. A favourite heckling stance.

'Penultimate stanza. Kelly. Sit up and read. The one before the final one.'

'*And thoughitin,*' begins Kelly. He stops and coughs. '*And though it in the centre sit,*' he tries again, spacing the words, '*Yet when the other far doth roam, It leans, and hearkens after it, And grows erect, as it comes home.*' Gaps as wide as Kelly's teeth, Miriam thinks, and smirks.

'What grows erect as it comes home? Miriam?'

'The compass leg?'

'The compass leg. The circle is drawn, the two legs come back together, yes? As *stiff twin compasses.* And what does that bring to mind?' Dr Cole casts around. 'Someone? Anyone?'

Silence. And now, surely, his classic line will follow. Miriam waits. *Thirty people here and only three of you thinking.* She can hear it, even if he doesn't say it. *That's how dictatorships start!*

Dr Cole levers himself off the wall and walks to the front. They sit sober, attendant in the heat. Miriam knows what he wants to hear but she's already answered enough. Too much with nobody in between and Dr Cole gets sarcastic. She grips the lip of her desk and tips her chair; her bum slides back, her feet dangle down like useless things. Warmth pushes through the open windows. The restrained drone of the mower and, beyond sight, a soft rumble like a skip emptying, sending the crows up from the Thicket. A hoarse complaint. She drops back to the floor.

'Nothing? Not – anything? Stiff, erect. Circles, holes? I won't labour the point.' Dr Cole raises a palm to his skull, rubs it about and chucks it down. 'I'm not talking about sex for the sake of it. I'm talking about sex because it's relevant. Kelly? Not usually so shy.'

'It's about doing it.' Kelly reddens.

'It's about doing it. It is. In part. An impending physical separation, the promise of a union. Reunion. Two human bodies hinged together by desire. One moves, the other responds, they come back together. A circle, a circuit of sexual energy. Of love. Do You Read Me?'

Nodding. 'Yes, Dr Cole.'

'Wedding rings, also circular for a reason, yes? Fidelity, unbroken vows, etcetera.'

Miriam's eyes drop, finding out his fat gold band. What sort of wife? Willowy, with crochet waistcoats. And the compass still snug in one fist.

'Because a circle is true, faithful to its mathematical premise in the sense that the distance from the centre to the circumference remains the same all the way around. Right?' Dr Cole turns on Nicolas.

'Correct,' Nicolas replies, one hand on his geometry tin.

'But let's be precise. What grows erect? Who grows erect?'

'The fixed foot?' Davy offers. 'The wife?'

'The woman. She does. Strange? Unsettling? Yes? No? Not sure? If we begin with a conventional premise – man leaves, woman remains at home – Donne's imagery pushes far beyond any restrictive ideas we might have about male, about female. Following?'

'Like they're merging bodies,' Miriam says.

'Excellent, yes. Exactly that.'

'Is this even on our syllabus?'

Dr Cole spins around, flinging his arms loose. It is Nicolas, his ruler raised. An oblique slice of glacial blue, the plastic liquid with sunlight.

'Every word written in the English tongue is on your syllabus, as far as I'm concerned. And, ideally, many words not in English.' Dr Cole lays his fists down on Nicolas's desk and leans his bulk towards him. His face, like a steak, hangs raw and heavy. 'If you mean will you be examined on this? No. You will not. But should you read it? Should you engage with these ideas? As a human being, as a young man or young woman wading, more or less innocent, more or less defenceless, into the great boiling sea of language, of literature, history, ideology, human experience and other effluents and intoxicants, yes, I think you should read it. I think you should. Because, one day, even you, Nicolas, might need it. Even you one day might find yourself grabbing at a poem like a man going under. Or not,' he concedes, meeting Nicolas's discomfort with his own imitation of a smile.

Dr Cole lifts himself up. He wrestles his jacket off and throws it at a chair. The compass, released from his hand, skids across the floor.

'Permission to take off our blazers?' Davy asks.

Dr Cole looks about him. 'Fine.'

They wait. Davy, with a sideways reach, retrieves Nicolas's compass and passes it backwards. Nicolas restores it to his tin and presses the lid shut. Dr Cole eyes them.

'It's just that Mr Gomme usually—'

'SHIRTSLEEVES,' he bellows, blasting the word over rocks. 'Okay now? Or do you need to see it in writing?'

They peel off their blazers, swinging them over chairs. The moving air breathes into the back of Miriam's shirt, carrying the cut green of the lawn, the resin of the twin cedars. Almost a whole day of sweat.

'Complexity,' Dr Cole resumes, turning and walking in the other direction. 'A certain level of difficulty. Donne pushes the circle, the image of the compass as far as it will go, until he brings us to a strange, a surprising conclusion. The merging of two bodies, as Miriam so aptly expressed it.'

'But isn't it elitist?' James asks. 'Donne's so-called difficulty.'

'To be literate is to be an elite. Then even more than now.'

'But Donne's work is deliberately opaque.'

'It's demanding. If you bother to follow it. It has subtlety, development. An unexpected kick inside. Its difficulty, as you, James, might appreciate, is part of its pleasure.'

'But should poetry be exclusive?'

'It shouldn't be any one thing.'

James gives this a moment of silent consideration and then leans forward and laces his fingers together, gearing himself up. 'And yet it seems to me that Donne, having made his suicidal marriage, having lost his job as secretary to Lord Whoever – and of course he's a Catholic, who converts to Protestantism for pragmatic reasons, and therefore a person of suspicion—'

'A packet of fags there's not a book on Donne left in the library,' Miriam offers.

'There was only ever one,' James tells her. 'But I confess I was reading it a bit between rooms and there's a possibility it went out from the hall with the jumble trash. We always empty ourselves out thoroughly for Our Lady's Whitsun fête. I've asked to be put on books and the tea urn, so if I spot it, I can claim it back. One year, my sister inadvertently donated her Rangers uniform – they're like

Girl Guides, but for people old enough to know better – and when my mother went around to explain, Sister Joan offered to sell it back for more than it cost. Even nuns, it seems, must keep abreast with inflation—'

'Enough.' Dr Cole kicks the door and turns.

'Can I finish my point?' James asks.

'If you have one.'

'My point is – and now that I'm making it, I realise that it is, broadly speaking, a Marxist interpretation – my point is that Donne is broke. No one will employ him. He has a baby coming every year and nowhere to put them. So I don't think he's elitist by nature. Necessarily. I retract that. He's a man pushed to it by despair. He's dug a deep hole and has somehow to talk himself up again and into some money. He does it – and I only speak for the first half of his life, by page a hundred-and-seventy-something I'd lost hold of the book – he does it by creating scarcity and therefore demand, in crude economic terms, for himself. Here's my poetry, he says, but I'm not going to print it. It's love poetry, but not the ordinary type. You can read it if you're one of my dearest friends, or if you're absurdly wealthy and well-connected, but only in manuscript, and even so you'd better be clever because it's more or less in code –'

James breaks off. He turns to Dr Cole. Startled grey eyes. 'It occurs to me that there may well be more copies

of this poem in this classroom now than Donne author-
ised in his entire lifetime. Thirty duplicates, Dr Cole.
Thirty-one, including your own. Donne would never
have sanctioned it, such wanton employment of an office
photocopier.'

Dr Cole leans his head back on the cushion of his
neck, his small eyes sharp. 'Mrs Poole in the office wasn't
wild about it either.'

James drops a hand, a substantial flesh-paper-wood
slap that makes Vanessa, a seat in front, turn around.
'To conclude, the complexity of Donne's work is an economic survival strategy: as long as only clever people
read him, the courtly will finance him. Because rich
people like to have what other people can't, or so I
understand. Therefore Donne prevents his work from
reaching the *layetie*, the jumble trash, those deemed the
Great Unclever, and restricts distribution to the intellectual elite – another form of aristocracy, equally insidious,
naturally, but one he has in part created – and those
considered sufficiently clever—'

'There's nothing wrong with being clever,' Vanessa
says, looking straight ahead.

Dr Cole slides his attention across the room. Miriam
watches a redness flare up the side of Vanessa's neck,
flushed out, it seems, by Dr Cole's stare.

'Meaning?' James demands.

'Meaning some people are clever and some people aren't.'

'It's more that some people are rich and some are not,' James says.

'No. Some people are just better than other people,' Vanessa insists. 'Like us and the other school.'

The hot words hang.

Tapping. The door opens and Miss Harper's face appears in the crack, followed by a red clipboard. 'Apologies for interrupting,' she says, her eyes skittering about.

Miriam, the bulk of the class, begin the push to their feet.

'I'm not coming all the way in,' she tells them, fanning them back down with her clipboard. 'Can I borrow you for a moment, Dr Cole? We're having to rejig the after-school rota.'

She ducks out. Dr Cole follows, banging the door behind.

'You think we're better?' James asks, addressing himself to Vanessa. 'We're not better. There are kids far cleverer than us in the other school. We all know that.'

'Why aren't they here, then?'

'Because being middle class, being English, we paid. I speak generally, my parents didn't, of course, they're a bit stretched as you know, but we all tutored ourselves here one way or another. By background, by family aspiration.'

James crosses the aisle and plonks himself down on Vanessa's desk. Miriam climbs up onto her own desk for a better view, her feet on her chair. For all his holiness, you can rely on James for a decent fight.

'Nessa's not middle class,' Kelly says, idling over.

'Get lost, Kelly,' Vanessa tells him.

'Well, you're not. If I'm not, you're not. And neither are you.' This from Kelly to James.

'No,' James agrees. 'Perish the thought. We're the educated proletariat, are we not, Comrade Nessa? Or are we Tebbit's aspirational poor? I'm a little unclear on the difference.'

Nothing.

'Not that I'm entirely English, of course,' James continues. 'Being Irish. And most of my extended family living in America. Would you like to visit America, Vanessa? Reagan's cursèd empire?'

Vanessa sits with folded arms and closed face. A resisting silence. Kelly wanders away.

'Well, never mind, perhaps you will. But whatever happened to your –?' From his perch on Vanessa's desk, James leans back, his eyes raking her hair. 'It was all remarkably . . . remarkably . . .' His hands bounce by his temples, an invisible firmness. 'This morning. And now it's gone a bit more . . .' He searches the air, finds twin finger prongs and strikes them up and out.

'Head of Medusa,' Miriam suggests.

'Charles the Second. But to return to our conversation, to the division of one small town in two by an ill-conceived and outdated education system, one might observe that there's more than one way to measure intelligence. Or that the very attempt to categorise a child at the age of twelve is gravely negligent, given that individuals develop at different ages, in different ways and, frankly, sometimes not at all. And, further, that verbal reasoning tests grossly disadvantage those who don't have English as their mother tongue – I refer to a highly specific English, that is upper-middle-class English, both written and idiomatic – the results of entrance examinations being –' He reaches out to touch Vanessa's sleeve. He is plaguing her now.

Miriam turns to Tin. A sudden drop in temperature. Her mood has changed, as Miriam knew it would. Tin is sitting with her elbows sharp to the desk. She is looking at something, but not at Miriam, and not at anything Miriam can see. Around her, the entire room, almost, is in cautious circulation. It is hard to know how to be when Tin is like this. Her stillness appears absolute, but there is nevertheless something mobile in her that Miriam fears to rouse. Electric scorn. No wonder Robin's done a bunk. Or is Tin only sad? Miriam doesn't know. She would like to ask what happened at lunchtime, with Jonah, what his letter said, but it might be something else entirely. Or nothing.

It is Mr Ardennes, Miriam sees. A sudden flare of clarity. What happened last night, this morning, pulling Tin back to the cold, ruined place she sometimes goes. Where Miriam is not allowed. The place that makes Tin desolate like this, scorching. Careless of herself and everyone else around. What will Miriam do if she's always barred from where Tin is? Turned away. If she's always left alone? She looks to Tin, the side of her face, the long slide of her cheekbone. But there's no reaching Tin here. And no hold for consolation.

Miriam stands up. James is still going – apartheid, the Berlin Wall, the island of Ireland, the small betrayal of our own results day, an unbridgeable – Kelly is shunting desks about, for God knows what reason, so that Dr Cole's path down the aisles will somehow be impeded, but Nicolas is refusing to move. He has taken everything out of his geometry set and is now putting it all back in, the correct place in the fiddly plastic tray.

'Moooody!' Kelly crows, but leaves him to it.

Miriam crosses to the windows, to Davy's desk. Always the Walkman. Lifting the headphones from his ears, she slides them small and puts them on. An acoustic guitar and a spare voice. A shoreline of pebbles, rolling up and down.

'Who?' Miriam mouths.

'The Jam.'

She turns to the lawns, the circling mower. Shadows of cedars felled by lowering light.

Miriam remembers results day. The envelopes, addressed to their parents, they were given but told to take home. Excitement twisting her gut, she had folded hers into her bag and gone to the park afraid. Turner, casual on the roundabout, had torn his open and wheeled away, choking into his arm. And no one had ever teased him. They knew what it meant. There were parents who wouldn't put their kids through it, who bussed them out to the comprehensive in the bigger town. There were kids who didn't try, who said they wouldn't come even if they got in. But Turner wasn't one of them. Or hadn't been.

Her dad's City efficiencies, her mum in neonatal. Pass or fail. Viable, not viable. It feels a ruthless process.

She turns back to the classroom, listening until the clunk of the tape, then unhoops the metal headband and hands it back. Davy opens the tray and turns the cassette over.

'Why should I donate my clothes?' Vanessa is saying. 'They don't need clothes.'

'They do need clothes,' James spits back. The argument has shifted. There is hard anger in it. 'And if you were displaced in a warzone, you might not have packed a suitcase either.'

'It's not the same,' Vanessa counters. 'They're not like us.'

'They're exactly like us. Only they're starving.'

'Then why should I donate my clothes? They're dying anyway.'

A bright treble of drums from Davy's ears. Miriam lifts his hand and puts hers underneath, its weight a comfort.

'I don't care because I'm not Ethiopian,' Vanessa says. 'And I don't care how socialist your big brothers are, we're here because we're clever. We passed and the kids at the other school failed. Because they're too stupid to pass.'

—

'Vale!' Dr Cole shouts, pushing back through the door and letting the through-draft slam it. 'Who does Latin?' He has a wedge of papers under one arm, Miss Harper's clipboard under the other. He throws them at the front desk and scratches his neck. The class quickly reconfigures, pulling itself back into lines. '"A Valediction", anyone? I'm asking what the title means.'

'Farewell.' Miriam drops into her chair. 'It means goodbye.'

'It's a farewell. Separation, both temporary – you have to go home for dinner, you'll meet in the park again on Friday, I can't bear it, I miss you, I love you, see you tomorrow, goodbye – and the other goodbye. For ever. Death. And why the other part. Why "Forbidding Mourning"?'

'Because all the Blessed will be folded together,' says James, 'in Our Lord's Immortal Embrace.'

'If you believe in God,' Dr Cole qualifies. 'Yes. The whole of eternity to look forward to. With your loved ones.'

'Do you believe in God?' Kelly asks.

'No. Do you?' Dr Cole's voice like a headlock.

'I was baptised.'

'Felicitations,' James claps. 'One fewer sinner feeding the fires of hell. There's still purgatory, of course. Some untold millennia. Oceans of—'

'Let's say you don't believe,' continues Dr Cole. 'What other options have you got? To perpetuate life. To achieve immortality.'

'Freeze yourself?' James suggests.

'Reproduction,' offers Davy.

'Reproduction, yes. Procreation. We began with death, the poem begins with death, yes? *As virtuous men pass*. We move from there to love. An orgasm, on the one hand, a little death – Cleopatra dying twenty times a day, the school play, remember? Yes, Kelly, smirking? – a short, unconscious swoon; at the same time, the potential conception of new life, a beginning. Death, life, death – the life cycle. So, religion offers one promise of eternity, to complete the circle. Human reproduction another. What else?' Dr Cole thumbs the photocopy up from Claire's desk and rattles it by the corner.

'Poetry,' Davy says.

'Poetry. A poem of this standing, or of any standing, as long as we choose to read it, lives. The voice remains. It's another way to circumvent death, literature, a different sort of child and significantly cheaper—'

'Do you have children?' Kelly once again.

Dr Cole comes to a halt. He places Claire's photocopy down on an empty desk, squaring it with the tips of his fingers. 'Poetry is intimate,' he says. 'Let's not make it personal.'

Kelly's pinched face retreats. Dr Cole lifts his hand and resumes his walking.

'Tin!' At volume. 'Are you with us?'

'Mostly against,' says Miriam, without meaning to.

Tin snaps her eyes open.

'Moving on. Rhyme scheme?'

'ABAB,' says Tin. 'A four-line verse.'

'Known as?'

Silence. Tin knows this, Miriam is sure that she does. And if she doesn't, she won't care if she's shouted at.

'A quatrain,' Tin replies.

'Why use quatrains?'

Tin considers, without any apparent urgency. 'A to B is the difference, the separation of the man and woman. A to A is the return of the rhyme, the coming back, closing the compass legs. The fidelity to metre, the coupling of lines describes the lovers' constancy. Or, if you really want to push it, ABAB, life-death-life-death.'

For a brief moment, Dr Cole stands still and silent, then: 'You should always push it. As hard as you can. To see if the poetry holds.'

Dr Cole walks to the front and throws himself down to his chair, feet to one side, legs out like planks. He eyes the fat stack of marking on his desk and elbows it away.

'Final line? Final two lines?'

'He goes home,' Claire answers.

Without turning his head, Dr Cole points to the pencil mark on the wall. 'He goes home. Full circle. The end in the beginning.' He drops his arm and casts his eyes down the rumpled length of himself, then bends his knees and turns to face the front. 'Okay. Enough. Off you go.'

'The bell hasn't gone.' Nicolas, half-lifting a wrist.

'It no doubt will. Eventually.'

A few of them stand up. They have been dismissed but remain uncertain.

'Go on, put on your gaiters, or whatever it is you do in the cloakrooms. Ten minutes, less. I'm giving you leave, the briefest of holidays. A communal exeat.'

'Exeunt,' says Miriam.

'Very good.' Dr Cole drags a hand down his face. 'Now go home.'

Miriam dives down for her bag. Coming back up, she finds herself unexpectedly close to Tin, the side of her face, to her hair hot from the sun. All around, people are stuffing bags with blazers, a shallow volume of chatter rising up around them. Dr Cole remains at the front, apparently indifferent.

'Did you see Jonah at lunchtime?' Miriam blurts out.

'No.' A sharp sound in the bare-walled room. The flow of voices stops and then continues, chair legs juddering.

'If he comes into our classroom again, I'll go at him,' Miriam offers. 'With Nicolas's compass.'

Tin pivots, a quick switch on her chair that makes Miriam jump. After all the turning her back, Tin's dark eyes are on her. She takes hold of the hem of Miriam's skirt with both hands.

'Do you want to know what Lyn Ardennes said about you?' Tin asks. 'After the school play?'

'Yes.' Of course, yes. Greedy like hunger. Mrs Ardennes, who actually knows. Except it can only be bad if Tin hasn't told her yet. Three weeks since the play.

Tin leans back to the white wall. The skirt stretches like a pitched tent, a full gown, something spreading out in water. Miriam watches it go taut, bracing herself. 'She said you can act. And when you learn to do less, you'll be even better.'

Tin releases her, letting the skirt drop. Miriam lifts a wrist and wipes her mouth, hiding her smile. An uprush of pleasure, a cork pushed down in water springing up again. Already on her feet, squeezing her bag to her front, she joins herself to everyone else moving to the door. Davy pulls it open – the thrilled gasp of the empty corridor – and they all cram through together.

26

In Detention

3.17 p.m.

Tin stays where she is, in the almost empty classroom, the almost stillness, a low beam of light warm across her arms. The air breathes in and out through the windows. Discarded photocopies lift from the floor, drift, and rest still again. A rounding quietness, full of muffled sounds and gradual shadows. She was up late last night. The hot sun too has emptied her out. The room expands around her, rocking slightly, scattering its furniture.

'What do you want?' Dr Cole, hauling his head from his hands, has seen her sitting.

World peace and a gold star. 'I'm in detention,' she says.

'Again?' He interrogates Miss Harper's list, crumpled on her clipboard, and pulls the corners of his mouth square down.

They sit for a moment, detached and silent, companions in inactivity.

'I didn't know how to mark your story,' he says, stabbing a finger at the pile of homework. 'I think it was very good, but –' He lifts his hand and rubs his head, the scalped whorls of black and grey.

'It's okay,' she says. 'It wasn't personal.'

He nods, as if weighing whether or not to accept this.

A babysitter, a drunken man, twin cocker spaniels. A lurid tale, in fact. 'I made it up,' she adds.

'Ah, fiction.'

'Fiction,' she agrees. 'Not truth, not lying.'

'Both truth and lying. And in different measures, depending on who is writing.'

'And who is reading.'

He expels his breath, letting her empty cleverness fall.

She doesn't make a pretence of getting out work and he doesn't ask her to. He sits with his marking, the heel of one hand to his chin. His head looks immoveable, a roughed-out statue. *Man Undone.* She slides her palm over the warmth of the desk and lays her head on her arm. The wood is glassy, polished by decades of woollen blazers. Even the compass marks at the edges, the gorges by ruler, are rounded over. Slow-moving ice, the worn stones of the weir.

Water folding over.

One ear down, she can hear the rumble from the floor below. Chairs moving, the bass of the geography teacher's voice. And through the windows, the air bringing the church bells from Castle Hill stumbling in over each other. The town lies in a ring of humpback fields, the trees rising and hedges surrounding. The small beyond. On the ridge – the road, cars flashing silver between the trunks. The road goes to a bigger town. In the bigger town, a station. From the station, a train to the city.

Now she is detained but nothing is required, and the trouble of the day is held at bay by the door.

From where she is, this place of suspension, she can't tell how deep things lie. Robin with Jonah, Jonah with Robin, what they have or haven't done. Perhaps it is nothing, all the sex and hurt and drinking she has to care about.

Because there is no one true in this world. Nothing constant. It is naive to expect that there is.

But her desire for Jonah had felt true. And she had loved Robin, not knowing how, from that first summer when she had appeared, sunburnt and scrawny, lost by the side of the roundabout, peeling off the paint.

Now one has cancelled out the other, leaving only complications.

And Mr Ardennes? The thought of him is like a sudden drop, deep and irrevocable. Her mind swerves away. She stands on an edgeland. A desert of rock and wind. Impossible to ever go home.

She doesn't want to go home. She wants to get out. As far away as she can. In some ways she already has.

What do you want? Speeches and a fireworks display? Your name in gold on the wall?

She shifts her head and sees Dr Harrington issue from behind the Headmaster's Lodge, walking the curve of the path with his cartoon doctor's bag. Two crows sweep down behind him, shuffle their feathers and stalk about, important on the grass.

This small place is bound like an island. It takes stamina to endure it. Patience. Neither of which she has. She wants to get to where she isn't known. To where the constraints of all the things that have happened here – to her, to all of them – entirely lift away.

Her brother had just walked out, a year, two years ago. Even Mr Ardennes couldn't stop him, although he had tried. A party every night like a lure and barriers fallen through. A roundabout of parties. The nights softening into the days, the days strung out without distinction, blurred by risk and pleasure, until the hold of the weeks, the months seemed to lose conviction and reality, lifting, had slowly listed sideways.

She knows where he is, but she cannot reach him. The roundabout continues. Some of its glamour has worn off; it has worn through a number of glamorous people, but it remains, reeling about itself, driving deeper into the same small town. Of all his decisions, the squander and the chaos, staying here seems to her the hardest to make sense of.

The last time she saw him, he seemed to be asking for something.

What do you want? Approval? A long sleep in a straight bed.

The air draws in and out. Dr Harrington, his bag arm swinging, passes the front of the school, the Thicket, and is taken in by the shade of the Lane.

The felted lawn and thickening trees of the school. The town with its soft, damp bricks and tilting stone streets. There is too much here that is rotten. And Gomme has made himself mad on it, his own vicious tenacity.

She cannot feel for Gomme. He has taken too much down before him. He has taken other people down.

The bell detonates.

'All right,' Dr Cole says. 'Off we go.'

Tin sits up. Dr Cole is looking at her, chewing the side of his mouth, a hard glint to his eyes.

'Stop wasting your time,' he says, 'making trouble for yourself.'

She shrugs.

'You can help it, don't pretend. It's wrong to be so negligent.'

She gets up, slinging her bag over her shoulder, and watches him strike a heavy line through her name, through Mr Dalton's poker-face minutes. He is not going to hold her to them. He drops the pen.

'Every single life. Fearfully and wonderfully made,' he says, his black eyes glaring. 'It goes fast, Tin. Take proper care of yours. Nobody else can.'

'That's – individualistic.'

'That's not how I mean it. Find something. Friends, work, whatever it is. Anchor yourself. Otherwise, yes, it's each petty milk-snatcher for herself. And the waste of everything braver.'

She salutes him, one hand at her temple, walks to the door and is pulled into the flowing corridor of bodies, the rushing tunnel of noise.

27

Dark Alley

3.30 p.m., home time

They funnel in under the trees, James first, Miriam and Davy behind, descending the narrow tarmac. At the bottom, buses to take them home, those of them who live in villages, which James doesn't. But they all go this way, down Dark Alley. The other way is for the other school.

The air is cool and still, like wading into water, a declining shelf. To one side a tall plank fence, along which Kelly trails a jumping stick, gaining on them; to the other the Thicket, old spruce trees overhanging. It is black in there. An absolute black, absorbing everything. Crows, deer, the cross-country loop. Gomme patrolling the night, comb-over up on end and eyes deranged by the flashlight. A soul plagued in the dark, James thinks, from all directions.

They flow down the hill, their bags over their backs. There is relief in it, James finds, this daily descent, as if in going downwards something, a burden, is borne away. They go faster, accelerating over the bumps of roots, ramming the third years in front. Kelly dropkicks his bag, sending it skidding down the slide of tarmac, overtaking on its own. Suddenly they pull up. A railing bars the exit, and it is here that they collect: smokers, fighters, couples from different years, a pool of bodies in deep shade. And today – Robin, surrounded. She has come the other way. She has bunked off the whole afternoon, after lunch at his house. But it is what she says, not where she's been, that has them crowding around.

'What's going on?' It is Tin, sauntering down. She is out much sooner than James expected, released from Dalton's purgatory detention.

'Are you talking to her now?' jeers Kelly, pointing a short finger from Tin to Robin and back again, peeling his eyes.

Tin stops above them, appraising. 'What's the excitement, Robin?'

A tight circle of silence, surrounded by a swell of noise.

'Mr Ardennes killed himself.' The words burst out of Miriam's mouth.

'No, he didn't.' Tin's face struck white in the dark.

'Er . . . yes he did,' says Kelly. He has caught up with his bag and begins to harry it between his feet like a football.

'Turner told Robin,' Davy explains, taking a soft step forward. 'That's what they told them. At the other school.'

A howl pulled thin from her gut into the golden afternoon. 'Will this cunt of a day never end?' Tin shouts, or at least that's what James hears in the stretched, distorting sounds.

Pain flows like water, finding a way. Sometimes dropped from a height in boiling confusion.

Tin starts abruptly towards Jonah's bus.

'He's not there,' Davy calls. 'I think he went into town.' But she is already spinning around. The sun catches her dark head, the flare-up of a lighter.

'Idiot,' Robin says.

Kelly kicks his bag through the railing. Goal.

Miriam is shaking excuses out: 'I didn't mean – I didn't think –'

Tin sprung from nowhere, needing no one. In the years since primary school the memory has dulled. But they all know. Miriam does know. Tin's mum took her own life. James watches Tin step off the kerb and walk away. A clarion protest of bus horns.

Mr Ardennes, a suicide. The word a drought in his mouth. What to say? James doesn't know. They stand at the bottom of Dark Alley, shifting their feet, the dry sand of their thoughts, waiting for someone to lead them.

'Somebody go after her, then,' Kelly says. But none of them do. Death has finally pulled them up.

Robin shoulders her bag and walks away, the opposite direction. The sun, lying the length of Chandos Road, turns her fine, floating hair red-gold. James feels a tug on his sleeve: Miriam, her eyes wild, a raw appeal for something. He finds himself lost, words sticking in his throat. She turns, follows Davy to the steps of the bus and climbs into its shadows.

'*You shall see heaven open, and the angels of God ascending and descending upon the Son of Man,*' James says. A chain of words, the only available ones. But Dark Alley is almost empty, the last buses pulling away, the crowd at the railing gone. Those who remain, alone, in twos or threes, spin off into the small town, fragments of the day's explosion.

James hefts his bag, sharp-cornered with books, onto his other shoulder. Miriam had looked to him. For what? Forgiveness? To somehow share the burden. He looks at the kerb, the dry silt in the gutter, steps down and walks away.

28

Ford

3.48 p.m.

Fuck it, thinks Robin. And stops. And turns. The middle of the quiet road. Tin is quick, but if Robin tries, she might still catch her up. She takes her hands out of her pockets, clamps her bag to her ribs and runs.

The empty length of Chandos Road, the corner shop, a huddle of third years. Robin's hot feet slap the paving slabs. And then she sees her, the shine of Tin's dark head passing the garage. Robin slows to a fast walk. Petrol fumes, oil stains, the long, dusty plate window of the car showroom. For a moment, they are both held in its glass; Tin, glancing backwards, fixes her eyes on Robin's reflection, then she pulls away and turns into Ford Street. Robin follows, gulping for breath. Her feet and legs feel fuzzy, uncooperative after the rush. The backs of her shoes slip off. She passes the side of the garage, the dark, clanging hangar of mechanics, and tries again to gain on Tin, hurrying along the narrow pavement and down towards the bridge.

She is only, now, a couple of paces behind. As she draws in close, the sun flares white on the flat of Tin's shirt and Robin is hijacked by the desire to push her, hard, between the shoulder blades. She shunts her bag around, bracing her palm; she is about to push when Tin accelerates away, swerves and drops down off the approach to the bridge onto the slip road below. Without breaking her stride, Tin charges towards the ford and explodes into the river, throwing water up into the air like a child racing through a paddling pool.

Robin stops where she is on the rise of the bridge. Water flies upwards like confetti, sparkling in the sunshine. Tin is crashing through below her, shin-deep, knee-deep, deeper. The ford is supposed to be shallow, gravel and stones. The odd bit of glass. It is where they all used to paddle, where Robin and Tin did, fishing for minnows, dipping for frogspawn. Tin splashes out the other side, jogs up the concrete slip and hauls herself, legs, arms, bag, over the railings of the bridge. She walks back towards Robin, an easy pace, stopping on the crown of the bridge a short distance away.

The river runs beneath them, fast, talkative and muddy. Above, a single cloud, thin-bodied, trails long, wispy tails behind like a jellyfish. Tin stands on the bridge above her. Having passed the turning to the football club, the gate to the park, Robin is railed in. Tin's shoes gleam like she's bothered to polish them, her dark legs glisten. Even so, she looks less wet than Robin thinks she should.

'Do you want something?' Tin asks, but with such hostility it translates to Robin as: You can fuck right off.

'I just want –' To push her, wrestle her to the ground. To put her arms around her. And a leg. She just wants everything to go back to how it was before. Last week. Or a year ago, a couple of years, before the weekends and the drinking. I shouldn't drink, Robin decides. Her conclusion is so obvious she is amazed she hasn't come to it before. It feels like the only certain thing she knows.

Tin waits. Her eyes fire and darken. She doesn't do actual fighting, Robin knows, but this feels like she might. A pulse of fear, then nausea and Robin feels herself slipping, sliding out sideways. It takes a force of will to remain where she is, standing her ground, facing Tin down. She wraps an arm around her front.

'Are you going to keep following me?' Tin asks. 'Wanting anything I have?' She takes a step forward. And then another step. 'Because it's all getting a bit close.' Another. 'Too close. Or do you like it too close?' Tin's voice is low, unhurried, like it's winding around the back of Robin's knees. Water lies in splashes on her arms, on her shirt, spreading like stains, evaporating. 'How close do you like it?' Another step. 'Like this?' Robin feels the toes of Tin's shoes to hers, heat from the bar of one thigh. 'Closer?' Another small push forwards. They are chest to chest, but not quite touching. Robin can see Tin's breath, drawing in and out against her shirt. The water on her face. So close, like she's going to kiss me – 'Because it starts getting dangerous,' Tin says. 'Too close like this and people get hurt.'

I'm not hurt, Robin thinks. Or does Tin mean – Can she mean herself? Robin hadn't wanted to – Remorse sweeps in from the side, unexpected, for what she did last night.

'Tinny!'

Robin jumps back, turning her head. It is only Kelly. Always everywhere you don't want him. Kelly looks at Tin's feet, her wet legs, but doesn't say anything. Instead, he thrusts a packet of Wotsits between them, shaking them at Tin.

'You all right now, then?'

That is what Robin had meant, the right question, what she had come to ask before the pushing had taken over.

'Yes, I am, Kelly mummy,' Tin says, looking at Kelly, or possibly above his head, along the flow of the river. Her voice is flat, each word even and colourless.

Kelly shifts his arm, the drum of powdered baby milk under his elbow. How has he had time to go home, Robin wonders, and already be sent back out to the shop? Kelly rattles the crisps at Robin. Robin shakes her head.

'Suit yourselves.' He retracts his arm, swapping hands, crisps, baby milk, and feeding a fist of orange, puffy worms to his mouth, dusting off his fingers. 'Bye,' he says, and walks off crunching. He is even cockier out of school, Robin sees, the bounce in his step, the gel in his hair. He descends the bridge, walking towards town, then just before the pub, he stops and calls back: 'No fighting over boys, ladies!'

'Fuck off, Mini Milk,' Tin says, but not raising her voice. Robin laughs and feels a drench of saliva fill the gullies of her mouth. Ice cream, even Mini Milks. Or more, Kelly's crisps, now they have disappeared around the corner. *Cheesy Corn Puffs. When You Know Wot's Wot, Wot?*

Two sixth-form boys and a girl come over the bridge, one of the boys swinging in close to Tin, saying something into her neck Robin cannot catch. Everywhere they go, always someone wanting attention. Lifting a wrist, Tin pulls it across her forehead, as if wiping whatever he said, the river water, the drag of everything else away. She drops her arm.

'Let's go back to yours,' she says. 'Play Pac-Man, pierce ourselves. Whatever it is we're supposed to do.'

Robin looks at her, not sure if she can mean it. Tin starts walking.

'Ok-ay.' Robin follows. She doesn't want to go home but she's not about to argue.

They walk side by side down the small hill of the bridge, up the rise to the garage, back the way they came. Is that it? Robin wonders. Tin doesn't do fighting. She doesn't do shouting, crying, hugging and swapping perfumed biros. But is it over now, about Jonah? About everything? Robin isn't sure. They turn into Bridge Street, crossing the road between cars. 'I've still got *Airplane*,' Robin says, a week overdue at the video shop. 'And an old tape of *The Tube*, three episodes.'

'I've got rolling tobacco and a tab of acid.' Tin pushes a hand into her skirt pocket, one side, the other, then turns them both out empty like a schoolboy. 'I did have. I've got full pockets and a hollow heart.'

29

Darkroom

3.59 p.m.

Jonah steps inside and turns the white light off. They are in darkness, but not blackness. A red plastic lamp, moulded round like a mushroom, glows on the bench. The air is close and hot, astringent with liquid passing through funnels, with chemicals poured into trays.

Mr Betts walks across, the crepe of his shoes quietly gripping and releasing the floor. 'One part developer, nine parts water,' he says, and glugs something nose-pinching like vinegar from one shadowy vessel into another. 'It's a new bottle, so we'll have to watch it. It's easy to give it too long.' He moves around in the dimness, measuring, decanting, returning things to shelves. The trays of liquid gleam, square and shallow, lined up by the sink.

Jonah gets soap and sawdust when Mr Betts moves. And when he speaks, an assertion of freshness. Mentadent P, a defensive pasting, or Trebor Mints, penetrating the dark. Jonah had asked in advance, but he still had to pull Mr Betts out of the staffroom. 'It's cool if you can't today anymore,' Jonah had said. Mr Betts had backed away, his hands raking his face, and come back out again with water in his beard, like he'd dunked his head in the staffroom sink. But he doesn't seem incapable. He seems, if anything, more attentive that usual to the accuracy of his percentage mixes.

'Have you got your negative ready?' Mr Betts asks.

Jonah has. He has done the threading of film onto a reel in a black felt sack, coaxing it in between the runners and switching it around; he has done shaking it about in a tank of developing solution like mixing cocktails in the dark. He has chosen his frame and lined it up in the carrier. He is ready now to print.

Mr Betts flicks the switch of the enlarger and its big white bulb glows up. He built the darkroom himself last holidays, Jonah knows, all the shelves and counters, and brought his own gear in.

'They have darkrooms at the college,' Jonah tells him. 'At Art Foundation.'

'Is that the plan? Next year?'

'I've applied.'

'And the running?'

He is supposed – the school want him – to go somewhere they can boast about with athletics, and a wave-through on his A-level grades.

'I can't handle it much longer,' he admits. 'The Saturday mornings. I can't get up that early.'

'We'll need some paper,' Mr Betts suggests. 'The semi-matte, second shelf down.'

The paper is in a cardboard envelope, and then in a thick black plastic wallet. Jonah sets a single sheet down at the foot of the enlarger, under its glowing eye, and folds the rest back into the dark. Something is showing; his negative, but indistinct. Black and white in a smoky sky.

'This one.' Mr Betts taps a dial.

Jonah turns it towards him, and away again. The image jumps to life.

'There's the queen,' Mr Betts says, and rubs his beard. The sound crackles in Jonah's ear, hairs scratching together. 'And the other one, that comes as a pair.'

'Like this?' Jonah asks. 'Is that –?'

'You judge. Your eyes are better than mine. I hope they are. But if you're asking, a touch towards you.' Focus. Its sharp, decisive bite. 'There you are.'

It is different to see the image like this, reversed out of the small, sheeny negative, thrown down onto the paper.

Tin is standing upright, her head and shoulders straight. Robin is behind her, around her with her arms, one ear down and her chin to Tin's neck.

'Good use of depth of field,' Mr Betts comments. 'The shallowness. What you want sharp is pin-sharp' – a shadow finger circling Tin's eyes. 'And what you want soft should have exactly this quality' – the buzz of Robin's mohair jumper and blur of her skin, the light rubbed into her hair – 'like fur.'

Jonah laughs. Because it is true. Draped around like that, her eyes lit and glassy, Robin looks exactly like a fox fur, shabby and old-fashioned with the head still on, and the points of her canines catching her mouth.

'Is it overexposed?' Jonah asks.

'What lighting did you use?'

'I didn't, really. There was a lamp on, two lamps maybe, but it wasn't fully dark outside. And we had a lot of candles. In bottles. That was the night of my birthday.'

'It's all the different light sources making Robin do that.' Mr Betts indicates the pale of Robin's skin, floating on the surface of the paper, the detached glint of her earring. 'Thomasin doesn't look very happy,' he reflects. 'For a birthday.'

'She hates dinner parties,' Jonah says. And birthdays. 'I should have realised. "What's the point of playing Happy Families and pretending to be forty?" That's what she said.'

'She has a point.'

But it had been a good night. Tin had been funny after she'd been hostile, affectionate even, and done her impression of Prince talking shy and flirty. There had been loud music and slow dancing, everyone swapping in like they were twelve at a disco. It had ended in two broken chairs and a sprained wrist, Davy's, although he couldn't now say how.

'I'm forty-five and not wild about dinner parties either,' Mr Betts tells him, stretching sideways to switch on the fan. 'I would run quite a long way to avoid one, in fact. And I'm not much of a runner.'

The fan gives a gentle stutter and then settles into its drone, a low thrumming, pushing the heat around. Mr Betts has shacked up with a twenty-year-old, Jonah knows. She looks more like thirty close up, in the queue at Spar, but that's the rumour. And that she's pregnant, which is probably true if Miriam's saying it, because Miriam's mum would know. All in all, Mr Betts is ripe for dinner parties, in Jonah's opinion, whether he likes it or not.

Mr Betts lifts something off the shelf overhead, a stop clock, and sets it down beside the enlarger. 'Ready?' Jonah nods. 'Ten seconds,' Mr Betts says and strikes the start bar down. Jonah swings the block out from the enlarger's lens, exposing the paper to light.

The seconds tick out fat and full in the dark. Jonah counts and then swings the stop back in. Mr Betts kills the clock and switches the enlarger off. The image evaporates, leaving an empty rectangle.

'Start on the left,' Mr Betts instructs. 'The left-hand tray.'

Jonah carries the paper towards the sink, a shining blank in the red dark. The image is there, held in the silver and salts, but entirely invisible. There must be other things we can't see. Things all around written in chemicals that no one even suspects. He lowers the paper into the developer and Mr Betts starts the clock. Jonah has done this before, once, rocking the tray like a cradle, the developer rippling forwards, folding backwards, over the whiteness. And now the image rises under the rolling liquid, taking blackness to itself. Tin's face, the dark shine of her hair, gathering heft and depth.

'That's sixty,' Mr Betts says.

Second tray, stop bath, swish it around with the tongs. 'Thirty seconds.'

Third tray, rinse. Jonah turns the tap on and directs the hose. He agitates the photograph around. Tin's eyes fierce and sharp under a depth of moving water. Robin liquid and unfocused, the water rolling over her head.

'Tongs. Above you, the squeegee ones.' Mr Betts rattles the washing line. And there above, pegged by one corner – Mr Ardennes.

Standing against the wooden slats of the technology fence, squinting into the light.

Mr Ardennes with his head tilted. His arms caught behind his back.

Jonah gulps. He feels himself gulping and he can't stop. He has to close his eyes.

'You're all right,' Mr Betts tells him. 'Keep it steady.' He steps over and redirects the hose from the floor to the sink, holding it there.

Pale, pummelled by water. Deep underneath. Robin's jumper, stretched like a net by the weight of the river. She had almost drowned them both.

Jonah gulps and keeps gulping. He tries to open his eyes.

Mr Ardennes. On the grass of the riverbank. His face drawn thin by the dark. A month ago, at a small distance, when he'd asked about the art-school form and asked again, until Jonah had got it in the post. The cloister, last summer, talking about the Tour de France, as they sometimes did, the bikes and teams and stages. Mr Ardennes standing, squinting into the light.

Turning off the tap, unhooking the tongs, Mr Betts takes the photo from the tray, clamps the rubber blades to the top and runs them down, pushing a wave of water out in front and into the sink. A little tide.

'What did you cook? I mean for your birthday dinner.'

Jonah finds himself unready.

The humming fan, pipes running. The irregular drip-drip of water. Drop.

'Bolognese.' A wavering voice. Jonah swallows. 'Celery, no carrots.'

'Nice.'

The water keeps running, somewhere low down, along the length of the pipes.

'And chocolate mousse. But that didn't really work. Less mousse, more hard scum and collapse in a puddle of brandy.'

'Easily done,' says Mr Betts.

They look at the picture. Jonah's party in a rectangle in Mr Betts's hands. Mr Betts weighs it up and down.

'It's good, the composition.'

Jonah straightens his head, pushing the slide of his hair to one side. His forehead is sweating. He narrows his eyes on the balance of light and dark and opens them again. He hadn't noticed Robin so much at the time, the instant he'd taken the photo, but he sees her now, how she makes it work. Two interlocking shapes, Robin blurring sideways, Tin up tall and alert.

'I thought it might be all right when I took it. The moment I pressed the shutter.'

A little silence. He hadn't meant to sound arrogant.

'Sometimes it is like that,' Mr Betts affirms. 'You do know. And things square up.'

He passes the photograph to Jonah, who hangs it up on the other line, a peg to each top corner. Standing underneath, looking up at Tin and Robin, Jonah feels under sudden, unexpected scrutiny. And worse, that they're both laughing down at him.

'There's time to do another,' Mr Betts is saying. 'If you want to.'

A sting to the heart, bringing its illumination. He has done something reckless, irreversible, hollowing everything out. But what? He's not even sure. The guts of last night swell up like nausea. He was out of it and something happened. Something with Robin. He kissed her. He does remember that. Her Dr Pepper lips. Or she kissed him. And afterwards? He has no idea. Until the river, everything is blackness. He feels both sad and surprised, like he has hurt himself badly by mistake.

Mr Ardennes. The floor of life dropped out. Grief vast and cold like a universe extending all around. For ever and in every direction.

He has no right to feel sorry for himself.

But if he has lost Tin . . . He feels like he has lost her, and a wave of sorrow rolls over his chest. Something good irrevocably broken. He has broken it. Had he hoped to

teach her a lesson in some twisted way? Teach her . . .
that she loves him. Why would she love him?

Except that he needs her to. He needs her.

And then Robin. What excuse does Robin have? He
would like to blame her, or at least blame somebody. But
Tin might easily side with Robin, he sees. She is capable
of that. And maybe she should. Because he has behaved
– He hasn't behaved well. And Robin, who is – Who just
happened to be there when he was off his face. He owes
her an apology. Robin as well as Tin.

He has given Tin the mixtape, but he made it before,
a week ago. An outdated appeal. He needs to apologise
properly. Have a conversation. He had tried, but when
she saw him at lunchtime Tin had walked away. Over the
grass. He hadn't had the courage to follow.

He runs the tap and throws the cold at his face. 'Sorry.'

'Don't be sorry,' Mr Betts says, tightening the lid on
something. 'Sweat it out all you like. You're in the dark.'

'Another one, then?' Jonah manages.

'Another one,' Mr Betts agrees. 'I'm not in any hurry.'

30

The Dairy

4.24 p.m.

Miriam stops at the farm gate. 'Can I come home with you?' she asks. She doesn't want to go back to her own house. By herself.

Davy unhooks the loop of baler twine and they walk up the track together, either side of a spine of green, the grass growing tall between the tread of tractor tyres. In the sun the track looks like a miniature desert. There are little outcrops of stone, humps and hollows, a black beetle labouring across. Miriam's feet kick up the dust.

They pass over a cattle grid, under the arms of a big tree, and cross the yard to the farmhouse. The back door is open. Swiping through the flies of the boot room, they enter the kitchen and drop their bags and blazers to the floor. It is warm inside but shady. Miriam hunts around for animals under the table, all the patchwork cushions, not finding any. The kitchen looks both clean and worn, like old bath towels washed and aired and folded. She watches Davy move about, humming, mixing Ribena, twin pints, then follows him through to the snug.

She likes the snug, its deep, battered chairs and heavy rugs, the smell of drifting wood ash. Rachel, Davy's sister, is already established on the sofa, the TV on and a full-ish packet of Jammie Dodgers wedged between her leg and the cushion. She lifts them out of Davy's reach, her mouth stretched wide, an unbroken circle of biscuit inside, and points under the coffee table. The noose of her tie and some custard creams. A third of a packet and the top twisted shut like rope.

Davy lowers the Ribena to the table and offers Miriam the creaky chair. She decides on the floor, sitting down cross-legged, her back to the chair arm. He stretches out behind her – a yawn of upholstery springs – and untwists the biscuits. Rachel is watching something BBC, men in suits pretending maths is fun.

A ginger cat idles in around the door. Thickset and thick-pelted, it has one tatty ear, like something sharp, a squirrel or a stoat, has taken a bite out. It moves in at

Miriam's side, bullying her hand for a stroke. Getting down on one elbow, she rubs its chin and scrabbles its ears, bringing the tip of her nose close to its blunt head, to the globes of its amber eyes. She is squeezing her eyes shut, blowing a cat kiss, when she feels a strike to her cheek. She snatches her hand back and sits up. The cat must have swiped at her, but it felt more like a blow than a scratch, a surprising force to it.

'Am I bleeding?' she asks, turning to Davy.

'Move your hand. No. Are you okay?'

Miriam looks at the cat. The cat looks at her, its front paws prim together. Her cheek feels hot.

'It's because he's a farm cat,' Davy explains.

'He's not,' Rachel says. 'He's a house one.'

'Mum paid Rachel to tame the whole litter. So we could sell them. But they're all like this, or worse.'

'What's his name?' Miriam asks, bending up her knees, pulling her shins in.

'Satan, Susan,' they say.

The cat spreads itself on the rug, recumbent like an emperor, and feasts on its paw, licking the pads and gnawing between the claws.

Davy's mum comes in, looks with sharp attention to the TV – harmless, just men moving number tiles about on boards – and then says hello.

'We're doing homework,' Davy says, spraying crumbs. 'Just about to.'

'You mean you're going to make Miriam do yours,' says Rachel, standing up and walking out. Their dad is calling her from outside, through an open window somewhere.

'Have you got much?' Davy's mum asks.

'Only art,' Davy says, which is maybe what he always says.

Miriam considers. 'No one really set us any.'

'That can't be right.'

They don't argue. It seems unlikely to them too. Except – Miriam looks at Davy to see if he'll explain. Miriam doesn't want to. She doesn't want to bring today into the snug.

'In that case, you can come and help.' Davy's mum lifts a lean brown hand to the edge of the door. More rings than Miriam expected. Big stones. Gold watch and bracelets. 'The heifers have broken through the fence in the top field. A different part of the fence.'

'I'll help,' offers Miriam. But Davy's mum is already out of the room and along the corridor.

'You don't want to,' Davy tells her. 'They look soft from a distance but up close they're massive, like the side of a van. And if they come for you at a run or plant a hoof on your foot –' Miriam knows about this, the various encounters between Davy and the cows, the concussion and the crutches. 'And once they're in the spinney, they don't want to come out.'

'Why?'

Davy stretches forward for his glass. 'They like barging about breaking sticks. Actually, they like eating something that isn't grass. Undergrowth and young trees. They'll reach right up for the branches, the new growth.'

'Like giraffes?' Miriam is thinking of Whipsnade Zoo, the stilted legs, the long grey tongues browsing, rolling around the twigs and leaves. Every summer term in primary school, her favourite trip.

'Sort of. But they can strip a sapling down. A hundred saplings between them. And we're trying to establish the top wood. My uncle is.'

Miriam nods and holds her hand backwards for another biscuit. Davy has a number of uncles, all with conflicting enthusiasms. 'Shall we go upstairs?' His records, she knows, are in his room.

'Better not,' Davy says.

She cranes around, but his eyes shift to the empty fireplace. She turns back to the telly, cartoon numbers jumping around to the comedy 'boing' of springs. Davy's parents are religious. Evangelical, in fact. She forgets that, and that sometimes he's not allowed out, or has to make up lies for parties. Even so, Davy's parents are the only ones who have ever organised something for them on purpose, setting up a PA and a barbecue in a half oil drum in the barn. And everyone had come, most of them had, and tried to behave, pretending that they didn't drink or smoke or swear. At least in front of Davy's parents. Or fuck. Because everyone likes Davy.

Actually, she doesn't fuck or drink much.

'I was alone all lunchtime,' she says. 'After you disappeared.'

'Sorry.' Davy stretches an arm around and puts his Ribena down. 'Tin was upset.'

'Why?' And then: 'What did Jonah's note say?'

The collapse of a biscuit between his teeth. Miriam knows that he won't tell her. 'What did you get up to?' he asks, through the rubble in his mouth.

'I stood in the corner and wept.' In fact, she had sat in the library in her favourite alcove, her back to theology and feet up in psychology, reading plays, until Miss Fernside had made her come and stand at the desk and stick in new labels. '*A man is not an apple!*' Miriam tells Davy. She likes the play with the demonic girls in best, the witch trial and hysteria, but she had started the other one in the same volume and odd lines have anchored in her head. '*You can't eat the fruit and throw the skin away!*'

'You can't,' Davy agrees, as if he knows what she's talking about.

Except that you can. Because that, more or less, is what Miriam's dad does all day. Streamlining. Relieving people of the burden of their jobs. Or getting other people to.

She delves into her skirt pocket and lifts what she has out on the tip of her finger, swivelling around to show him.

'Where did you get that?' A slow creaking of chair springs.

'Tin's pocket.' They look at it, the tab of acid, Snoopy's face blurry on the top. 'Olly doles them out. Or he gives them to Tin, at least. She doesn't usually take them.'

'Olly in sixth form?'

'Yes, Oliver in sixth form. The one with the flat-top and drainpipe trousers,' she adds, because Davy is interested in fashion. 'Want half?'

'Now?'

'Yes now. Or shall we wait for the 1960s?'

'No thanks,' he says.

She opens her mouth and lays the dry square on her tongue. Before he can stop her. Because he looks like he's ready to try.

'Shall we see what else is on?' she asks.

Davy pushes himself up and turns the dial to ITV. A helicopter. A dog running in circles and the grass blown flat in every direction like hair splayed out by a hairdryer. She loves *Lassie*.

'Hello, young lady.' It is Davy's dad, carrying one end of a trestle table along the hall. He disappears backwards – an interval of wood – and Davy's sister appears walking forwards with the other end. The weight bangs down and they both return, red-cheeked, to the snug.

'And are you staying for dinner?' Davy's dad asks. He looks like Davy, only redder and more wiry. The same wide smile.

'I should probably go home soonish,' Miriam says. 'But thank you.'

'Ring your mum. Tell her you've been invited.' He dusts off his hands, one big palm brisk against the other.

Rachel looks at her dad. 'I thought the phone was Emergencies Only.'

'This is an emergency. An acute need for some refined and glittering company.'

'I'll be quick,' Miriam says, standing up. At home she uses the phone whenever she likes, there being no one to police her.

The front-room farm office smells of beeswax, Miriam remembers, pushing the door open. And flowers, a china boat of hyacinths standing on the windowsill, the plump blue stars curling open. The phone sits squat like a frog on the busy desk, on a landslide of papers, its cord twisting into knots. Beside it, a bumper tub of green jelly with no lid on. She picks it up: a sharp smell and a gorge down the middle like a bear has got its paw in. *Swarfega*, she reads, the label smeared black with grease, and a book on the desk underneath, *Calorie Counting, Your Pocket Guide*. Davy's sister does that.

She puts the tub down, steadies the phone and dials Tin's house, the see-through disc reeling around. They hold a magic for Miriam, these six numbers, as if each time she pulls the wheel back, she's casting a spell on the future. But not today. Today they bring a winding snake of dread, coiling in tighter. She hadn't meant to blurt it out like that, after school. The words just flew out of her mouth. She waits twenty rings, her stomach elastic, before putting the receiver down. Tin will never speak to me again, Miriam tells herself, and does her tragic face. And then she tries what she saw, Tin white-stretched, ugly with horror, howling down Dark Alley. The distortion falls away, wiped clean, as she passes out through the office door.

'No answer,' she announces, returning to the snug.

'You can try again later,' Davy's dad tells her, and spreads out his arms. 'The afternoon is still young. On the other hand,' – turning to Davy, clapping his palms to the sides of his legs – 'cruel time gallops ever onwards. Have you checked the levels?'

'He hasn't,' says Rachel. 'And it's nearly five o'clock.' She picks up a glass and gulps down what remains of Davy's Ribena.

Miriam follows Davy out. It is bright in the yard after the shelter of the house and the cobbles look clean-polished, each one shining in the sun. Miriam glances across for Rachel's horse, for the breathy snort and push of its mouth into her palm, but the stable is empty, only flies hanging, gold and lazy, in the air. A flash of water draining in a fine, straight line from a barn to the middle of the cobbles, and something big and unsightly in the dark angle of the yard. A turkey. But it's not at all a turkey. Davy doesn't have – and here's a chicken with a head ruff shooting around the corner. And another with the same fluffy puff-head, racing right by her legs.

'Vanessa,' Miriam cackles, pointing. But Davy doesn't laugh. He usually won't at other people.

Two men come in over a gate, conferring. Wellies up to their armpits and braces to keep them up.

'More like a stopgap,' says one as they pass, raising a looming hand to Davy, his brown arm slashed with pink.

'Ditch up channel stop,' answers the other, and is sucked under an archway.

Davy leads her across the yard, along the vibrating heat of a brick wall and around to a low wooden door. He holds it open, bows inside and pulls it softly shut behind them. She stands just over the threshold, letting her eyes adjust, while he washes his hands in the dark; then she moves further in, to beside some pipes, and sits down on a step. Davy's shadow walks quietly around, disappearing behind things, reappearing. He comes across, tilts a clipboard on the wall beside her and writes something down with a biro hanging from a string.

'What are you doing?' she asks him. 'I mean, how do you know what to do?'

It is lovely in here in the dark and cool. She hasn't been inside before. It smells hygienic. Like yoghurt. And also metallic, all the tubes and vessels. Davy is standing up on a stool, reaching an arm over the side of a drum. The drum is enormous, big enough to have a bath in, to swim about in, almost. He moves at the shoulder, making watery sounds. 'Is it like at school?' she asks with a shiver, getting back to her feet. 'You make all the numbers up but write them down very neatly?'

'Here,' he says, stepping down and coming over. He offers her a metal beaker.

She looks at the milk, rising white in the dimness, and takes a sip. And another. A gulp. It tastes like nothing she has ever had or imagined. Three-dimensional. Restorative.

'Ambrosial,' she whispers.

He frowns, as he does when he's confused. 'It's untreated.'

'Give me some more.'

Miranda: You shouldn't drink this. This is for cows.

Miriam: Yes, taste it. Just a sip. See? It's delicious. Drink it all up.

Miranda: It's disgusting. It's not for humans. No one should steal this from baby cows.

'Who are you talking to?' Davy's voice, somewhere in the darkness. Miriam had forgotten about him.

Do you see nothing there?

'It's Miranda,' she tells him. 'Say hello.' She died such a little calf. But how can she die if we're exactly the same and she's my chromosomes and I'm still alive? 'It's not true,' she adds.

Why, look you there! Look how it steals away!

How did Miranda get over there? On her own, by the door?

'Tis here! 'Tis here! 'Tis –

Miriam: Don't you dare. Don't you dare go off without me.

Miranda: Don't be so dramatic. Where am I supposed to go? How possibly could I?

'It's okay. We're still twins,' Miriam explains and starts to laugh. There are daisies pushing up all around them from the tiles of the floor, open-faced and crisp, pure picture-book flowers. The soles of her feet tickle.

Miranda: Don't you ever have babies, Me-Mi, will you?

Miriam: Angel, you know I never will.

'Fresh as a daisy,' she says, or thinks. But growing giant. Triffid daisies. And then, dropping the cup, seeking Davy's hand: 'Stay with me. In case things get too weird.'

31

Lounge

5.02 p.m.

Claire thumbs off her socks. Stiff this morning, they are soft now, after a day of wear, and smudged on the heels from the dusty pavements. She drops them in her laundry basket. They'll be back in her drawer tomorrow or the next day, boiled white, the punctures of the running patterns ironed flat and the hems turned together.

A garage door rolls down. Her house probably or maybe next door. The cul-de-sac is not as quiet as people pretend it is. There are always drills and dogs and engines going, and everything loud like it's inside your house. Even the ice-cream van, which stops at the end, plays from the bathroom. 'Oranges and Lemons', playing inside her head.

She looks around at the white walls, at the ceiling, the white pleated lampshade. She has white sheets and an off-white carpet. A bank of fitted coffee-cream cupboards so she doesn't have to look at what she owns. And all the light of the day, drained from the back of the house, has come in here, into her room, driving away the edges. The walls are radiant, each alight, the ceiling swirls like crests of royal icing. She doesn't believe in any of it. This thin-walled house, the bleach and starch. The whole confection of this family.

She hears the kick of an engine starting, its hungry revving, and crosses to the window. A view of the driveway. The top of her sister's head and feet, a grass divide and another driveway. A yellow hose, half coiled, half twisted. Beyond, identical sets of houses, paired like twins, with double garages and driveways backing into the fields.

She unhooks the latch and swings the window open. 'Mitch!' – in between blasts of petrol smoke – 'Michelle?'

'What?' Mitch is on the saddle, lowering her helmet.

'Where are you going?'

'What?' Mitch yells upwards, helmet paused at her nose.

Claire moves a step back, feeling the tears begin.

Mitch stares up at the window, her gloves in one hand, like she doesn't know what comes next. It is too hot for gloves and engines, is Claire's feeling. And shouting down to the drive.

'Jesus,' Mitch shouts up and stands off her bike. 'You'll dissolve.' She throws her gloves to the concrete and lets the engine cough itself quiet.

Claire is by the settee, the back of her legs to its soft arm. Mitch stops on the threshold of the lounge, the lip of the pale carpet. She is not allowed in with her motocross kit on, the invasion of mud and engine oil.

'Is it Mr Ardennes?' she asks. 'Because it's fucked up about Mr Ardennes.'

Claire moves her head like no and slips her hand into her skirt pocket. The ribbon loop, the soft crumple of cotton. Tin gave it back but has left uncertainty on it. Distaste. As if it belongs to someone else. She frees her hand and crosses the room, stopping in front of the mahogany chest of drawers and pulling the top drawer open. They both know about the hidden drawer. It's not a secret. It's just that it's not for them to open it. Claire stretches her arm in now, up to the shoulder, jabbing around, until a narrow panel at the very top of the chest pops open like the tray of a cash register. She walks back to the settee, not meeting Mitch's eye. Mitch pushes her boots off and sits down beside her.

The envelope is thin, light on Claire's legs, a tepid, institutional brown. Nothing written on the front. She turns it over and slides the photograph out. A small picture of a baby, cut from an album, with part of a coloured page attached. Uneven, greenish margins.

Carol Spicer. Written in black ink. And underneath, in different writing: *Claire*. Which doesn't tell her anything.

'Carol,' says Mitch. 'Mum and dad did something right. You should be grateful for that at least, the beautiful gift of not being Carol.'

It isn't right, though. Claire wants to say so but her throat narrows on the words. Unsafe to try and move them. 'Not feeling yourself?' Matron says, gripping the neck of the Milk of Magnesia bottle. Thin leather watchstrap, thick red wrist. No, she's not. Because she doesn't know how to feel herself. How to be Claire. And she doesn't know how to be Carol either.

Her eyes become unfocused. Rage and not knowing, filling up to the top of her lungs. Her questions. The question of herself. Her real mum, real dad. Whether they're living or dead. How can she have one name and it be taken away again? Who has that right?

Who Am I? Twenty guesses. No fucking clue.

'Why don't they even let me see this?' she gets out, unable to see it. She wants, for a short moment, to rip the photograph up. Instead she throws it down on Mitch's knee.

'Because they're old,' Mitch says. 'And scared. That we won't love them.'

A little silence, in which Claire ignores the liquid mess of tears. Cheeks, chin, hands, skirt.

'Yes, you do,' Mitch tells her, knocking Claire forwards, putting her arm around. She rocks them slowly side to side, her motocross leather creaking.

A baby, small, crescent-eyed, curled like a leaf on a blanket, her hands and feet joined. Something hatched, still in the shape of its egg. And smiling. Laughing, even.

'Is this even you?' Mitch picks up the photo. 'It looks like a baby from – I don't know when. Prehistory.'

The knitted pixie bonnet, the crochet booties tied on with ribbon, a sepia fade. It isn't like any of the photos they are allowed to see, the two of them older, in matching Womble nighties, in stiff lampshade dresses, Claire shrinking, Mitch squirming, and party bows stuck to the sides of their heads.

'Always pretty, though,' Mitch adds. 'And very well fed, for an abandoned orphan. I don't even have one, note.' The flick, flick, flick of an oily fingernail, fast and hard to the corner. 'Already at birth too ugly for a photo.'

They sit side by side. A small gold clock chimes on the mantelpiece. Claire leans back, pressing her eyes shut. Her eyes are always sore.

'Don't you even want to know?' she asks.

'Yeah,' Mitch says. 'No. I don't fucking know.'

The second tinkle of the clock, gold and delicate in the bones of Claire's ears. Mitch stands up. Claire has made her late.

Gold to airy thinness beat.

Can that be true? Something stretching out and out, molecule-thin but unbroken, one person to another, even if you don't know where they are—

'Mitch?' Claire shouldn't stop her again. Mitch is zipping her boots back on, short, efficient tugs. 'I spoke in class today. Out loud.'

Mitch looks at her boots then straightens up, stamping her feet. 'What did you say?'

Claire had laughed in assembly. It had been the weird way that Gomme was acting. Her body had spoken for her by mistake; it had shocked her as much as everyone else. But she wants to speak for herself.

'I said, "Stop it." In chemistry,' and that had been what she meant.

Mitch laughs, then does her big smile, eyes, mouth, teeth, tongue. 'Put the fat baby away before Mum gets back,' she shouts from the hall. 'And shut the drawer.'

But Claire doesn't care if she's caught with stuff where it shouldn't be. This is something that actually belongs to her, whoever she is. This small, round beginning of herself.

32
Art Cupboard
5.14 p.m.

Sue Sharpe is sitting down at one of the tables, about where James had been this morning. James and Thomasin and – the other one. Miriam. She has the small board in front of her, her beachscape, and with a fine brush is filling in the pebbles one by one, the faint pencil outlines. Colouring in, more or less. And yet it is soothing. It is calming to do something bounded and unchallenging like this.

She has got through the day, the bleak expanse of each lesson, this room holding the shock above her head. Only now that the building has emptied, has rid itself of all the noise and bodies, the sweat and sensitivities – desire, betrayal, raw exile, the whole teenage comedy, reeling around and around these desks – only now can she begin to collect herself enough, hand, mind, eye, to feel herself arrive. In person. Now she alone sits here in the presence of loss. A short interval of time, her own small task, and trying to bring herself to what has happened. Even so, the question arises: how has she come down so small? Reduced herself to this?

She cleans her brush in a jar of water, ringing it from side to side. It makes an unlikely, swimming-pool blue.

She had worked differently once, large, substantial canvases tipped to the wall, blank and unplanned, the floor around thick with paint. But that scale, its emptiness and scope, whole territories exposed – it requires courage. Physical, yes, as well as holding your nerve. Yet she had once regularly confronted herself like that, driving her fears to the wall.

She draws her brush across a puddle of green, picking up a small amount of adjacent blue to round the edge of a stone.

The thing about that kind of painting is that you can't put it down when the bell goes, when a flood of kids come in. She hadn't been able to. It is wanker painting, really, that demands you turn your back and lock the door. Because if you are interrupted, required to attend a staffroom something, you stand miserable or seething, fixated on what you can't do until you can get back and do it; and then, by the time you are free, you find yourself incapable, overwrought, your concentration shot to bits and pieces. She can't undertake that here, the hourly frustrations, the stubborn resistance required. That is what she had concluded. Not in a school day. But she could at night. She could when everyone else has gone home. And that had once been her plan. Only – What? She has never held herself to it.

She sets her brush down and considers, looking around at the walls, the floor, the light at her disposal. There is space. But there is an inertness, she sees, somewhere in this room, this box on stilts. The walls are institutional, encumbered with pinboards, the lino polished bald and colourless. A few dusty sheep's skulls, a collection of blue, green and brown glass, bottles drained a decade ago. Assorted jumble-sale objects, all metal, with more and less reflective surfaces. This is not a place to make art. It is a holding space, a garage. A hospital store. And yet she has seen work made even here of great delicacy and power. Once or twice in the course of her teaching career. Once.

She pushes herself up and walks into the back half of the room, to the cupboard, shouldering the door, flicking the light switch. There had been oil paint. She had ordered a big box of it, a year, two years ago, in error. The wrong code on the order form. She no longer uses oils. She paints in gouache, which is by nature contained, whereas oil paint is slippery and hard to control. It gets on things, spreading itself indiscriminately across any surface – board, floor, canvas, skin – and can't be cleaned away by water. And it is costly. It has no place in a school. In her life as she is living it now. Nonetheless, there was, somewhere here, a whole heavy box of it, which, if she remembers rightly, she had opened but never handed out.

She starts to look into the darker recesses of the cupboard, the back corners at stooping level, the unfathomable depths of tall shelves. She goes out for a chair to stand on and comes back in. As she searches, she sees the shelf of fixative, the cans standing upright, lying sideways, and picks one up, shaking it gently to test its weight, the liquid content. The canister is cool in her palm, but lighter than it should be. Another one, empty, and another and another, all empty, fourteen, fifteen cans. It is more than she had thought. It is too much. In what? Two, three weeks.

She steps down, having spotted what might be the box she wants through the slats of the shelves. Airless, this small cupboard. Tar rattling her lungs. She clears her throat. Chicken-wire armatures shoved and abandoned. Parts of a paint gun, which the kids had lobbied for and broken, or maybe just dismantled. Props for *Antony and Cleopatra*. The set had been designed to look like *Dynasty* – not her idea, Sophie Callaghan's, and a good one, the spectacle of power as unashamed, as flash as it is – but she fears she will never be rid of the rhinestones. Self-adhesive, but not sufficiently. She pulls things away, making a path, and tugs the box out of the cupboard by two corners.

Standing up, one hand paused on the light switch, she considers the door. There is the key in the lock, where it always sits. Where it sits but is not used. She pulls the handle to her and turns the key once – all the richness of the world lies behind closed doors, the hungry locked out by the greedy – holds out the pocket of her smock and drops the key in. She starts to drag the box towards her desk, running over the grit of the floor, the fine rubble of charcoal and chalk, but abandons it halfway, heeding her back. Unbending herself, she looks out at the afternoon, high and pale over the trees of the town. A discreet, dispassionate blue.

She has several hours of daylight. More, probably, than she has energy for. She has a board, a big one, that Roger Betts cut for something, for one of the sixth formers, which has been primed but forgotten. What, then, does she lack?

And there it suddenly is, the word that Mr Ardennes had used a week, two weeks ago. A rare – their last – proper conversation.

Conviction.

She had gone to his office to complain about something and crossed with Thomasin coming out. The third time in two days, he had said, having closed the door, that she had been sent to him. Yes, Miss Sharpe had told him, lowering herself down to a chair, because Thomasin is always sent to your office, because none of us dare to send her to Gomme anymore. Because if anyone will, she will make Gomme crack and lose control. Finally and catastrophically. And although it is Thomasin who is driving them all demented, they still wouldn't wish that on her. Most of them wouldn't. Mr Ardennes had stood by the door, his head on a tilt, his eyes almost shut, listening.

He had a new print and pointed it out, a William Blake. *The Tiger. Tyger.* They looked at it together, at the fine branches of the tree holding the lines of the poem out, at the animal's huge, padded feet. What he had noticed, he said, was the expression in the tiger's eye, which he had taken as hurt before, but now, having it up on the wall, seemed to him something more like doubt, or, strange as it might sound, a lack of conviction. They had peered at the little framed image, their heads close together. 'Yes, you are right,' she had said. 'A lack of all conviction.' And then something had started up outside, shouting in Gomme's corridor, and Mr Ardennes had excused himself, inviting her to wait, but she had left his office and then the building, exiting through the foyer doors and sitting down on the guest bench, where no one ever sits, and had lit a fag, its shield of smoke rising up between her and whatever was firing off inside.

Conviction is a sort of energy, she can see, a force of life in itself. You can't get far without it. Things diminish, shrinking to the size of a square foot of board and painting by numbers.

And yet she has known conviction. The sense that she was doing exactly what she was meant to do at exactly the right time, the coordinates of time and space snapping into place around her. A rush of rightness. The brush landing true, charged with colour, the only possible one, to tighten all the rest.

It had only ever been painting. And only a handful of times, rare enough to count on her fingers.

But perhaps that too is wanker art. The desire to be right and right at the centre of things. Or is it happiness, simply, that she is recalling? In any case, she is not now concerned with her own coordinates. She prefers to stand in a wood surrounded by old trees, and lose all track of herself.

Even so, to wake up to something difficult and unknown. That, she suspects, is one way to feel alive. Because is it not, after all, more frightening, more disorientating not to even try?

Miss Sharpe lifts one foot off the floor and then the other, easing the stiffness in one hip, both knees. The sky from the height of the art room rolls out and out, ticked by small, bright clouds. Planting her hands on her hips, she sees Thomasin once again, turning her head, raising an eyebrow at her as she had this morning, lodging the doubt in her chest. What indeed does she know? Having lived most of her life alone, decades and decades, having engaged in her dry pencil sketches, her small gouache studies. She sits down on the nearest chair and rubs her failing knees.

Mr Ardennes had said something else that day, standing in his small office, the shadow of the cedar trees brushing the floor. What occurred to him about Thomasin, he had told her, was that she hadn't entirely lost heart and that, given everything, seemed to him remarkable.

'Yes,' she had replied, 'but how to tolerate the brutality of the girl, her rudeness and defiance day in, day out?' He smiled, as if considering the difficulty for the first time, but had only raised his hands. What Miss Sharpe had asked was obvious, or perhaps unanswerable.

Never reductive, Mr Ardennes. And that, perhaps, in the end was why everything grew too much.

Then finding it in her locker this morning, his *Tyger* glowing in her rubbish of spilt teabags and spent lighters, for that moment – It had been beyond her comprehension. But not beyond her anger. At some point, between her leaving school on Friday afternoon and coming back again on Monday morning, he had taken the print down from his office wall, walked up the stairs to the staffroom and shut it in her locker. She couldn't fathom it, the thought process involved. It hurt even to try.

The Tyger is now in her overloaded bag, in one of them, somewhere on the floor by her desk. At some point she will take it out and look at it. She can't imagine when. A decade of numbness away.

Who will clear his office? His other prints, his books. All the small, lost things he gathered around himself. Feathers, flints, arrowheads. Anglo-Saxon beads. The care he had taken to collect them, to understand what they were and meant. Who can pack that box?

The swing and crash of the outside door, the treads of the stairs sounding; someone coming upwards fast, acting on her like a shake to the shoulders. She pushes herself to her feet and walks across to her desk.

It will be sixth formers, a sixth former, Jonah, in all likelihood, who often comes in around this time and rattles about, pretending to draw. When he comes with friends, they hang around in the other half of the room for an hour or so, throwing jokes about. When he comes alone, he gradually drifts to the front, chatting, asking about what she is doing, how she is doing it, reluctant, it seems, to quite leave school. She busies herself gathering crumpled papers, notices from the school office, unopened envelopes, and stacking them together. Really, she should throw it all away. She has no clear idea what any of it is and no intention of reading it. She hears the glide of feet in the back room, the drop of a bag to the floor. And then the trying of the cupboard door, the shaking of the handle once, twice, and a firm kick to the wood. She looks down, at her short thighs held in denim, her desert boots planted, the pocket of her smock with its small weight, the cupboard key, hanging inside, and feels guilty, like she is being unfair. Given what she feeds into her own body. Given whatever they're all up to outside school. About which she knows more that she would choose to, because, for some reason, their talk around her seems more or less uncensored. It is her own weakness for fags, for booze, all too evident, that makes her seem neutral to them, perhaps. The rattling stops. An empty pause. A passage across the room. And then a class drawer slides open – rummaging, sifting paper – and is pushed shut again.

There are kids at home, her shut-down village, with not enough. The whole street piled in together to save electricity, one house until bedtime. There are kids in the world with catastrophic nothing. And here we sit on top of the plenty, awash, replete. Pools of milk, silos of wheat. Cupboards full of our own particular weakness. Miss Sharpe stands up.

'Okay if I take my sketchbook home?' Jonah, calling from the back, and then swinging around the pillar. 'Hello, Miss Sharpe. Don't work too late.'

'I like working too late.' A term's supply of fixative. Doing God knows what to his brain. She feels unmoveable, stubborn against his charm.

'Yeah, I know what you mean,' he says. But standing between the two halves of the room, his eyes wavering, he looks uncertain, like a child in need of a hand to hold. Perhaps Thomasin has done whatever she was threatening to do this morning. Chuck him over for someone else. Oliver in sixth form. His gaze drops to the box in the middle of the floor, the beached oil paints, and he is drawn down to it, lifting the flaps. He picks up a set of paints and turns it around. 'I didn't know we had these.'

She looks at him looking for a moment, the bones of his hands long and articulate, his shirt the thirsty blue-black of night, and then goes over, squatting down opposite and shaking out some tubes. She twists the lid off a yellow, a little squeeze to see. Student colours. 'But not terrible,' she says, opening another, a viridian green of sorts. 'Useable, in fact. With careful mixing.' And even in these polite measures, in play-sized tubes, the smell stirs in her gut.

'Can I try some?' he asks, looking down from his height. His eyes are green, flecked with light, but the skin around the rims is dark, as if smudged with kohl. She hands him a second and a third box, and two clear plastic bottles. He doesn't often hear no, is what she thinks.

'Wipe your brush on a rag,' she instructs. 'Then wash it in the turps. And don't pour any of it down the sink.'

'Yep, nope,' he says. 'Okay.'

Or drink it. Or set it alight. And don't eat the white because it's poisonous. Or used to be.

He stands up and does his handsome smile, his hair slippery over his eyes. 'Is that spare?' he asks, pointing his stacked hands across the room. The big primed board.

'Yours,' she says, and turns her back. The safe ship of her desk. Her brushes all in rows. Her bags spilt on the floor.

The Tyger is a watercolour, she points out to herself, sitting down. Jonah is thanking her, making his long-leg way to the door. And small in scale. The size of her hand. But intensely strange, intensely brilliant in colour. A blazing magnificence. The door bangs, leaving her alone. A small thing set on fire.

33

The Cold Room

5.27 p.m.

'Thank you for coming,' the man says. 'And so quickly.' He glances up at Dr Cole and then back at his desk, at his pen, removing something from the nib with tweezer fingers.

Dr Cole has come because he didn't want Lyn Ardennes to. He came straight away because he didn't want to anticipate coming. He had not been aware of where the morgue was. That the town even had one.

The man begins to write. The bald passage of a pen across a hard surface. He has one collar point tucked into his jumper, a burgundy round-neck, the other sticking out, folded up, like a cat's ear bent back. Why suffer a jumper? Dr Cole thinks, and yet he himself is sweating under his suit jacket. A useless weight of armour. From the corridor, the jingle of a fax machine. It stops to think, and then continues its compressed scramble of information. The man caps his pen, stands up, and leads Dr Cole through an inconvenience of small, joined buildings. Doors, ramps, unexpected gaps; steps up and down. He stops at a door, knocks, waits and then holds it open. Dr Cole walks a few fast steps in. Not fully into the room but close enough.

He'd expected someone, the man, an assistant, to come inside, to fold a sheet back. But there is nothing. Nothing covering. No ceremony. There is just a length of what had been, until recently, a man. Dressed in what looks like a tent bag. Even under the strip lights his skin looks tanned. Hand, wrist. Cheekbone. Like leather. And delicate around the eyes, the fine skin creased.

Dried by the cold of the Andes. Preserved by the grip of a bog. Prehistoric, an ancient held in time.

Mr Ardennes' head is bent to one side, and seeing this brings Dr Cole sudden and precise recognition. Pain to his heart, a quick, ruthless rip.

The cold begins to register. The tips of Dr Cole's fingers, the back of his neck where his hair's been cut. An infiltrating cold.

'People expect more – puffy,' the man says, wiping his feet on the tiles. 'But they got him out pretty quick.'

Not pretty quick enough.

'It was two people in a parked car, a van, who shouldn't have been in a parked car at three in the morning, if you know what I mean.' The man steps aside from the door, spreading a palm to its blank face to keep it from closing. Dr Cole steps through. 'They drove off, but then she made him turn around and go back. She must have had a notion that something was afoot. It was them that pulled him out. Not scared of getting wet in the dark, apparently.'

They retrace their path. Dr Cole signs the paperwork, lumbers out of the wrong door, an open fire exit, and sweats back up the hill.

If there's anyone left in school, he intends to drive them out, but he finds the whole place swept clean, not a soul, after all the bodies pressed in, passing through the day. Only the smell of the floor polisher remains, hanging in the corridors, its overheated rubber belt.

He ransacks the office for the spare keys. Coming back out, pausing in the darkness, the narrowness between corridor walls, he takes stock of the up-thump, thump of his heart, the black gash in it, then leaves the main school by the back staff exit, locking it behind him and crossing the car park to the old stable block. *DerekMaintenanceHq*, the door reads, in slanting, adhesive letters. Even from outside, he can hear Derek talking on his CB radio. Inside, the air is dim and loud and crackles around him. In his ears. A confusion of wires and tools and things taken apart. Derek twists around, a handset, something else held to his chest.

'All right, chief?' he says, and points a plugless cable at him.

'Go home,' Dr Cole tells him, looking around. Desks and chairs turned upside down or on their sides, part-sanded, propped, missing limbs. At his feet, a rusty spill of tacks. Jam jars on shelves and all over the tables. Full of something – string, drill bits, sedimentary paint. And the unaccountable smell of toast, a sweet, singed edge. Toasted fruit loaf.

Derek shows Dr Cole a raw thumb. 'Ten-four,' he shouts at the static. He stands up still talking, a chain of words and numbers, and pats the pockets of his army greens like he's lost something. 'Rubber down stay loaded,' he adds, or something else Dr Cole cannot catch. Cannot make any sense of.

Derek sits back down and snaps the radio off. The air goes quiet. He picks up a small brown fuse, reads the amperage, then taps it down, tock tock tock, the soft metal cap to the wood of the workbench. He looks at Dr Cole. 'I never saw this coming.'

Knock, knock.

'No,' Dr Cole says.

'I saw his Mrs, Friday night on the Lane, coming out of her school.' Derek's gaze drops, then steps across his scrapyard table. 'She told me they was moving to France in a couple of years and she was looking forward to it.' He looks back up, his eyes round. Knock.

Dr Cole nods. He hadn't known that. Looking forward. 'I'll finish locking up,' he says, shaking the keys, his fist of jagged metal. He pushes out of the door.

'You go home,' Derek calls to his back. 'Have a drink with your wife, go to bed. And then tomorrow, today will be over.'

Gym, music room, art block – hot and empty, only the resident smell of Sue Sharpe's Benson & Hedges – slamming doors, turning keys, rattling handles. Computer lab, laundry, home economics. Science labs, dark as bitumen. He stops and lays his forehead against the window: long charred benches, sinks and gas taps, tall stools tucked in close. No one inside, no Emma Harper, darting around in the murk like the floor's on fire. Coming back along the path, over the bite and roll of new gravel, Dr Cole veers away onto the grass, out over the playing fields and onto the rugby pitch.

A sudden breadth and height, a surprising focus, under the pale dome of the sky. From here the chalk lines run crisp and white against the green. The goalposts, like scaffolding, stand square against the blue. He reaches the middle and, with a heaving lurch in his lungs, swings himself around.

'Come on, you spineless fuckers!' he shouts. 'Come on, blow your fucking whistles!' Gomme, Ward, all their high-pitched, packed-in lies. 'God Almighty, you twisted bastard Tory grandee! You think I can't whistle? Ten-four fucking five I can whistle. I can shout. I'm going to shout and shout my fucking head off!' A mouthful of fingers, a pitchy alarm, whooping up and up – and a strong, throat-widening fountain of vomit thrown down, splashing up from the dry ground. Free school meals. For worms. For the crows.

He spits, wiping his fingers on the front of his trousers, the top of his shoes on the back. All the truth and the lying. Poetry, our great, life-saving fiction. But the body will speak for itself. The man had been his friend.

Straightening up, seizing the air to his lungs, he bellows, a long, hollow blast of fury. A cow parted from her calf, articulate with loss. When he runs out of breath, he throws himself down, his back flat to the hard, warm earth. The sky is massive. The sky is all of his vision. His legs and arms flung out, a pile of Derek's broken junk, he closes his eyes, breathing like a man who can't, scorched in the lungs, bitter in the throat. He feels the earth pound against his back, his heart thrashing. When he is ready, he hauls himself up and staggers away, the school behind him, the Divide his horizon, across the wide green grass. Reaching the fence, following it along, he cuts in around the swimming pool to the back gate, where he stops, leaning his head and chest, one shoulder against the metal upright of the gatepost, his hand flat to the heated bulk of the padlock.

The Wheatsheaf, Sue Sharpe had said, a recruiting finger stubbing into his arm. But first he should go home. Make some sort of appearance while it's still daylight. For once.

Unhooking the padlock, its weight square in his hand, Dr Cole lifts his head and launches his arm sideways, hurling the black lump into the scrub by the bike sheds. It strikes something, stone or metal, a ringing clang and a thud to earth.

He is not going to pretend that he can lock up an entire school. Fields. A wood. Two woods, Dell and Thicket. A long, broken-hedged fence. Dr Cole draws himself up, hanging his arms by his pockets. Life flooding out, flooding in. Let it come. And go. The whole human mess of it.

34
Looking In
5.43 p.m.

'Do you want to do homework together?' Kelly asks, lifting a hand to the outside of the house and dropping it again. Sharp stones, what's it called? Pebbledash. Vanessa stands above him in the hall, on a doormat. Her house looks big inside, like he's heard it is. The carpet rolls away behind her, a protective plastic strip down the middle. The smell of hairdressing rolls out the other way, surprisingly forceful, even standing outside.

'No,' she says.

She is wearing tight jeans and rabbit slippers, and a grey sweatshirt with pink cuffs like sweatbands. It's the jeans that make him think of the Durex, which he had forgotten about most of the day, lost in his bag, not blowing a single one up. Double denim, except he is still in his school trousers.

'Since when do you do homework?' she asks.

She's got a point. He doesn't waste his time. Because he has no intention of staying on for sixth form. He intends to get an apprenticeship at the Austrian bakery, like his eldest brother Dale. Because people will always need bread, if you think about it.

'And? Anything else?' she says.

Kelly is listening. He can hear Americans fooling about behind her and a blast of TV laughter. *Different Strokes.*

'Do you want to come and walk my dog, then?' he asks.

'Why would I want to walk your dog?'

He didn't want to walk it either. 'I have to, or I don't get pocket money.'

'I thought you were putting up stalls.'

'That was just carrying poles. Between the van and the market.' He hadn't been tall enough to do the actual construction. And he hadn't lasted long. 'That's finished now anyway.'

'Who is it, Nessy?' Vanessa's dad, sitting all the way down the hall and keep going, at a table. The kitchen table probably. Stacked with files and paper. There are spotlights, Kelly can see, even from the doorstep, and up-to-date kitchen fittings.

'It's Kelly.'

'Kelly! Ask him in, you donut.'

Nessa steps back.

'Should I take off my shoes?' he asks.

'Yes,' she says like he's an idiot, and points at an empty shoe rack. *Guests: Kick Back & Relax!* painted on the side, and footprints to show where to put each pair.

Kelly stands in his socks, near where the carpet goes up the stairs. They don't have stairs in his house. It's all ground floor. Beside him is a mirror and a shiny table. A fishbowl of sweets almost full to the top.

Nessa's dad is walking towards him, rubbing his eyes and wearing slippers, leather ones. 'Accountants and more bloody accountants,' he says. 'They'll be the death of me.' He puts his glasses back on. 'They can all add up, but none of them can take away again.'

Kelly smiles and nods his head, and then shakes it, sympathetic. He hasn't seen Nessa's dad in a while and he looks a bit different. His hair is darker, but the brown doesn't match his eyebrows. Even his eyelashes, big behind his lenses, have turned whitish.

'Nice of you to look in,' Nessa's dad says. 'How's the football?'

'The boys don't do football,' Nessa tells him. 'That's the other school.'

'We were doing tennis,' Kelly says. 'But now we've got to do cricket.'

'I bet you're good at cricket.'

'Not really.' It's the pads that annoy him. They're way too big to run in. But mostly it's how Mr Ward bowls. Hard balls and straight at his head.

'Hair's looking good, though,' Nessa's dad tells him. 'Turn yourself around. Where d'you go now?'

'Hair Today, Gone Tomorrow.'

'Nice clean job. He's good with men, Tommy.'

'That's what I think,' Kelly says, doing a quick sort of Chaka Khan move and fake-combing his sides back, but without really messing with the gel. Actually, he's not supposed to joke around with Nessa's dad. Not after what he did to Nessa's mum, her real one. 'That Lying Creep' is what Kelly's mum calls him. Even so, Kelly for one thinks he's all right really, and he looks less weird now that Kelly's got used to his hair, so what's the point of falling out?

'Have you seen the new salon?' Vanessa's dad asks him.

'Nope. I haven't stepped foot in here before.' Kelly looks around the hall as if to bring himself up to date. There are doors on both sides of him. Two front rooms.

'You show him, Nessy,' her dad says, heading back down the hall to all his bits of brightly lit paper. It's glass, the kitchen table, Kelly sees. With metal legs. There's a microwave.

'Have you got a cocktail shaker?' he asks her.

Vanessa detaches herself from the hall wall, turns the handle nearest to her and pushes the door open. 'You can go inside if you want,' she says, snaking an arm around to switch on the light.

He walks in while she stays outside. It looks like a room, with a chair in the middle.

'Wow,' he says, stepping back out. He shuts the door for her. 'Do you want to come for a walk, then?'

'Why would I want to do that?' She opens the door again and turns off the light.

'Fresh air and exercise.' The house, after all, has a very strong smell. Especially now they've let the salon out.

'I was going to do a hair mask.'

Hair mask? He has no idea what that is. 'Do it after,' he says. 'You never come out.'

She turns to the hall mirror, as if she needs its help to decide. She has some sort of padded thing, a headband with yellow and white candy stripes, on top of her head. It all looks fine to him. Why bother with the extras? If he was a girl, he would just grow his hair long and comb it once in the morning and once at night and forget all about the packets of bleach and perms and Wash In,

Wash Out. Because from what he's seen with his mum, whatever happens under a plastic bag always ends in the wrong colour and dribbles. And his towel full of holes and stains.

'Dad! I'm going to walk Tina!' Nessa calls down the hall.

'You what whaty?'

'I'm going to walk Kelly's dog. Can I?'

''Course you can, teddy bear. Just don't go too far. And not the adventure playground. Kelly, can you hear me? Not the adventure playground. I don't like the look of those climbing things. The trunks are rotten.'

Nessa opens a cupboard and a light comes straight on inside. Fully automatic. Kelly picks his shoes up – *Kick Back &* – he follows her to the doormat. She pulls open the front door and put her shoes down on the plastic. They are slip-ons like plimsolls, with an anchor stitched into the side and a row of small blue buttons on top. A sailor's suit for your foot.

'Are they new?' He puts his shoes down beside hers.

Nessa is staring straight out to the road, one hand on the door latch, pushing her shoes on without looking. 'Have you known anyone else die?' she asks.

'Not really. Only Louise.' His brother Jason's girl-friend, who never really came round. Something about the epidural.

'If you had to choose, would you choose Manda or Manda's mum to be alive?' Vanessa asks.

What sort of question is that? He looks down, her shoes clean white like they've never been worn. Jason would have chosen Louise, maybe, when it first happened. And Louise had been quite nice to Kelly. But now there's Manda. He can't imagine there not being her. 'You don't get to choose anyway,' he says, squatting down to unknot his laces.

'Not usually,' she agrees. She turns back into the house, steps off the plastic runway and picks up the fish-bowl from the hall table. Plunging her hand, she rustles about. 'Not the gold ones,' she says, walking towards him. 'They're for clients. Hard toffees in case we need to stop them talking.'

'These would be gone in five minutes in my house,' he says, straightening up and helping himself. Just a fistful. Whatever comes.

'Because there's more of you living there.' She sets the bowl back down, tipping her head at the door for him to step out, all her big hair, the curly crown, staying put where it is, even on its side. She pulls the door. A quiet clunk behind.

The sky is high and pale and pinkish. It's nice to be outside in the air. They cross over the main road and walk into his close, down the middle of the soft tarmac, and then turn into the side alley to go around the back. Everybody's teas smell burnt, like a surprise surge of electricity.

'I'll just get the lead,' he tells her, opening the back gate. The dog is flat out by the back door, its head on its paws, its eyes on the window. 'Walkies?' he says, to make her tail thump. He looks in through the window. All Manda's bottles lined up on the sill, standing upside-down on a clean tea towel. He looks in through the bottles. His mum exactly where he left her, learning her Highway Code, the book for driving coaches, and the narrow table going wavy through two, through three layers of glass and plastic. He steps over the dog and opens the door.

His mum looks up, her face sharp with information. She's a night bird, is what she says. Come six o'clock, her brain starts working. Come midnight, she can memorise anything, any fact you care to throw at her. Which is true, because whenever he tests her, even boring, irrelevant stuff she's learnt after he's already gone to bed, she always knows almost all of it the next day.

'I'm taking the dog,' he says, reaching around the door to the hook where the lead should be.

'*Every bus must carry a fire extinguisher*,' his mum tells him.

'Correct,' he says. 'And a fully up-to-date first-aid kit.'

'*Make sure you know where the fire extinguisher is located,*' she continues, without looking down to cheat, '*and how to operate it safely and effectively in the event of a fire.*' She groans down under the table and unravels the lead from around the legs of a chair. Manda likes to do that, to wind it round and round. 'Thanks,' she says, sitting up pink in the face and passing it to him. 'You're a good kid.'

He glances through the kitchenette towards the lounge floor. Manda's farm book. His dad's legs at a low angle, propped up on his heels and holes in his socks, both big toenails poking.

'Don't look like that,' his mum says. 'I put her down a bit early. She was worn out from all the sunshine. And going to the paddling pool.'

He had meant to say goodnight before he went. And do cash-register tummy to make her laugh.

'I'm glad we've got Manda,' he says. 'Mum. Are you?'

'I am,' his mum says. 'Yes. We all are. And you can get up with her for me in the morning. Nice and bright and early.'

Kelly clips the lead to Tina's collar. She's not that old but has one bad foot and a lumbering walk.

'Hello, Tina,' Vanessa says, and takes the lead from him. 'Do you remember when she was a puppy?'

'Yeah,' he says, but he doesn't clearly.

340

'Don't you remember, because you came round to mine with her, and she was so tiny you weren't even supposed to put her down in the park in case she got germs, and your mum went to put her down on the lounge floor and my mum said don't you dare put her down in here, my floor's filthy, worse than the Woolpack bogs? And she didn't have a name yet. So we called her Piddle.'

He tries to think back. That would have been when they were five or six and had just started school. But it sounds about right. Nessa's mum, her real mum, still works in the Woolpack and she likes it known that she doesn't give a stuff about housework.

'I think we called her Widdle,' he says.

'Widdle,' Nessa calls to Tina, who looks back up at her.

'She thinks you've got a treat.'

Vanessa unwraps something and holds it out, but not so Tina can reach.

'What one's that?' Kelly asks. 'I didn't get one of those.'

'You can have it.' She offers her palm. 'I don't really like them, the mint creams.'

He takes the lump of chocolate, already soft, smudging his fingers. What if he asked her out now? He could just ask her out right here, at the end of his close. He looks at her, his heart gone berserk and his mouth full. It might be too soon. But they're having a very nice time. And she had sat with him at lunch, all on her own and without him even asking.

He swallows twice, toothpaste, chocolate and syrup, and feels the lack of water. 'Shall we go to the adventure playground?' he tries as a warm-up.

'Are you deaf? My dad said no.'

'So?'

'So we're not going.'

'Roundabout?' But they both know they're not going to the park. The roundabout's where the other kids go. Kelly has seen them get it spinning, Turner, Robin, Tin on occasion, the way they jump on and lie down with their feet in the middle and heads over the edge, as if they want to get thrown off.

They stop together on the corner, just before the pavement runs out. Tina lies down, tangling her front paws up in the lead. There's the new supermarket on the ring road. Kelly's only been in once, but they have an aisle for toys and one for clothes, all in the same shop.

'We could just walk along the old railway,' Vanessa suggests. 'And then walk back again. They've made a new path and put in benches. It's supposed to be much better.'

'All right. Let's do that.' Kelly undoes Tina's feet, which are hotter and heavier than you'd think.

They wait for a lorry, and then cross over. He goes to take Nessa's hand, but she swaps with the lead and he misses his chance. Better not anyway, he reflects, skipping forward a bit. Not yet. They step down a kerb and then step up again. The air is a nice warm, not so hot as it was earlier. He looks at her, but she is looking straight ahead, holding the lead, her nose wrinkled up. She looks happy, as far as he can tell, her hair big and up and freckles beginning all over her face like she gets in summer. It makes him smile, an inside grin. He could tell her about Gomme's office. Or the party last night, Robin and Jonah all over the street. Or not tell her. Because they're just walking along like this with the dog, close together, somewhere done new they haven't even been to before.

35
An Empty Place

6.30 p.m.

'How was school?' Nicolas's mum asks.

Nicolas looks up. He doesn't know how to answer. He wants to tell her about Mr Ardennes but is unsure whether or not it counts as gossip.

'It was good,' he says, and lifts his glass of water, the meniscus, to eye level. 'My viola lesson was cancelled.'

'I'll still have to pay for it,' says his father, tucking a napkin into his collar.

There is an empty place at the table, his sister Diana's. She has dyed her hair but that is only the latest outrage. She is already grounded for having a second earring without asking, and a boyfriend. Now, it seems, she has to eat on her own in her room.

Diana goes to the other school, but she wants to leave without finishing the last year properly and work full-time in the Midland Bank, where she has a Saturday job. No one knows why. Nicolas's dad blames his mum and his mum shouts at his sister and then goes to her sewing room for a long lie-down. When there are only three of them at dinner, Nicolas faces a wall.

They eat in silence, as his father prefers. On the wall, a painting of a boat, grey like a tin can, very slightly off true. Nicolas thinks about getting up to straighten it, lining up the sides of the frame with the verticals of the wallpaper. His nerves twitch with his desire to.

'Sit still,' his father says. 'Or have you got worms?'

When Nicolas's father chews, his nose moves. He keeps his hands up between bites, his forearms braced against the edge of the table and his cutlery pointed at the ceiling.

When they were small, he and Diana used to count how many chews their father did before swallowing to practise their numbers up to fifty. Sometimes Nicolas still counts, without really meaning to but not out loud.

'Davy's got a Walkman,' he says, after a while.

His mother looks at his father. His father chews. He points a knife at his ear but says nothing. His mother turns back to Nicolas with a very small shake of her head.

Your father has a lot on his mind, is what his mother says when she wants Nicolas to stop being chatty. But Nicolas has concerns of his own today. He has concerns about his bike, even if he isn't about to raise them. Diana took it after school without asking, and then brought it home with a puncture in the back tyre. He doesn't really know how to fix it and knows he cannot ask. Because his father has shown him once already and won't show him twice. Even though it feels like a very long time ago when his father had pushed something, the inside tube, into a bucket of cold water and a gasp of silver bubbles had risen from the hole. There is more to it than that, he knows, than the bucket, but what that is he's forgotten.

Diana said that it wasn't her fault, that he had a slow puncture already. So perhaps it had been Tin after all, her weight on his saddle. Or something sharp she pushed into the rubber. Tin, or maybe the sixth former who had laughed. Either way, he'll have to fix it somehow or his dad will notice. Maybe Kelly knows how. No, not Kelly. Maybe Mr Dalton? Would Mr Dalton help him? If he gets up early tomorrow, he can wheel it in and see if Mr Dalton has time at break.

There are other matters he needs to raise with Mr Dalton. The chess club fixtures list, most pressingly, which was supposed to go up last week and already hasn't. It will be a good opportunity to clear the air.

He carries the plates and knives and forks to the kitchen and comes back for the glasses. Walking carefully back, crossing the tiled floor, he stops like a shunted train right in front of the sink. Because he has remembered about Tin. What they had all been told in primary school. Well, that certainly, that puts – That is two people, then, in fact, that he knows who are dead. Or knows of, rather. Because he can't very well now, at this distance, remember Tin's mum, what she looked like or indeed anything about her. But that is not entirely to the point. The important thing is that Tin's mother is no longer alive and, as a consequence, Tin must be sad and therefore allowance must be made, he can quite see, and must remember, and he is, without reservation, willing – But not to the extent of a flat tyre, surely. That is too much to reasonably ask. He lowers the glasses down and turns around. A new carton of crème caramels ready on the side. Or even to that extent, yes, even two tyres, because a tyre can be repaired, after all, although not by him, and not, therefore, without some considerable inconvenience. No matter. Allowance must be made, and generously, because no person is very easy. Even people more usual than Tin –

Nicolas picks up the carton and returns to the dining room. These crème caramels come in individual fluted plastic cups. When you invert one and break the little tab from the base, and thus the vacuum, the crème slithers out onto your plate in an after-rush of caramel. Ingenious. The birth of a pudding!

'No pudding,' his father decides, standing up, and Nicolas clears the spoons as well.

Nicolas used to do his homework on the card table in the sitting room, but now he's allowed to do it in his bedroom, if he brings his homework diary down afterwards to sign. Even his viola, now, he's allowed to do upstairs with the door closed.

He goes to get his briefcase from the hall, straightening his shoes on their square of yesterday's newspaper as he passes. He has wiped the dust off and rubbed on dubbin. He just has to leave it to soak in overnight so he can brush it off again in the morning. He wore the shoe-cleaning gloves, but he still has one oily finger, black around the nail, which may well need another scrub with the nailbrush. Given that dubbin is colourless, or at most the shade of beeswax, it is more than possible that it was the gloves themselves that made his hands dirty. Which he might have said, had he thought of it at dinner, if anyone had raised it, the state of his nails. He is thankful that nobody did, and also a touch disappointed, now he has a ready answer for them.

On the other hand, he had come across a very good article in the shoe-cleaning newspaper about the inventor of the Rubik's Cube, Mr Rubik, and group algebraic theory, which is advanced mathematics and therefore worth reading twice, which is why he cut it out to keep for A levels. There are some things which you can draw but you can't build, that was one interesting point. Architecture impossible in non-theoretical space. The other was a photograph of a Rubik's Snake, which isn't actually a puzzle you can solve, like completing a cube, but more something infinite without solution. With infinite solutions. Or, now he considers it properly, perhaps not, strictly speaking, infinite, but with more potential configurations than one person can exhaust in a lifetime. Which might get tiring. He likes to solve the Rubik's Cube. He can do the whole thing, six sides, and fairly quickly, in under three minutes usually, but not as fast as some people in maths club in the year below who have their own to practise on. Davy even did a side, yellow, one breaktime, although that might have been a fluke.

Nicolas picks up his briefcase. He will scrub his nails, but first he'll do his homework. Because now it is time for homework, only he doesn't really have any, which presents him with the problem of a number of hours before bedtime. He climbs the stairs, two at a time. He is up to date with his revision timetable, but he could borrow a slot from tomorrow, physics say, and do it today instead. And naturally there's always viola. He opens his bedroom door, steps inside and closes it again. He stands for a moment in the stillness of the room and then, laying his briefcase flat on his bed, he pops it open and extracts his ruler with a flourish, a sword from a sheath. He has an idea. A very good one.

He sits down at his homework desk and takes a pad of squared paper out of his maths drawer. It isn't dark, but he turns his desk lamp on for extra illumination. He wants to do a face. In blue biro. A portrait face. He stares down the page for a moment, taking in its solemn emptiness, and then starts in the middle, the nose, to avoid smudging, measuring so that it is symmetrical and taking care to curve the nostrils around the corners of the printed squares. Small and neat. Claire's nose. He adds eyebrows either side, counting the lines, and then ears, one round pearl stud in each with cross-hatched shading, quite successful, and a discreet size suitable for school. Claire might also like clever boys, he thinks, leaning back to consider his progress. It is true what Kelly said, he hadn't ever even thought of that. He attempts her eyes, straining to get the upward tick at the corners. He adds hair, but the more he does, the darker it looks, and that is wrong. Her real hair is mouse-ish gold. A neck, but a bit too straight like a tree trunk, a mouth that looks enormous, or might in fact be too small – no, demonstratively not too small, perhaps he ought to have used pencil first – a mouth which looks like a slice of apple his mum cuts up if it's Fruit and not Sweet for pudding.

It is Claire, but she looks like a monster. Mr Potato Head. And she has Tin's eyebrows by mistake. Too wide, too dark altogether.

'Nicolas!' his father calls. 'You've left the bathroom light on.'

He looks at his drawing, the horror of it, rips the sheet out of his pad and screws it up. If he had matches and a fireplace, even a small metal science-lab bin, and if there wasn't the fire alarm, he would set it alight and reduce it all to ashes. Instead, he pushes it into the inside pocket of his briefcase, where the photocopy from English is too, he sees, folded into quarters. He doesn't need that either. If it's not on their syllabus he's certainly not going to waste his time revising it. He will throw them both away tomorrow on his way to school. Into the river. Over the railings of the footbridge. Even so, he pulls the poem out, opens it up and glances down the lines, at his notes cramped around the edges. Only the first half of the page; after that he'd given up on annotating. Circles and death and virtuous men. Women merging, or is it emerging? His writing is unclear. An eternity baling hay. No, he can't see it. It doesn't matter how much Dr Cole shouts and attacks the walls with Nicolas's own property.

'Nicolas!'

'Yes, doing it.'

He shoves the paper back into his briefcase. His fingers meet sharp corners. The packet. His hand closes around. How had he forgotten about this? He swallows. And his briefcase all afternoon standing there in the hall.

'Nicolas!'

He jumps up and runs across the landing to the bathroom, tugging the cord of the light.

'Done. Sorry,' he calls over the banister.

'Viola! Or can I stop shelling out my money? Orchestra fees, instrument hire. Lessons that never take place.'

Standing still, a few breaths, Nicolas listens for more shouting. For any downstairs movement. Not another squeak. It must be the *Telegraph* and washing up quietly without banging plates. On his sister's door, the blue Perspex 'D' and pink 'I' she made at school and stuck on with Super Glue, and then took off, but had to put back on again to cover the holes. He knocks softly and eases the door open: gravy and acetone, which is a common household solvent, employed to break down oils in paint and remove ladies' nail polish.

Diana is not crying. She is sitting on her bed, concrete-faced, surrounded by coloured plastic straws, which she likes to plait together to make things that attach to other things but which she is not plaiting. At some point she has been given a tray, but the food has congealed on the floor, three different browns overlapping. A cold Venn diagram. 'It's not just colouring pie charts in!' That's what Mr Dalton had said. And good riddance to that, in Nicolas's opinion. Although he does quite enjoy colouring in, from time to time.

He looks up at his sister. He is not sure whether she is angry just with their father or angry with everyone. He looks at her hair, at the skin around her forehead. Purple-black trickles where the dye has run. The colour is certainly striking.

'What?' she says, as if tired from waiting a very long time.

He shuts the door. 'Do you want these?' he asks, holding out his hand, but with the fingers still wrapped around.

'Probably not. What is it?'

He steps closer, feeling his palm prick hot. 'Rubber johnnies.' He opens his fingers. That is the slang name he'd heard and couldn't remember.

'Jesus. No.' She stares at him, frowning, shaking her head, and he sees he has made another miscalculation. A misunderstanding. 'Where did you even get those from?'

'I found them at school. In the boys' cloakroom. They haven't been opened.' He turns them over to show her. Unbroken cellophane.

'I don't care. Yuck. No. I don't want them.'

'Well, I certainly don't want them.'

'Why did you take them then?'

He can't say. He'd just liked the picture. The attractive man and woman, shiny and yellow. He'd just wanted to put them in his briefcase pocket and do up the clasps. He moves his foot. He is standing on something, a crumpled tissue flower, stained red with nail-varnish remover.

'Jesus. You are such a weirdo. If mum and dad find these . . . Where am I supposed to hide them?'

He drops his hand. 'Don't worry. I'll put them back where I found them. Or throw them in the river. I've got some other—'

'Give them here. I'll throw them.'

She holds out her hand, staring down at the packet for a moment to appreciate the picture, before pulling her bag up from the floor and pushing the box into the strap, a Velcro pocket he didn't know was there, which must be useful, particularly as a hiding place. He begins to retreat, edging around the door.

'I'm sorry about your bike,' she says, sliding her bag to the carpet.

'It's okay.'

'It's easy to fix. I'll ask Gareth to fix it.'

'Okay. Thank you.'

'Nicolas?'

He waits. Her face, set hard before, has gone crumpled. In her hand, a bundle of coloured straws. She hits them against her covers, making a complicated, hollow plastic sort of sound, but muffled. Jazz-style drumming.

It is no surprise that Diana gets gloomy. There are animals on her walls in cages. They are not allowed Blu Tack, but she has evidently found another solution to the problem of fixtures, and very effective. Anti-vivisection literature has very small type, it strikes him, although *The Comsat Angels*, he can read that, who are men in a group, he assumes, despite their lack of instruments, mostly standing about in the cold, staring at the ground, and looking none too happy about it.

The drumming stops. Diana looks up at him. 'I feel really sorry for Mrs Ardennes. She's actually a very cool person.' Mrs Ardennes had been his sister's form teacher last year. He had forgotten that.

'I feel very sorry too,' he says, and knows that he is inside.

'And he had kind eyes,' says Diana. Then, after a moment: 'You're a kind person too, sometimes.'

'Thank you.'

'You can go now. I just wanted to say that.'

'Yes. Goodbye.' He begins again to retreat. 'So are you,' he adds. He means sometimes too.

He is out, not banging the door, and creeps back along the landing. Safe in his own room, he stands in the middle of the floor, a small, empty square, the sky vaguely gold, vaguely pink in the rectangle of his Velux window. He doesn't see it, actually. He doesn't comprehend why it's necessary for his father to flatten everything down. Why shouldn't Diana be happy? Her and Gareth, whoever Gareth is. Why not? Nicolas would like them to be happy. In matching denim jeans.

He looks at his viola, its worn brown case and threadbare corners. He should do his practice, one hour fifteen minutes, all the major and minor scales twice and plucking arpeggios. But there is a crack. Even if nobody else can, he can hear it. The body of the instrument is fractured somewhere.

Why even bother with the viola? Why indeed? Good question. He's not going to bother! He'll do something else. He'll do another drawing, he decides, sitting back down at his desk. A portrait. Because, thinking about it, he can certainly do better, given that the other one was only his first ever try. He'll do one that makes her look nicer, like Claire actually is. Or maybe he'll just do someone made-up. Yes, that's what he'll do. More human, less monster this time. And with appreciably less dominant eyebrows. There are countless possibilities. There are things you can draw that can't ever exist!

36

Undergrowth

7.49 p.m.

Robin looks at her feet, pale and narrow, unaccustomed on the warm brick floor. She has peeled off her tights and thrown them in the corner, a black coil in the leaf dust. She looks at Tin's shoes, the same as hers, almost, but without the broken backs. She wants to put her feet inside. Maybe she does want everything that Tin has.

'Golden Virginia Shag,' Tin says, having said not much for a quarter of an hour. She sets a second, perfectly even roll-up down beside the first, two white sticks of chalk, and pushes her hair back. Robin's deckchair creaks, the canvas adjusting.

They are in Robin's summerhouse. She likes to be here. It is not really a house, not completely the garden and it is warm. They sit on long chairs, the table unreliable between them. The doors stand open, flaking paint.

This is where they used to come to do Ouija board. Before that, urgent meetings of unclear aim, unclear at least to Robin. Survival Club. Something about a book Tin had read and read to bits, until she lost all interest. That was a time of activities and distractions, Robin reflects, before they'd narrowed it down to smoking on the roundabout.

From where they sit, the floor extends outside, a baked platform of bricks, weeds growing in between. In front, a view down, the river itself hidden by what used to be shrubbery, what used to be gymnastics grass. To either side, midges bump the dusty windows. It has been elegant, grand almost, this glass and brick building. But even here, bottles.

'A bed day,' Tin says, looking back at the blank of the house.

Robin knows what it looks like. So many windows, curtains neither closed nor open. She gives her yes-no hum, holding her eyes to the herringbone floor. Forty-five degrees, each worn, slender brick keeping its place. In truth it's been a bed week. She has barely seen her parents for four, five days.

'Golden Virginia shagged,' Robin says, and starts to laugh. It seems to describe the state of her parents exactly.

The frayed, colourless hair and yellow eyes, the rattle of ice in shaking hands.

Tin strikes a match. In the dry air, the sound swallows itself. 'Let's smoke these by the river.'

Robin agrees, casting around for her own shoes, tugging them on, but she knows they can't get down. They cross the terrace, the loose, see-saw bricks, its dip and rise, and push themselves in where the lawn once was, threading through the shrubs and thistles. But it is too high all around, too dense and savage, the dry brush of last summer, the assertion of new growth. Instead, they stand where they have reached, apart, elbows raised, and look down towards the hidden river, their smoke butting back a crown of midges.

'Of everything, this is the bit I mind most.' Robin half-reaches an arm over the prickle of undergrowth. 'Or maybe I quite like it.'

'Miriam thinks you've created a habitat.'

'For what?' Robin asks.

'Big game. Small, furry things.'

Robin looks. Only a dragonfly, clattering, manic royal blue, displacing a pulse of midges. And a fine length of spider's silk, the light bending along it, unanchored, as far as Robin can see, floating in the air.

'You can still hear it,' Tin says, holding up a smoking palm.

The soft pull on willows. Reeds rustling aside – something low, making its small way through. From nowhere, the plump splash of a fish. The river running full and liquid.

'I did say sorry,' says Robin, looking up, not daring to look over. 'At break.'

The sky is a saturated baby blue. Sheets of pink, of gold hang at angles to each other. She hadn't noticed the high, hotel-brochure evening coming on.

'I don't care about Jonah,' Tin says.

Robin feels something unclench. A stomach fist. 'No-ooo,' she agrees. The relief of it, if it's true, as if all the anxiety of the day can at once evaporate. Holding her ear, she finds the holes, two burrs in the soft lobe, another in the cartilage which never really heals. No earrings. Because who can ever find the ones you're allowed for school? Robin squeezes hard. 'He is sexy, though,' she adds.

'Even unconscious?' A sudden distance, vast as a waste.

Robin has gone too far, she sees. As she often does. And where to go from here? She swallows. 'We didn't have sex. He just talked about you and then passed out. And nothing really happened.'

Clouds transporting light. Two tall plane arcs crossing over, melting sideways.

'Are you still angry, though?'

Tin breathes slowly out. Smoke gliding up and over. 'Wasn't there a boat at the bottom? When it used to be a garden?'

'I don't – Did there used to be a boat?' Robin asks.

A silence, in which Robin checks the backs of her knees – scratches, but no new bites, not yet – and Tin detaches something from the grasp of a thistle. She holds it up, a dark dart, a feather, its down buoyant in the light, then sticks it behind her ear. Survival Club. Caves and melting snow to drink. Somehow Canadian.

'I'm not angry. I'm –' everything difficult, a long horror, occupying the mild air, 'only always sad.'

Robin looks, but can't see what she thinks she hears, a smile of disdain. Inward only, then. Yet Tin has admitted something. 'About?'

But Tin won't say. And Robin knows, deep down, the trouble with Tin, the black hole in her heart that can't be filled with words. O. Tin would never have dragged it out. The coincidence, what has happened, has brought it around again.

'Not sad about you,' Tin says. 'Although I should be.'

'You should be,' Robin agrees, accepting Tin's stop, her turn. 'Because I'm a fucked-up state of affairs.'

She feels Tin's eyes suddenly on her, dark, alert, questions in them, but Robin cannot say. She can only stand here holding her fag, one earlobe, until Tin looks away.

'You are. Some days,' Tin says. Her lullaby voice. A cool hand home to Robin's forehead.

And Robin's chest expands, springs pulled to their limit, like she can finally breathe. She needs to move and waves something big, a wasp, away, a quick panic taking up, throwing out her arm. Because Tin doesn't hate her. What she has done, what Robin has actually done – She hasn't been exiled. She has tipped a plank over the worst and braved it to the other end. All around the air is thick and warm, hospitable with light, tiny rising bubbles. And Robin's heart lifted high, all the fish jumping. She wants to tell Tin about Mr Ardennes, the weir. Come entirely clean. But she doesn't see how. Not without bringing Jonah in.

'I saw Mr Ardennes last night,' Tin says.

A snag in Robin's chest. No one can read thoughts. Except when they can. '*You* did?'

'I did. Up on Castle Hill.'

Robin doesn't know what this means. Whether she has, after all, somehow been caught out. 'Did you talk to him?'

Tin moves her roll-up around, unhurried, against the persistence of the wasp. The tip flares orange, a lazy rush of oxygen. 'A bit.'

'About?' Robin waits, but Tin doesn't say more. And no point asking twice. Above, two swans fly over, improbably big to be airborne, their wings wheezing like bike pumps. Swans mate for life. Or is that true?

'If I knew how, I'd move out now,' Robin says.

'Marriage or the army?'

'Ye-es. Both are quite tempting.'

'Or become a nun,' Tin says.

'A filthy habit.'

'A Goth nun, in black, so the dirt doesn't show.'

Tin bends a knee and twists her fag out on the sole of her shoe.

'You could clear all this' – skimming the undergrowth, a mic-arm over a crowd – 'with one careless flick.' Dropping the butt, she undoes a button, pulls her shirt over her head and throws it across to Robin. She looks smaller without it, her shoulders dark and round, unarmoured, her bra straps phosphorescent in the floating light.

'Are you going swimming?'

'I'm going home. If I can find my blazer.' Tin turns and begins to wade away through the height of the grass.

Robin holds the shirt to her face. The smell of Tin in it. Salt and matches. A bimetallic strip passing through flame. She takes her skin into her mouth, the shy inside of her elbow. *The steel still expands. Listenin'? Just not as much.*

Robin lifts her head. 'I can't wear this. It's white, with faint blue lines on.'

A low sound, rolling away. She has made Tin laugh.

'You can't wear what you're wearing. Something died on the back.' Tin stops, her bare arms spread above the grass. 'You know you can always stay, if you need to.'

'Won't your dad mind?'

'Maybe. If he notices.' Tin starts walking.

'Bye,' Robin shouts.

Will you call for me tomorrow? That is what she really wants to know.

Then quietly, distinctly: 'I missed my last period.'

Tin is already beyond hearing. Passing through the summerhouse, emerging in her blazer, she cuts across the side path and walks out under the darkness of the arch.

Robin turns back towards the river, launching her roll-up, the last few drags, into the undergrowth. It might be nothing. Or it might account for the ache in the back of her head. Thickness everywhere. She waits. Light floods gold in the sky, the river pulls but nothing catches. Her fag has put itself out. Well, anyway, she knows how to get rid of a baby. She has seen her mother do it many times. And she does want to. Or she doesn't.

37
Across the Fields

8.28 p.m.

Davy takes Miriam out the front way, the steps, the path, which nobody ever uses. They have been in the barn climbing the straw bales, looking for kittens he knows are no longer there, that the mother cat has already moved. Even so, it has been a sweat to keep her.

'It's not pampas,' Miriam says, sweeping an arm, raising the clarity of lavender. 'It's softsoftsoft. It's squirrel tails waving.'

Davy doesn't know what it is, but he catches a stalk as he passes, the grass head running supple green between his fingers. They pass through the lavender, under the oppression of yew and into the avenue. Here the air alternates – thin blue shadows, bands of warmth and busy insects. The trees are smooth and spaced, two lines of stone pillars. They walk between them, scuffing the gravel, and emerge opposite the Green. There are still children on it, a roaming pair and a little discussion group, heads together, over by the telephone box. Davy waves. One of Darren the dairyman's kids.

A handsaw in a drive, something resistant. Radio 1 car repairs from the old blacksmith's shed.

'I'm fine, actually,' Miriam asserts, when he steers her away from the pond. She points up: three birds, short-necked, fast-winged, water birds of some kind. He nods but feels unsure. She is unusually quiet and blanched around the eyes. But she has stopped talking to her twin, testing her, line after line from a play. He circles the bench, Miriam riding the dip they've worn hollow waiting for the bus, and they take the hurdles of the Green together, sideways, stepping onto the tarmac and crossing the road.

'Keys?' But they have left her bag, her blazer on his kitchen floor. He knocks, the small brass hand hot in his, the heat of the day in it, and hopes for Toby, Miriam's brother.

'*They work all day and they work all night,*' she sings, hopping, knocking left at a stand of wellies.

'If we're lucky.' Davy steps back: low sun firing the windows. Miriam's dad is one thing, but there'll be no fooling her mum if she's at home. The door pulls open.

'All right?' Toby in cut-offs, Levi's, and the sides of his t-shirt open to the waist. The Stranglers play behind, dirty bass on decent speakers. Dropping his hand from the latch, Toby walks away. No longer so thin, Davy sees, and his skin tanned. All their French summers sunk in deep. Miriam greets the hall mirror and takes herself upstairs.

Miriam's bedroom is huge and dim, and another shadowy room attached just for clothes.

'Try lying down,' Davy says, pulling back the duvet. 'And I'll stay with you.' He looks around for a lamp, crosses the dusk to a chest of drawers and follows a cord for the switch. A ceiling of stars rotates above his head.

'Yes, lovely Magic Roundabout.' The crash and bounce of mattress springs.

No, he decides, and turns it off.

Miriam lies pinned, her shoes on the duvet. Her room in the dark looks the same. Still the poster of Babar, three-piece suit and bowler hat, always a well-dressed elephant. She starts rolling from side to side, kicking. As he walks across her legs accelerate, the duvet heaping at the foot of the bed then sliding off in stages. When she stops kicking, she bends her legs and begins scratching her shins. Holes in her tights. Well, she's right, Davy thinks. It is too hot for duvets. Kneeling, he unlaces her shoes and pulls them over her heels, setting them side by side on the floor. Minute, they make a giant of him. He captures her hand, hot like the brass knocker was hot, hoping to still her.

'Get in,' Miriam commands.

'No.'

'Yes.'

Silence like a provocation.

'I'm just here,' he says, squeezing her hand.

'And here for Miranda?'

He shifts his weight. Something unaccommodating under his kneecap. She pulls her hand and stretches her arms wide.

'He won't get in. He's saving himself.' A bitter tone.

Davy can distinguish the two voices now. Miriam's lighter, stretchy with laughter; the other dry and short, with edge, the lost twin, Miranda.

'Old maid.' The cutting tone, Miranda.

'Milk maid!' Miriam, and Miriam's cackle.

'Don't shag him.' The bitterness. 'Virgin boy.'

Laughter.

'Chubba, chubba. He's a chubby bear.'

'Don't be mean. He just wants Tin.' Miriam's voice. She points her small chin at him: 'Don't be cross, it's not Miranda's fault. She blurts things out. Come to bed.'

'Not like this.' He just means not.

'No, because Tin won't like it, will she? Because Tin likes to have him all to herself, even if she doesn't like to have him.'

There is too much twin in this.

Davy stands up, pincushion feet. A while not talking. Miriam lies flat, staring. The window above her bed is full of sky, as his own is full of tree. He pushes his hands into his pockets. He still has Jonah's folded note. He hadn't meant to keep it. *Please meet me* – the gates at lunchtime, where Tin hadn't been. And underneath: *Don't shut me out*. He will give it back tomorrow.

'I should go.'

'Should you, darling?' Neither voice, or both of them together. Someone from an old film. 'We all love you,' Miriam adds. 'Everyone does. Tin too. Or she might, when she realises that she can.'

'Just try and stay in bed,' he says. 'And don't talk to your mum and dad when they come in. Pretend to be asleep. Are you going to be all right?'

'Oh yes,' she says, joyful, but thrashing around again, then, kneeling up, she pushes her face to the window, palms spread silhouette.

He stretches around and turns the window lock. 'Okay. See you tomorrow.'

'He isn't dead.' Davy has reached the middle of the room and stops. Miriam continues: 'I don't believe it.

Because if Miranda isn't, why Mr Ardennes?' She turns to look at him, her small eyebrows pulled together in the centre of her forehead. An oblong of golden light wavers over her chin and makes her teeth gleam. 'Anyway, I saw him this morning. In the cloister garden. His wife will know. And she said I was good.'

Her voice has flooded with satisfaction. Davy doesn't know what she means. She speaks like this sometimes, in stagey pronouncements, a fairground oracle. 'Don't think about that now,' he says.

'I don't believe it.' Her voice is ecstatic. 'I don't believe we're ever going to die!' She throws herself down on her bed, her small, rigid frame bouncing back up on the springs of the mattress. A slab of blackness hollows out her eyes. Her alabaster chin points up. In the dimness, the pale blur of her hand moves to her front, and then the other hand, crossing over. Her arms vibrate on her chest. She is laughing, a silent, rib-shaking cackle. *'He is dead and gone, lady, He is* . . . But off you go.' She lifts a hand, a scribble of chalk in the dark air. 'I'm fine, darling, honestly. I have never been finer.'

He doesn't like to leave her like this. She's not going to lie still for long, he can see. He doubts she will even stay in her room. Unless she is quieter without him. Which she might be. Or which might only be the excuse he gives himself to go. Closing the door, he finds the curve of the banister and descends the dark stairs. Guitars, a dry drum, a voice coming in like a rush of adrenaline. Talking Heads, propulsive from the sitting room. He drops the window key in the bowl by the mirror, not looking, the dim bulk of his reflection, and lets himself out.

Sun glowing pink, spreading orange just above the line of the fields. Pylons striding, the air gone milky. Davy stops at the end of Miriam's path, his shadow long on the road, its head in the ditch. Three, four gulls sail over, silent, their undercarriages pink with light. The growth of the hedge, of the garden trees around, is lit up gold, each fine twig, the curve of every branch distinct, the new leaves flushed with sap. And as he watches, the sun melts itself down and the church tower, cut from the air, goes sheer blue insubstantial.

All day, the compression of heat, its heavy rub. And now the air sweet with hedges, the sun's clamp released, his skin let go.

He hears a car take the bend – its big engine, a streamer of music – and two searching lights stroke the hedge, the Green, bringing the darkness, and swing into the drive, Paul McCartney cheerful from the window. It is Guy, Miriam's dad. Davy waits for the car to stop, then moves around to the side.

'Hallo, old chap.' The tape cuts out with the engine. 'All well?'

'I'm fine, thanks,' Davy says. 'How are you?'

'Coming or going?'

'I just walked Miriam back. She wasn't feeling great.'

Guy's eyebrows jig about but his eyes lock. 'What sort of not great?'

'It's been a difficult –'

'I heard about that. Him. What's his name?'

'Mr Ardennes.' Was. Davy feels instantly treacherous.

'So not feeling great, emotional?' Guy pulls his ignition key and holds it up, eyeing its teeth. 'Or not great in the way of drinking?'

'Drinking? No. She just had milk.'

Eyebrows.

'But unpasteurised. It can make some people –' Hallucinations would be pushing it.

'Can it?'

Miriam's dad gathers his keys and extends his elbow into the drive. He is a wide man in a blue suit in a wide car, the same midnight blue. Davy can feel the slats of the gable end in his back. Something in the flesh of his thighs, with thorns.

'Because if it's any of my top-table wines, there'll be tears,' Guy concludes. 'Mostly mine.' He drops his hand and turns the ignition, buzzing the window up. Another blast of 'Temporary Secretary', which won't improve, Davy suspects, with listening.

A hand on the hot, ticking armour of the car, a salute to the window and Davy moves away before Guy can get himself out. He takes the verge, passing the Green, passing the lane home. He'll go the long way, up the track and across the fields. He's late anyway. Or maybe not yet, given his parents like to eat at midnight. He pauses at the corner of the bottom field: the heifers breathing in and out on the other side of the hedge. Big animals, the smell of sweat in their coats, torn grass. The dry of the field stamped up. They snort and jostle, then bolt a bit as he starts up the track, the rattle of his feet over the cattle grid.

In the semi-light, he feels more than sees the way the land is, the small drops and steady lift, the oaks standing the boundary one and then one and then one. Robert's cottage, held in a dip by two rolling fields, an upstairs light and then, as he passes, extinguished. Bedtime, Robert's ancient mother. In autumn, mist inhabits this fold, thick like wool, soft like feathers; in spring, a waking tide of green. He loves the farm. He only doesn't love farming. For farming it needs two of you, all day and your night, and the steel to face down ruin and bank managers. Swift animal hurt. Not getting back up.

They have given their lives, his parents, his grand-parents, back and back, and he will give it away because he won't take it on. But maybe his sister will. She is more cut out like that.

Calves and cows. Calves and cows and calves, over and over. This is what he knows about death. Not Miriam's ghosts. Not his parents' radiant heaven. A country boy, as Tin said. Not born in Watford. Born in the farmhouse, the bedroom next to his.

He climbs the track, the aisle of green and whitethorn. A month of rain, then heat, and the hedges are exuberant. Robert will cut them back, but now there are wrens in them, nesting robins. Voles. In the ditch, the glint of water running cold to the stream – sticklebacks, bull-heads, waterweed – spreading the pond – tadpoles in soupy jars – and out again, channelled into the Ouse. His feet stir the shallow greens, the medicine of nettles. A single foxglove, floating, luminous, sways slightly as he passes, like a candle.

He enters the top field, cracking over a shingle of beechnuts, and squints to see. Almost imperceptible, the deer from the spinney grazing the rise as they do each evening, faint like shadows of clouds passing over and just where his uncle doesn't want them, all his tender saplings. Davy crosses the brow of the field, high above them, grass thick at his ankles, a slug of dampness in it.

Slowing his pace, he closes his eyes, soft shadows grazing his eyelids, and offers what there is, his open heart, the particular beauty of this broad, quiet evening, holding Mr Ardennes in mind, in a green and passing moment, and then he opens his eyes and looks about with a sense of life rolling over. Crows survey from a height, from the crowns of trees, one from the post by the paddock gate, its feathers disorganised. As he nears, it dips its head like a weight has fallen, turns around and lifts away, voicing its feelings.

This is the highest point of the farm, the viewing post. School, Davy thinks, not seeing it, the proud side of the hill three miles away, swallowed by dusk. Instead, he sees the water tower, the odd, upturned structure, holding its volume of water high, glowing as the light thins. Something built for a moonscape. The sky, immaculate this morning, looks tender now, as if it has lived through something. He climbs the paddock gate, creaking the hinges. Darkness in the air like brick dust, red in the hairs of his arms, and high above, clouds carrying the remains of the sun. This gate is one of the old ones, which should be replaced and might be soon. Another few stampedes. He sits on top, palms to the weathered wood, and feels a sort of elation like freedom to be outside in this plenty. Fields thick with life. A rich quietness all around.

It doesn't matter if Tin doesn't love him. How much he gives, how much he wants in return; he can't do it, weighing it up like a quadratic equation. He just does love her. Through any imbalance. And she needs someone to love her. Without calculation.

But is it true that Tin will love him when she realises that she does? No, not true. Always precise, she wouldn't want him like Miriam says and not know yet.

Tin doesn't love him, not that way. Not perhaps in any way. *You're obese.* Hard and sharp like a puncture. But for a long moment before, his body spread afloat, Tin's hot head on his chest, he had felt only happy.

Across the lane, his sister's horse turns in the stable, a hoof, the weight of a flank thumping the wooden wall. He has seen the barn owl here many nights, up from the clay pit, the disused sheds, where it sleeps out the day. He scans the dusk, the oak by the house for its white span, its cracked, woodwind call. In that instant, the colour of the day withdraws from the sky, a greyness comes in and the clouds, emptied of light, thicken up like smoke.

He looks across, under the arms of the tree, into the house: Robert, his sister, a few other people move around in yellow light, his parents lifting saucepan lids and grabbing adjacent elbows. They like to talk before they eat, they like to stand around stirring things, pouring people gin, and dinner going over.

The darkness moves around like silt, granular and silky.

But where does the warmth, the closeness go if Tin doesn't want it? His need to screw like a rush of adrenaline? He has to keep it to himself, full like a water tower, alien in the landscape. And if the weight grows too much, the walls can't hold? They will have to hold. Because he is the bulwark, the strength in the scrum. That is what he is.

He drops down, crossing the baked ruts of the lane, and enters the yard. The fuggy malt of feed bins. Stone-green water in troughs. And something stewing, wine and onions, rich through open windows. He pushes the boot-room door. A rumbled joke, Darren's, and a ring of laughter spreading. And then, unmistakable, from the tree behind, a scratching hiss. The owl's dismissal. He turns, a brush to the side of his vision, powdered snow, the white underneath of wing before the door bangs shut.

There'll be dumplings if it's rabbit stew. And he will eat more than he should, a weighty softness to soak the longing up.

And then another wide night, his window open. He will try to sleep, to lose the hours under his inheritance of bedclothes. He will try not to think about Tin, not to dream about her, whatever it is she is doing.

38

The Wheatsheaf

10.14 p.m.

A tingling start of recognition. 'What are you doing here?' Miss Wright asks. Her husband, beside her on the pub carpet, an intruder from her other world. *More Blacks, More Dogs, More Irish*, she reads. A new badge on his donkey jacket. It's still too hot for jackets, she says to herself, and aloud: 'Have you come to drag me home?'

'I've come to drive you, if and when you want to go. If and when you want to get as drunk as a sailor.' He squeezes her shoulder and sidesteps around the circle of chairs. A doubtful hand to a stool, its leatherette marshmallow, and he sits down, raising his glass and looking at everyone in turn, clockwise, in the eyes, even those she knows he doesn't know, before he takes a slurp.

'Foul,' he smiles, backhanding the foam. 'The abomination of shandy.'

He turns and starts up with Roger Betts about dry rot. The next time she checks, it's Velázquez with Sue Sharpe.

Miss Wright slides her hand down the silk ties of her dress, upturning the little silver bells, a cluster of seeds, and watches Dr Cole duck in under the low door and stagger to the bar. He is not drunk, or not necessarily. He just walks like he is.

'Pint?' he shouts, pointing at her. 'Pint?' at Miss Harper, Mr Austen. 'Three, four – everyone?'

He arrives with a rattling tray, laying it down with uncharacteristic care. Dragging a chair, he throws himself down.

'Are you in one piece?' Miss Sharpe asks him, offering Benson & Hedges. He waves them away then snatches them back. She pats herself down and pulls another packet from her smock.

'Always prepared,' Roger Betts says, thumbing a Zippo.

Miss Sharpe accepts his light. She throws the new pack open to the table.

Everyone is smoking. Smokers and non-smokers. Even Roger, pipe lit, holds a cigarette in the other hand. He considers them both, pipe, fag, contemplative, one worn, corduroy knee over the other. There is a lull; the noise of the room washes in and around them, lifting and dropping, kind in its normality.

Mr Austen, Miss Wright sees, is getting drunk, his neck flushing redder and redder. Being new, he is unsure, perhaps, whether or not he should be here. Not all of them are here. Some of them just went home. But Colin Austen came, rounded up from the staffroom by Miss Sharpe's gruff invitation, and his big black shoe now bounces up and down, jeopardising the drinks on the table. Miss Wright watches, counting the weeks before the summer holidays, losing track, beginning again, until Miss Harper stills the jumping shin with her hand.

'What's your favourite animal?' Miss Harper asks him.

'Warm or cold-blooded?' Mr Austen asks back.

Miss Wright loads a tray and carries it across to the bar. She would like to take her heels off and she does, ordering from a few inches lower to the floor and meeting the drop of the landlord's eyes down her front gamely, with a lingering glance to the bald shine of his head. She kicks her shoes sideways for men to trip over and comes back across the carpet on stockinged feet. Her toes spread, small and broad, free from the restraint of shoes. *Les pieds, les pieds sont libérés!* She passes the door. A breeze meets her from the pub garden. Finally, the coolness of the night coming in. Bugger tights tomorrow. And bugger blazers. Let Gomme implode.

'Absinthe,' she announces.

'No!' Emma Harper says.

'No.' She offers the tray around. 'Pernod. To sober us up.' Roger Betts stands and everyone follows. They touch glasses, a chain of clinks. The Pernod goes down cold and clean. Aromatic. It is what Mr Ardennes drinks, drank, which some of them know and some of them don't. Which Roger certainly knows, Miss Wright sees, his face stricken.

'Can we just start whatever it is we need to do?' he asks. 'Tomorrow. And be rid of him?'

A bellowed affirmation and Miss Wright's husband jumps a foot, his Pernod leaping out of his glass like a fish. 'I'll get you another,' Dr Cole offers, glaring at the wet patch.

'No, no, I'm not really drinking.' Her husband puts the empty glass down. 'It's just you scared the living—'

'And get rid of Ward,' Roger Betts adds. 'And Matron. And Dalton.'

'Dalton's all right, isn't he?' Mr Austen asks. 'He isn't?'

'It's a revolution,' says Mr Betts, softly. 'We clear all the bastards out.'

'You're drunk, Roger,' Miss Harper says.

'I am.' Swirling the remains of his bitter. 'And have been since about ten o'clock this morning, on and off.'

'You're holding a decent wake,' Miss Wright's husband says. 'Good man.'

'How do we do it, getting rid of Gomme officially now?' Miss Harper asks.

Dr Cole scrabbles his hair. 'Some hellhole of procedure. We'll have to ask the forces of the office to gather the paperwork.'

'Good luck with that,' says Mr Austen, and giggles. Once he starts, he finds it hard to stop, it seems.

Miss Wright's husband wanders in the direction of the Men's, hitching his trousers. She looks around the ragged circle, her colleagues talking and not talking, and wonders what Lyn Ardennes is doing now, who she's with, who's with her. It seems inexplicable that he's not here. His drawn smile, his creased, considering eyes. And Lyn, the tonic of her wit. Aye, aye, aye, the first raw night, how to get through?

'Paola's expecting a baby,' Roger Betts says, frowning vaguely at her.

Miss Wright blinks. She can't, just now, do the politeness.

'I'm forty-two. Actually, I'm forty-three,' he tells her.

Her hand runs the cords of her dress, shaking the little silver bells. Old. But not too old. 'You're good with broken things.' She means he'll be fine fixing kids' bikes.

He raises his pipe and dips his head, modest even in the face of this stray compliment.

The air is soupy, boozy around them. Miss Wright breathes it in and sighs it out again. Roger stares mildly through her, rubbing his corduroy knee the wrong way, flat again; she nods back, humming along to the jukebox.

'It will . . .' she says, but loses focus.

'Yes,' he agrees, eyes liquid in his sawdust face.

They are floating in the shallows of the night, Miss Wright, Mr Betts, the others, bobbing in its placid warmth, even with death scouting about outside. What else should they do? It all so blatantly continues. But she is singing along to Genesis, Miss Wright finds, or at least to solo Phil Collins, and abruptly stops, sitting herself upright. Can she have raised the ghost of Stephen Jenks like this, by jilting him a second time in front of a classful of teenagers? Well, there's no running away from your past. Her nan was fond of telling people that, one wagging, waxy finger. Especially people too young to have any chance at running.

A small burp, a great heartburst of affection. Her class. Tin's undefended smile. All her brave and shaky teenagers.

'Because I'm spent,' Sue Sharpe is saying, not without irritation.

'So why not retire now?' Miss Wright's husband asks, back on his mushroom. 'Get down to your own stuff. The drawing and the painting.'

Sue lifts a hand and rubs two stout yellow fingers and a thumb together. 'And anyway, I like the kids.'

'No you don't,' says Emma Harper.

'No. I don't!'

A round of laughter.

'Good one!' Mr Austen puts a hand on Emma's arm, his big foot bouncing.

Miss Wright looks at Dr Cole. His small eyes glint back. Broken glass. She had passed them in the car park, Emma Harper and Colin Austen, pressed like teenagers against the dusty flank of his Escort. It's the scramble to be happy, to feel alive that carries people away like this. In wrong directions. Or is it just that no one on this whole wild earth knows what the precious fuck—

The bell hammers last orders. Miss Harper looks about like she's forgotten where she is.

'Nightcap?' Mr Betts suggests, drawing a hand down his beard and standing mostly up.

'I'll help you carry,' Miss Wright's husband says, and rights the fallen chair. He side-squeezes past, his jacket buttons catching her dress, his smile breaking over her skin. *Nucléaire? Non Merci*, his other badge. The one she gave him. A spiked red sun with slits for eyes, squeezed shut – *le soleil brille* – turned upside-down in unaccountable happiness.

Roger Betts is back, wet hands and fullish pints. He slops them down. Her husband arrives at his side. Three more streaming glasses.

'It's fast. And deep,' Roger says, taking a grip on her husband's shoulder.

Her husband shakes his head, then nods, then stops nodding.

'He was a good friend,' Roger adds, dropping his arm and sitting abruptly down. 'What more is there?'

39
Stairs

11.27 p.m.

'I hope that's not my phone bill.' Jonah's dad stops half-way up the stairs, one long arm hanging over the wooden ball of the banister, a crowbar and a dripping towel in his hand. Another flood, Jonah sees, inaccessible under the floorboards. His dad's eyebrows, his sailing-trip beard have grown wild, which makes everything he says seem unlikely.

'It's not,' Jonah tells him.

'Good. Because you've been on the phone for nearly an hour and not said one word.'

Jonah hears Tin laugh, and the silence, taut between them, goes slack in the darkness. It is his dad's, his parents' bill, in fact. He had phoned Tin. And she had called him a fucker but she hadn't hung up.

Jonah sits down on the bottom step, propping his elbows on his knees, and spreads the fingers of his free hand out. Oil paint in his nails. A lurid green. He is waiting for Tin to say something. Or for his dad to go away so he can. He looks down the hall, at the inside of the front door, a battered undercoat pink, at the walls flayed of paper but never painted, and the prints and photos and coat hooks gone up anyway. One of his mum's old band posters, her hair long to the waist, parted down the middle, the plump, swirling writing; a wall of hunchback coats, his leather jacket, one grazed cuff where he came off his bike, thick zip, and the cat stretched flat on top like a fluffy orange jumper. On the floor, under the weight of cat and coats, an avalanche of shoes.

'Are you still there?' he asks, as if she's left him off the hook and walked away. He tries to hear her breath. He tries to imagine her standing by the phone, her straight body, long legs, the high, stark echo of her hall, and feels a tug of longing. There is nothing in Tin's house. When you walk around, it booms like a grain silo, an emptied-out swimming pool.

His dad moves upwards, circling the landings, creaking the top flight of stairs.

'I misunderstood,' Jonah says. 'I thought you were already seeing other people.' Because that is what she'd said. But not, maybe, what she'd meant. Because she hadn't done it.

Silence.

But he had. And if she had been testing him in some way, his loyalty, he had failed her, as he was always going to.

Jonah turns his head. Beside him, telephone numbers scribbled in pencil, in biro all over the plaster. Wheels with many spokes. A field of doodled flowers, daisies, the petals round like children draw. A horned devil with an arrow for a tail. The scattered Ms of birds.

'I thought you didn't want me anymore,' he tells her, moving a pencil from the floor to the ledge of the skirting board, nudging it along, which is true but doesn't sound it.

He looks at the shoes. His running spikes, grass wrapped around the prongs, at his dad's walking boots, which his mum wears for digging up the allotment, soled with dry mud. And that one, not even at the bottom, a flat, dusty Doc Marten. That belongs to his brother's old girlfriend, who moved to Canada three years ago.

He is waiting for Tin to tell him how to be, how they will be. He's not sure what she's waiting for. He pushes his thumb across the pad of his index finger, rubbing the grease of the paint into the grain of his skin. He has made a painting like a roughly plastered wall, long grass brushed flat by light, by shadow. He has no idea if it's any good.

He just spread the paint about with a butter knife, green and yellow and blue, and stopped when he'd emptied the colours he liked and come to the end of the turps.

His dad bangs back down from the top of the house, pauses on the first-floor landing and hisses Jonah's name. He is holding something up like a trophy: an old alarm clock, a transistor radio, a teacup with roses, all three gaffer-taped together.

'Very good,' Jonah tells him, and then down the phone: 'My dad's made my mum a Teasmade.' His dad nods, grinning somewhere under his beard, and climbs back upstairs to deliver his gag. At least he finds himself funny.

'Did you listen to the tape?' Jonah asks.

'What tape?'

'The one I gave you in French.'

'*Mais non.*'

'You should play it,' he says. 'It's good.' But it's possible she never will, he knows. She is negligent of things, leaving them behind, renouncing them, as if she can't imagine how they have anything to do with her. All objects, not just things he gives her.

He picks up the pencil, turns to the wall and writes sideways onto the plaster, his neat, crabbed script: *my heart hammering your heart hammering my heart*. She had written that on his arm, all the way up the inside skin, lying on the grass one hot lunchtime last summer. It had made him hard, the passage of the biro to his armpit. Her concentration.

His skin, her skin. A strong pull of desire.

'Is your dad in?' he asks.

'Just come anyway,' she says, and puts the phone down.

All day, the bond between them dragging, because he had broken it, or she had let it drop. And now both ends pulling in tight.

'Bed,' his dad says, banging back downstairs.

Jonah spins the pencil around and rubs Tin's words from the wall. A soft, metallic smudge over the plaster. He stands up, dropping the pencil.

'Aye, aye,' he says. 'Night, Captain,' and runs lightly up the bare treads of the stairs.

But Jonah has the fire escape in his room. And if his parents find his bed empty in the morning, they'll assume he's gone out running. Because athletics has started, the white nauseous mornings, and athletics, as Jonah has often been told, covers a wide range of activities.

He reviews the trousers he is wearing, pulls a shirt from a hanger, rolls it into his bag and turns his light off. When he was twelve and promising, he used to be up and out by six o'clock each morning.

He has run it before, the distance between his house and Tin's. Under twenty-five minutes. But he wants to be there faster. Before midnight. And the last time he cycled over, another late night, a different kind of phone call, he hadn't made it off his bike before she'd kissed him to the ground. Bruises proud on his shins and the rare feeling of being wanted. All of him. All of her. The frame of his bike in between.

He presses open the door – the big darkness of trees. Mr Ardennes had taken himself from his life last night. While Jonah staggered home, wet and in the dark. This car crash of a day. Tin walking across the grass away from him, with Davy. His queasy regret, coming in like waves. Even the oil paint, spreading itself inexactly. He wants to find resolve. Hold true. Not idle away what's important, let what he loves leak away like smoke. He taps quietly down the metal stairs, creaks through the garden door and unlocks his bike from the lamppost opposite, not clanking the chain. He is ready for this chance, if that is what this is, not to lose everything. He swings his leg over the crossbar, shifts his bag to his back and pushes off from the kerb.

His heart is already hammering, starting to race. And here comes speed, sweet and unfamiliar after the day's slow heat; acceleration, pulling in strong and clean, a slim dart. To be fast and in his element – the headrush of it. The headfuck, cockrush speed of his heart through the dark.

40

In Doubt

11.42 p.m.

James lies on his bed. He believes in God. If he doesn't understand Him, that is only his fault and only to be expected.

A sexist fag.

He is not, he believes, a sexist fag.

And yet the disgust he had felt – His disgust had been genuine. Tin's thigh. Woman's fallen flesh.

And what about the flesh of man? His mind veers away.

St Augustine insists on the actual existence of Adam and of Eve. Their sin and their shame. Can he believe that? Believe, absolutely, in the material reality of Adam and of Eve? Two physical bodies, specific in time and geography. Not a parable. Not fiction. Our named first progenitors. Is that what God is asking him to do?

He doesn't know. If he prays, he believes He will tell him. In His good time.

But the waiting. Held on a small, jagged rock. The cutting lash of doubt. If things can't be bridged? Praying for a leap of faith.

James hears the front door bang. A rumble of voices, in the hall, in the kitchen, his mother and father and Francis talking. Tap, kettle, stubborn lid, directly below his head; the getting up a steam and the switch clunking itself off again.

'And so!' his father cheers. The revelation of an automatic kettle, it had delighted them all for weeks.

A scalding hiss from the spout and spitting into mugs. He might as well sleep under the kitchen table for all the solitude his own room affords him.

James turns his head to look out of his window and up at the sky, the town's almost-darkness, and turns it back again. His ceiling is mildly orange, the borrowed glow of the Close's single streetlamp.

It is a sin to take your own life. As it is a sin to take another's. And yet his father had gone to tidy it away. Pragmatic. His father lives pragmatically and not according to principle. James refuses to live like that.

But was he, Mr Ardennes, a man of principle? James had always felt that he was. Perhaps he'd been a man only of wrong, of mistaken principle. Or of no genuine principles at all. Certainly a man without belief.

Even so, James had felt it deeply, Mr Ardennes' goodness. He thought that he had. And Mr Ardennes will have had his reasons, no doubt. Reasons which were to him imperative, however mistaken. Looked at this way, his act might be understood as unavoidable, involuntary even, if those reasons, the particular circumstances that drove him to it, were understood. Because who knows what strange turns the mind can take, when it is tired, when it is backed up by misery, by confusion, until only one channel appears to remain open. One path. A false inevitability born of old defences that seem fixed, but which could, in fact, with effort be shifted. Sandbags from a ditch. And that being so, the full, transformative force of His compassion is surely due. And ours.

But no. It is James's own reason that is mistaken, shifty, trying to blur the edges, when the teaching is clear. It is against commandment. There will be no circumstances weighing, no reasons borne in mind. The deliberate destruction of a life, the obliteration of God's light in a soul is a mortal sin. Without equivocation. A blow to the wounded side of His Son.

He suffered all temptation, an agony unimaginable, voracious, the wilderness and the cross, so that we might live. Not cast life away. Thorn-eager, nail-embracing.

Dante locks the suicides in trees. Seeking release, they are entrapped. Heavy lumber. At Judgement, barred from wearing them, they will drag their bodies around or hang them up on branches. Our inescapable flesh.

James listens and does not listen. His dad's talk is flowing on, around the obstacle of Francis, his mother's interjections. His own mind drifts backwards, bumping against the stones of the day, turning itself around: Dark Alley, Tin like a struck child, the golden desolation of it; the stark denial of English 1, throwing the world to the dogs; the benighted labs, their invasive tang, fish and scorched metal, the casual aim of cruelty at Miss Harper, at Gomme, all adult weakness; and on the art-room table, the morning raw with knowledge, the graze of charcoal, the rounded back of his stone which would not come right, rubbing itself out through his paper.

They have lived a strange day. Untruthful. As if not one of them had heard the announcement, Gomme on his stage, top-heavy like a lectern. As if all of them by proximity had had their minds muddied. Had no one heard? A buoyant, Judas giggle. Vanessa whispering to Claire, Nicolas fussing about his possessions, Miriam's performance. And Tin, wasting herself in her own lurid drama. A day pretending to proceed as usual, the same path they always take. As if it is still here, held high like a bridge above disaster, and not in fact as it is, a crumbling slide of sand and dust already washed away.

And, worst of all, James himself, lost in a sinkhole of pride. How clever I am. How singular in faith. Sins of the intellect. His conscience, brittle as a wishbone.

Only Gomme had had the courage to speak, to try directly. A madman slopping out words on the stage, across the polished floor. And no one else able to stand forward and say anything coherent. About life. About death. Dr Cole with his fist of alternatives, all equal, all equally worthless. Rudderless, all of them, a stage of cowards, mute before the primary question of our existence. What it is to be mortal on earth, a child of sin and heaven. How to live and die in truth, and keep the heart pure, in order to live again?

James is hot with disgust and his eyes are smarting. He is wasting his time on the weakness of the world. Except is it not, in truth, his own weakness that is making him burn? His fierce, fast, hungry disgust for himself.

Well, he will speak now. Even if he failed to speak before. Especially because he failed. He will speak to God. The only true interlocutor.

And yet, all that he has spoken to Tin, that she has spoken to him, discussions without boundary or divide. That is worth something. The pleasure of thought.

Or is it only monstrous, the way they drag ideas up between them? The weird and unruly, the unspeakable and implausible, ideas like freaks taking on life. Yet sometimes, a thought between them comes out clean and brilliant, like the shock of poetry. Newborn. Unless this is his particular temptation, the exhilaration of crossing lines with unbelievers, believing himself audacious but untouched. Worse than his dad. And today, a different violence in what he had said, Tin had said, that felt like hate. Or love. He had wanted to lash out. Which now he is sorry for.

James hears the locking of the doors, front and back and side, and his dad's pushing test against the bolts. Doubt, when he's only just locked them. The trooping up the stairs, one set of feet and then the others. Splashing, tooth-scrubbing, the plunge and jangle of the loo chain. The hinges of his brother's bedroom door and the answering creak of the floorboards. Bed springs.

And so it begins, the long darkness. He is unsure how to start. How to speak. And more, he is afraid of what will come, the depth of it, the grave silence. Nothing coming back. He must listen and endure it.

He finds his eyes are closing, are closed, and stares them open. He will keep his vigil. He will pray to Our Lady, Mother of all forgiveness. He knows how to speak to her. And how to say nothing. Her envelope of peace, soft cloak.

Because some compassion is due, surely, in all this horror and evasion. He does not know. A lost man, locked-out soul. His eyes smart but his mind is clouded.

He sits up, gathers his legs around and kneels down on the lino. His blankets are a neat rectangle on the floor, away at the foot of his bed. A hard repentance. Sin and shame. The inheritance of Eve, of Adam.

He will not sleep, the pity's length of the night. He will keep on his knees in a desert of saltwater, on sharp, blasted rock, and pray for understanding.

41

Outside In

11.54 p.m.

Tin stands in the dark hall and looks at the clock. A moon. Miss Wright's full-blown face.

If Jonah comes on his bike, he'll be here just after midnight. Or maybe just before.

All day, a concussion of hours. More than she wanted to be awake for. But now she is awake, and the TV-static darkness is live all around her.

She watches the clock, the long, slender hand approaching the stubby one in jerks. *Bergen*, it reads, painted on the clockface. Something stray from her mother's side. There must have been more, other things, and then at some point a stripping-down. Early, before she was old enough to register. But not the clock. It, perhaps, was nailed too high to take down.

399

Her dad is two floors up, behind a wall of books and John Coltrane. They share more rooms than they use, and a distrust of home improvements. Soft furnishings.

Inconceivable. That is the word her aunt had used, the last time she had come for a visit. 'I think the English word you want is "inconsolable",' her dad had said, swiping his fags up and leaving the restaurant. She can't remember being that. Just a numbness as far back as she can see, sound and colour fled from the world and a blankness facing.

When the house had flooded, and her dad's study was still on the ground floor, this hall had been awash with paper. Essays, pamphlets, index cards – small rafts tilting, making their own way out.

Critical theory, not as dry as you might think. A joke she hadn't made.

She unlatches the front door, which swings itself open. A cold embrace of air, the outside pouring in.

So, this is how the day will end. Like this. The two hands of the clock aligning, taking each other in, the low strike of the church bell shaking the dark, its reverb to her feet, and stepping out of the house.

ABAB. The day come home to the night.

Tin stands on the lift of the threshold, a shoulder to the stone of the doorway. At her feet, a dark channel of running water. Above, a height of black sky, the drift and shimmer of stars. It had only been last night, sometime in this same quiet stretch of darkness. She had gone for a walk, avoiding the streets near the party, climbing Castle Hill, and had ended up between the pillars of the church. When she'd heard an approach, the soft disturbance of gravel, she'd assumed it was the vicar – tidy hands, blunt wooden crucifix – doing his round-up. But then she'd seen the tilt of his shadow, the slim hunch of his shoulders.

Mr Ardennes had come to a stop, swaying a little, and after a while had begun to speak about earthworks and early settlements, things lost or dug up, broken and unbroken, pointing out the way the river, running black through the town below, bent around the hill, protective. One hand flat to the flank of the church, he had seemed like a boy, his voice bright with the fact of motte-and-bailey castles.

She will miss Mr Ardennes, as Davy said she would. However incidental he was to her life and she to his, like walk-on characters.

But that is not the thought.

The thought has dogged her since morning, hidden in full sunlight, pulling away around corners, a daytime of evasion. In the swimming blackness, she makes ready for it. The straight hit of its conclusion.

If she was the last person to see him, to speak to him – the horror of herself. And for a second time.

Her mum had put her to bed. She had told her a story, without a proper ending, and Tin had got back up. The girl is never satisfied, is what people say. She had felt a distance, a wrong space opening out like a cut when the air gets in. She had met the dark, her feet bare and hot on the polished hallway. Sweat prints. Stairs and stairs. One foot, the other, the very top of the house. The lodger's bathroom. A spill of electric light. The window pushed up high. 'O,' her mother said, falling away forwards. A transport of water, flowing, pooling. Feet islands, hump-backed. Warm water folding over.

A lazy image for a story. A terrible ending.

The story starts again and starts again and she can never finish it.

Is it my fault? she had asked. Today. Everyday. 'No,' Miss Wright had said. No. But that had been the sort of forgiving mood Miss Wright was in. The way she likes to let things blur. And what she said is no more true for being kind.

James had felt it, flinching away.

Tin lifts her shoulder from the stone, pulls the door shut and steps down onto the unlit street. Parked cars, stars sparking in the blackness, the liquid taste of night.

She starts walking. The edges of her, cut hard and clean, are taken in by the cold. The end of this day, the start of another. The dark and light of feeling alive. This is all there is. Dim, soft hours, sharp and passing pleasure. Grief rolling over and over the days, covering itself in anything that sticks. In things that happen.

If she had gone to the party, the day would have happened differently.

Tin walks out under the dark, its silver field of stars.

It is up to her to bring it back to life, her life. A jolt to the heart, love pumping down on her chest like resuscitation, the hot spread of frostbite and any way she can to make it vivid.

Her heart sparks, broken and unbroken. She walks and she keeps walking.

42

Afterimage
solar midnight

Mr Ardennes continued walking, leaving the park by the north gate and following a length of empty road. His feet carried him. His intention limped behind.

He had a circuit he did at night, a number of different, widening circuits, around the town and sometimes beyond it. Sometimes he crossed, quietly, with other non-sleepers. The drinkers and the dog walkers and those who couldn't sleep in a bed. Who couldn't sleep. And sometimes, as tonight, with kids from school. It surprised him how late he saw them, and this a Sunday night, Robin and Jonah. But just because they were out late, even wet as they were, fugitive in the dark, didn't mean that they were up to no good.

Because who was he to know what no good looked like?

He stepped aside for a car, its slow approach, its rough negotiation with the kerb, and back out onto the road.

Because he had come more and more to see that he had lost his footing. Even that he had come to stand with the wrong, in the way of what was good and right. He had, twice last week, been required to tell a child something he did not believe. Then to stand to one side and try to absorb their confusion.

So it came, he found, in traitorous middle age, for your working body, your legs and arms and effort, for your waking hours and then your sleeping ones, and it came for your throat. Progress. Competition. Individual goals. He could not swallow these words and he would not voice them. To kids who knew, deep down, that they knew better.

He stepped up onto the pavement, around the railing and took the narrow ascent towards school. Dark Alley, its deep, absorbing blackness. Either side, the uneasy shift of evergreens; under his feet, tarmac rippled by roots. He was walking against them, all the kids pouring down year after year. The brush of ghosts, light, thirsty, in swift hundreds against his climbing effort.

They had escaped through a bedroom window perhaps, Jonah and Robin, or walked straight out of an un-adulted house. Even so, he was glad to think of them, in this respect at least, as free. Kids will find each other, mostly.

Mr Ardennes emerged at the top. The back gate would be locked, but walking the wrong way down Springfield Lane, passing between the concrete blocks and into the other school, it was possible to cross their football pitch, climb the dividing fence and enter onto the wide, flat expanse of the playing fields. This he did, knowing the beauty above him, night opening like a flower, like fireworks over his head, not looking up but heading straight across. Reaching the Dell, he moved with care through its quiet shelter – the still air warm, ripe like mushrooms, and a swimming whiteness, cow parsley, high and blurred in the dark, spreading like a hem – and out the other side. He descended the bowl of the lawn where he paused, sensing the school untenanted behind him, and then continued across the hush of grass, placing a hand on the pillar of the attendant tree and climbing the stile. Beech, his skin knew, its smooth, metallic leather. Above, a broad green breath, its own rustling universe.

He stepped down onto a spill of coniferous woodchip. Desolation caught him up.

A new path had been laid here, a sinuous descent from the boundary of the school to the old railway track. *Woodland Way – sponsored by Taylors: Your Home, Our*

Pleasure, it read, at intervals, on large, reflective boards.

There had been moths, uncommon ones, Roger Betts said, that might come back.

Long before municipal improvements, before the arrival of trains, drovers had walked here, Mr Ardennes knew, down from the fat fields all around. Many days, driving sheep and cattle, walking as straight as they could. The kids continued that way, the old, direct route, and had beaten it back in through the new planting, through the saplings and unrolled turf, ignoring the benches on their little panoramic mounds, the arcs of wooden posts directing them to paving. He too went their way, straight to the end, then turned into Hunter Street and began to climb the hill.

He always climbed Castle Hill, every night and in all weathers, up to the church and around. A hill to him was a promise, the rushing up a shorthand for a mountain. But now he had to drive himself along, one foot then another, his hands riding the bones of his thighs, reminding them to try.

Mr Ardennes was surprised to find himself out of breath. He had walked for a couple of hours almost without stopping, but now, reaching the top, an unsteadiness overcame him, the gravel shifting beneath his feet, his body weighted but his head growing light. He came to a stop between two pillars of the church, a sheltering alcove, and looked out. Weary, a sentry keeping watch. From here, the close and scattered lights of the old town. Beyond, the new road, light-industrial units, the Enterprise Centre with its floodlit line of diggers. Poured concrete, heavy machinery in daily progress over the floodplains.

A motte-and-bailey castle was a simple form of defence. Almost impenetrable, with a good hill and a deep ditch.

He felt the sky above him, interrogative. Bracing himself, legs, spine, he looked up and looked around, his balance rolling back: a darkness vast with stars, its north and south immense over the small town, implacable, its east and west.

What use standing sentry now? Had he not already failed to be vigilant enough?

The steeple rose behind him, tall and sharp, its stone seamed with copper, a chalky line running upwards many feet, a hundred and more, warding off disaster. The sky reeled around. The Plough, Ursa Major and Minor, the Great Bear and the Small.

And so, it seemed he could not, in the end, believe in God. Not even brought like this to his knees. Not even lifted up on a hill, this ancient mound, to the vast black possibility above. An unscalable beauty. He could only believe this: that everything had its proper span, a modest chance and an ending, more or less abrupt.

Who would claim an eternity? An eternity was a naked horror.

Yet here was the steeple, its vane, a promise heavenwards, a flash of gold turning slightly in the air. It could be seen for many miles around, a pin pushed in the map.

He stood at its foot, a man in darkness, held between sharp gravel and exact stars. A scattering of bright salt, the middle of the night.

Mr Ardennes lowered his head and waited for the spinning to slow and level off. In the back of his skull a queasy vacancy, then a giving way. The wings of a small bird fluttering and shutting in. Gathering his will, his limbs together, he moved on, out of the gravelled bay and around the body of the church. The stone ribs flew up beside him. From the boundary, the effervescence of the lime trees coming into flower; their trunks, dense in the blackness, holding the circumference of the land down. The bell was striking, in the membranes of his chest, in the solid bones of the earth, and was broadcast by the carrying air. Three quarter strikes.

Rounding the south transept, he was met by the flare of a match, a shadow jumping the flank of the church, ten feet high, and then falling low again with the flame shaken out. Tin, Thomasin, leaning backwards, her shoulders to the towering stone.

Perhaps she had lost her friends.

'Hi.' The coolness of her voice.

'Hello, Tin.' He came to a stop. Her mother, he thought, as he often did, and tried not to look at her like a clue, a point of debate he could not grasp. 'I hope I didn't scare you.'

'I thought you were the vicar. Come to establish some ground rules.'

'Why, what have you done?'

She waved her cigarette around by way of explanation. Because it was late, she meant, perhaps. Because it was a church.

'But it was something else before it was a church,' he said. 'For thousands of years something else.' He lifted his hand to the stone, accepting its support. 'Why shouldn't you be here?' You should be exactly here.

'"Because I'm sick to death of picking up fag butts. If you have to come, you're welcome Sunday mornings. Teens of Jesus. And biscuits are provided."'

He smiled, despite himself. The vicar had precisely this flat-footed tone and, when other people talked, a sudden way of dropping down for litter, spent cigarettes, bottle tops, sweeping them up from between the buttresses.

'But you like to come to the church?' he asked. 'The building.'

'No. I like the hill.'

He began to talk about the hillfort, the find of Iron Age gold, bracelets nested in a broken pot. It was the age and depth of the mound they were standing on that spoke to him, its long geology, its richness in layers in the soil. Centuries of weather, many forms of human attack and activity – to resist so long was in itself a small miracle, however incommunicable. Instead, he described how coins had been struck here, not ten feet away, which was unexpected, a mint being rare and this one early, Anglo-Saxon, and the surprising fact of the bell foundry, a later date, but perhaps not coincidental.

She listened, an occasional lift of her chin. And then, as in a dark room, a projector clunking round, delivering a change of slide, he saw her mind wide and alert, sharply focused, an unfamiliar landscape, and felt the clear and immediate imperative not to walk across. Not to impress anything. He stopped talking, his conscience heavy. A clumsy stone dropped down a well.

A minute, two minutes, quiet drawing in and breathing out. Tin smoking, without apparent hurry.

She had often sat in silence in his office, staring at a wall, out of the window, in the opposite direction to anything that might come through the door and down on her head like a ton of bricks, as Gomme frequently threatened to do. A space to be so she didn't walk out, in which he listened to her silence without comprehension.

That was the extent of the help he h d given her.

Darkness. The quiet trees breathing together, attentive.

A drift of nicotine entered his head, lifting his brain from his feet. A different lightness. It was years since he had given up smoking. When he and Lyn were trying for babies.

'French, your cigarettes?'

She showed him the packet. Sky blue, maybe, in the dark. The gleam of torn cellophane.

'Not just because I'm pretentious. My dad's a wanker too and I nicked them from him.' She crumpled the packet – empty – but extended her other hand, offering the cigarette over.

There was every reason why not, he knew, his eyes drawn to the orange ember. And every reason why. He took it and was appalled. A wrong thing to do. And yet the smoke buoyed him up, a pump of spiralling air. It was of no importance now. Already he felt no longer a teacher. No longer even a man.

'Finish it,' she said, when he offered it back.

Two, three more breaths, his head in orbit, his stomach in empty rebellion. With care, he extinguished what remained on the sole of his shoe, the dusty leather, and dropped it into his jacket pocket. He was grateful for it, the end of this cigarette, grateful beyond reason. Looking up, the stars white like gulls, high above, circling around, a carousel of stars, he was surprised by a hand light to his upper arm, a brush to his cheek; a kiss, one side and the other, Tin's quick, dry heat in it.

'*Bonne nuit*,' he heard. Tin, or maybe not Tin. She had already released his arm and walked clean away.

He allowed the shock to pass through him, not moving himself at all. The rough reek of nicotine and a lost era of his life brought back. In the squares of Rouen, friends meeting and parting just like this, the same slide of cheekbone, halo of thin smoke. Girls, boys, sober and silent, each disengaged kiss formal like a benediction.

He had no idea what it meant. It was not characteristic of her, to the extent that he knew her, a person so physically contained. Yet he had felt it before, the way she had of leaving him on changed ground, unsure if it was ridicule or an instinctive understanding she had shown. And uncanny, her knack for picking up a word, a gesture like this. As if she could take hold of something forgotten and take its full measure, returning it in a strange form, made luminous and telling.

He had bricks in his pockets and felt their oddness, but she had set him on his feet. At ease. His head was clear, opening out. His head was all the bright black sky.

He would go then down St Rumbold's Lane, the steep side of the mound, and return via Bristle Hill to his original route. His legs moved of their own accord, past sleeping cars, a rattle of loose stones coming with him; his mind scanned and sped, plotting the gradient. Contour lines stepping down and down, looped close like fingerprints. The scattered rain of scree.

He could not help it. At some point he had taken in the shorthand of the map, its lines and symbols, and begun to carry it everywhere with him. Like a sheet of acetate, his mind lay over the land and he annotated as he walked, marking in the site of a spring, a *tumulus*, a trench. There were other signs too, a rough code he had made as a child to record his own small world, places he'd been taken to. Vertical sticks for a wood |||||, crossed for undergrowth ††††, a bundle of twigs for a fire. Chevrons like stacked arrowheads; two for a hill, three a mountain, a single dart, a shelter ^. He had seen marks like this in a cave in France, or imagined that he had. And horses, bison, deer galloping over his head.

What an odd child he must have been, copying things into notebooks. Moss and lichen and other indications of depression, of altitude. Air growing soft and warm or thin and cold. The staged formation of a glacier. And incapable, for a time, of passing a sharp flint without picking it up to test its blade, trying the idea that someone, thousands of years before, had used the same worked edge to shear hide, slice meat.

Cattle grid, boundary stone, sheepfold; horizontal lines, a single stick, one ring inside another. A child's scratches and scribbles. Quarry, barracks, power station. But not here. Not a military enclosure, offshore rig. Mr Ardennes closed his eyes and opened them again.

Despite it all, he still felt kindly towards that boy, his measuring and recording. Checking the scale of the map.

Mr Ardennes slowed himself at the bottom. On one side the vicarage, its twisted brick chimneys, unaccountably beautiful, beyond all utility, turning in the dark; on the other a run of medieval houses, their doors no taller than his shoulder. He moved past on quiet feet, the upstairs windows just above his head and only the ancient mud of wattle and daub, hand-packed, between the sleeping bodies and the outside night. In front of him, the old graveyard. A dog with its leg to the boundary wall, then crossing the road behind him. Electronic music, its quick, frayed pulse in his ears, in the ends of his nerves, and gone. A car in the next street.

He stepped up and into a darker dark, charcoal black, smudging the edges of stones. Not a soul, all souls. Only the fall of his feet, the small darts of his breath, denting the quietness; old tombs, scabbed by lichen, resting slab against slab in the rolling ground. He followed the path through the yews, their soft gowns folded in, passed between two stone posts, a narrow jaw, and stepped back down into the wash of a lamppost and onto the street. A large house facing. Robin's, if he wasn't mistaken. Solitary and as if uninhabited, the fine columns of the porch giving way. She was safe inside now, he trusted. Held fast asleep.

Here the road turned back towards the park, its emptiness stretching out between the garden walls, the buildings of the Old Mill, occupying the darkness. And in the park – the river.

A black line indicates a weir, stopping at the banks. Two lines denote a footbridge, extending either side onto mapped land. Interrupted lines, black dashes, mark a ford. Neat tufts like broken clouds show marshland. Reeds, equally. Saltings.

Mr Ardennes approached the park and entered through the south gate.

He could already sense it, before he saw it, before he heard it even, the river ripe and loamy. Alluvial. The water ran off the fields, through the streams and village ditches, carrying the smell of farms, the stirred green clay of spring. He moved towards it, his feet finding the path worn in the grass with a sense of return.

He had learnt to swim somewhere not unlike this, and relatively late, as a young man. The water silty, the fine minerals suspended, adhesive; the banks unreliable and indistinct, overcome with reeds and nettles.

He followed the path to the right, the slight fall towards the riverbank. The second time tonight. Before, an hour or more ago, he had walked against the flow of the water, hair brushed against the grain. Now he walked with it. This ancient town, folded deep in the land, there was almost no place further from the coast; and yet, eventually, even this water found its way to the sea. A long path, many miles in one direction, to saltwater.

He heard its whisper, then in a rush the full uproar of its fall. Where the weir had been made, channelling the water, requiring it to pool and drop, the river seemed renewed, crashing down its protest. His pace quickened as it came into view, the stone bar of the weir, the white collision of air and water, a luminous chaos, and after the drop, a spreading out, flat and smooth, the quiet width, full liquid depth of the pool. Darker now, all the lights switched off, and the football club, the houses slipping away beyond the edges of the park.

A curving line: upright for smoke, horizontal for the carved path of a river. For a still body of water, pool or lake, a long dash —. A longer dash, the sea ———.

It was here, more or less, that he had come across Robin. Jonah.

And in this water, pike big enough to take your finger

off, or so the men who fished the banks told him. But the fishing had changed. Floods three springs in a row, and water high enough for sandbags all the way up Ford Street and furniture winched to the second floor. It was the development, the men said, maggots at their feet, the building on the floodplains and all around the ring road that made the change to their catch.

Mr Ardennes bent down to pick a bottle up – *Superior Vermouth*, sticky around the shoulders – and lowered it into a bin a few paces away. His head reeled around.

And there the heron suddenly was, stock-still on the lip of the weir. Grey like ash. Larger, always, and more un-human than expected.

An intelligence with acute focus. A body motionless on the dark glass slide of the weir. Magnificent. Unearthly to behold.

One long, obstructing leg. Was it possible to sense the interruption in the gliding water? Not for him above but for a pike in the battered pool below?

Mr Ardennes stood on the bank. The heron stood in the water. The breeze roused the leaves of the willows and moved his clothes, its head of feathers around.

He had brought himself here.

He had brought the rest of the sleeping pills, if he needed them too.

His wife slept, smooth as a clean-washed sheet.

He looked up again through a dance of midges, his vertigo head. The air moved in the trees. The black sky shone, its great beauty spangled. Ursa Major, Minor, the Great Bear and the Small. Each life in the silver palm of His hand. Had he believed that once? He had never really believed that. But what a boy he had been, even in marriage, in adulthood. A man with a boyish blindness. And all the time, men running rings around, digging roads, mining, pumping chemicals out. Enterprise and profit.

Pylon, landfill, firing range. Red flags blasting the heath. American army base. Not here but close. Not here but all around.

'Don't frown,' the nurse had said, when he had been compelled as a teenager to lie in the dark, month following month, his eyes bandaged. She had pressed a cool hand to his forehead and smoothed the wrinkles out. 'It's not your fault, whatever it is you're looking so guilty about,' and she had changed his bedclothes. Brisk tugs and swipes.

But that, after all, had turned out not to be true. The destruction of whole peoples, whole geologies for his comfort. The scale of it far beyond comprehension. We might not understand, and yet be responsible for it. Be vigilant, keep watch and still it did not stop. We were the thugs of the world, pushing everyone around with the blunt fists of our money, our army. It struck him as wrong, as childish, to always be claiming otherwise.

He had seen and stepped aside. He had walked and kept on walking.

He considered the heron. Its stillness a judgement.

He knew there was a van. Across the water. The Old Mill car park. Lovers, maybe drinkers. Someone alone and thoughtful, or driven out of the house. He would wait for them to go, that was best, he would wait, standing by the sliding water, the concussion of its falling, light-headed on his feet.

And somewhere, underneath the wet clay of his shoes, the deep bell striking the half hour. And again, the three-quarters.

And later, the hacking of a fox, a sawblade catching.

And later, the delicate rearrangements of a bird, low in a nest of water grasses.

The heron standing, visible invisible in the grey moving grains of the night. Mackintosh wings. Paperclip neck bent, unbent.

The heron gone.

The heron back again.

And after that, the liquid gulp of a jumping fish.
His hands and feet in accord in their numbness.

|||||| a bundle of twigs of bones; a man made of shaking reeds.
———— the long gash of the night.
A curved line, a soul, lost ghost.

———

Mr Ardennes opened both eyes. To the east, the faintest softening, a rise into paleness. The presence of fine clouds, indistinctly pink, the very brink of visibility. The clean shine of the morning star. Not yet dawn, an indication of it, before the whiteness coming in like milk, drifting snow, tilting dark to light.

Then his mind, his eyelids falling down. A heavy slide like gravel.

A lull. The day at rest in the night.

The sweet precision of a chance meeting. Lost girl, found heron. The quick life of another being, warm to his cheek.

Impossible the heron was still here. All the quarter-hour bells sounding underwater.

A single line for weir. Two for a footbridge, reaching over. Scree thrown down on a map. Lead hail.

Tadpoles once, somewhere at elevation, scattered in the ice like shot. A tarn spilt out and frozen. Swollen heads magnified, tails ticked or straight, swimming motionless. And three sheep standing by, brown and white and maybe thirsty. He had broken the ice with his stick. Passing back hours later, bright afternoon sun, all melted; the tadpoles gone, picked off by crows. But talking afterwards, a man on a quad bike, the next valley, frogs as well as tadpoles survive intervals frozen. Even their organs. A high concentration of glucose. At altitude they overwinter, he said. They can do. After a spare summer. Not much food, no warmth.

Mr Ardennes stood with his hands on his pockets. He had taken down the garden wall, the sandy dust of bricks and mortar, and not rebuilt it, preferring the view, fields and sheep, and deer wandering in.

Grass held in frozen water, fine licks of green in toughened glass. Then the green swords released, swaying like seaweed, pushed this way, that way, supple in the air.

An expanse of grass is called a sward. To itself a world.

Once, here, a singular Arctic morning, a bottle iced in upright. A breath of silver bubbles rising, arrested.

Necklace constellation.

Message in a bottle. The Superior Vermouth.

Then the thaw. A world washed clean. And nothing inside.

That was the floodplains before. Spring released by winter. Before the building-over.

—

Mr Ardennes starts. Something dropped, soft-footed, from the van in the car park. An oiled paper cloud, chip papers to the ground, and the effort of ignition. He had been waiting to hear just this, his body inanimate, his mind afloat, a slow rolling over gravel.

And still the heron standing.

And now? What other caveats remaining? Nothing between him and what he came here for.

Only a shadow. Tin leaping the wall of the church.

How many silent hours and never once spoken? What she understood about her mother, she had never told him. He had not asked. He had only kept her in when she wanted to walk out. He had been afraid. That she would see her mother in him, her intent in his, and suffer for it. That in knowing about her mother, he would further undo himself. But tonight, an eloquence of silence. The living fact of her. The adult world had set a trap, a deep covered pit in her young life. She had somehow to climb out. And he should be ashamed.

He was full of shame. Hollow with it.

But then a parting like a blessing, a brush with forgiveness, its light and smoky wing. Or was that wrong? That had to be wrong.

A chance meeting on Castle Hill. Not in any sense permission. A coincidence only.

He had not helped her enough. Anything useful at all.

The river slid metallic, the swim of stars defiant in the thin, cold glass.

Mr Ardennes shifted, his bones lightly balanced on the assembled sticks of his feet. He had the letter in his jacket pocket.

No. He had the pills in his pocket. The dust of bricks, soft like silk, like love is soft. Newborn skin. He had ash. Flakes of spent tobacco.

A weir was a fine black line, stopping at both banks.

The letter was in his wife's jacket pocket. He had put it there. For her to find tomorrow.

It might already be tomorrow.

He wanted her to be free. As she had been, coming and going, the stone squares of Rouen. He had tried not to arrive here. For most of his adult life he had tried. And his wife had helped him try.

His scatter of bones, the smoke of his head, his pockets full of rubble. It will come back and come back and come again and again. It will always come back.

To put a stop. Think of his wife. How to think of his wife? The least possible kindness.

He had dragged himself around, he had dragged himself around, he had dragged his wife around. He had failed and tried.

A very long time. When he could barely breathe. Sharp and dark, mocking the lungs' effort. Chest-high. Rising. Morning like a hail of darts. He could no longer. When he could not speak, not walk. It was too much to keep failing.

I want you to be happy. That was what he had written. And burnt. *The ties that bind us, which have drawn tighter and tighter and which you have with such kindness and courage suffered* – It was too much weight slipping, pulling her down. If she might be released.

She had taken him in. Deeper than he imagined possible. His heart into hers. He had tried to hold her safe and close. *I'm sorry that I failed.* What she had given him, filling his life, spilling over. What he gave in return, reduced, dry-mouthed, always too heavy. *Set the burden*

425

down. Love remains, light as air, as spring. *My love goes with you everywhere.*

That, in the end, was all that he had written.

He could not have asked for more. Than her. Forgiveness cannot be asked for.

He had never really learnt to swim. Not well. She had tried to teach him. He had tried but she had never been fooled. He had bricks in his pockets. A demolished garden wall.

He had only ever been walking here, to the side of this river. The hurling down of water. A rough concrete ledge——

43
Under

3.17 a.m.

The heron stands in the water.

The man stands on the concrete, tilting.

The river moves through clay, under stars. Silt and silver.

A faint milk lift in the sky.

The whooping up of a fox.

Taillights, the retreat of a van.

The quarter-hour bell.

A step forward.

The heron spears the river.

A soft-limbed frog.

Pearls of water roll from its oiled neck.

Two soft bricks, weighing down each pocket.

The squall of a baby, a house across the park,
Fine and raw, born to the night of the world.
The river pulls, rattling the willow leaves.
A cold step in.
Snow in the mouth.
The small alarm of a coot.